The Grosvenor Gallery

The Grosvenor Gallery

A Palace of Art in Victorian England

Edited by Susan P. Casteras and Colleen Denney

YALE CENTER FOR BRITISH ART

YALE UNIVERSITY PRESS
NEW HAVEN AND LONDON

Published in conjunction with the exhibition
The Grosvenor Gallery: A Palace of Art in Victorian England,
organized by the Yale Center for British Art.

Yale Center for British Art · *2 March–28 April 1996*

Denver Museum of Art · *1 June–25 August 1996*

Laing Art Gallery, Newcastle upon Tyne · *13 September–3 November 1996*

The exhibition at Yale and Denver is made possible by the generous support
of the National Endowment for the Humanities, a Federal agency,
and an indemnity from the Federal Council on the Arts and Humanities.

Designed by Frank Tierney.
Set in a specially drawn Walbaum type by Yale University Printing and Graphic Services.
Printed in the United States of America by Thomson-Shore, Inc., Dexter, Michigan,
and Cromwell Printing Company, Inc., Cromwell, Connecticut.

Library of Congress Cataloging-in-Publication Data
The Grosvenor Gallery : a palace of art in Victorian England /
edited by Susan P. Casteras and Colleen Denney.
p.   cm.
Exhibition at the Yale Center for British Art, March 2–April 28, 1996;
at the Denver Art Museum in Denver, Colo., June 1–August 25, 1996;
and at the Laing Art Gallery, Newcastle upon Tyne, UK, September 13–November 3, 1996.
Includes bibliographical references and index.
ISBN 0-300-06752-6 (cloth : alk. paper)
ISBN 0-930606-77-9 (paper: alk. paper)
1. Grosvenor Gallery (London, England : 1877–1890)—Exhibitions.
2. Art, Modern—19th century—England—Exhibitions.
3. Aesthetic movement (British art)—Exhibitions.
I. Casteras, Susan P., 1950– . II. Denney, Colleen, 1959– .
III. Yale Center for British Art. IV. Denver Art Museum. V. Laing Art Gallery.
N1165.G76G76   1996
707'.4'42132—dc20   95-50255
CIP

A catalogue record for this book is available from the British Library.

The paper in this book meets the guidelines for permanence
and durability of the Committee on Production Guidelines for Book Longevity
of the Council on Library Resources.

10 9 8 7 6 5 4 3 2 1

Contents

Preface

THIS BOOK, along with the exhibition which accompanies it, strives to remedy a hereto neglected gap in nineteenth-century British art—namely, the extraordinary contributions of the Grosvenor Gallery to late Victorian art and culture. Aside from a few dissertations and Christopher Newall's valuable reference compendium, there has been very little written about this influential institution. This project marks both the first in-depth scholarly publication about the Grosvenor Gallery and the first exhibition devoted to its content and history. During its fourteen-year lifespan (1877–1890), the gallery served as a microcosm of art of the period, encompassing the conventional along with the avant-garde, a combination rarely seen at other venues at the time.

Located in the heart of the art market district at 135–137 New Bond Street, London, the Grosvenor was ideally situated to participate in and shape the forces of contemporary taste and culture. Indeed, it exerted a formative influence on many aspects of contemporary life including art patronage, the position of the artist in society, class consciousness, the role of the popular press and critics, the status of women artists, the attitudes of audiences and consumers, and changing theories and practices about artistic display of works of art in gallery spaces. In examining this largely ignored chapter of art history, the book addresses the intersection of late Victorian art, life, and culture at a juncture in British history which witnessed a shift both in art patronage and in the relationship between the artist and the critic as well as the viewer and patron.

The contributions of the Grosvenor Gallery to the realm of exhibition history alone constitute a compelling aspect of the Victorian period which has never been properly explored. A fundamental goal of our exhibition is to display, according to a combined thematic and chronological framework, a selection of paintings and watercolors that were actually on view at the gallery during its fourteen-year existence. In order to highlight the contemporary art movements and artists to which the gallery drew attention, we have chosen to focus primarily on the most advanced artists. As suggested in the introduction and in chapter 3, the gallery not only displayed progressive "modern" artists but also offered exhibitions of old masters. However, this exhibition concentrates mostly on the contemporary artists on the gallery roster because their inclusion was the chief reason for the Grosvenor's success and its notoriety. The Grosvenor was perhaps not the first gallery to be called a "palace of art," but this label reflects its founders' efforts to invoke comparisons with aristocratic mansions and their sumptuous interiors. But this palace of art was much more than an elite enclave, for Sir Coutts Lindsay was a visionary whose notion of artistic integrity, museum amenities, audience needs, and aesthetic display ally him more with the modern-day museum director than with a Victorian counterpart. The goal of this exhibition is not to replicate specific rooms or exhibitions so much as to distill and evoke the gallery's main achievements and key exhibition reforms in terms of major works of art, contributors, and issues.

The Grosvenor Gallery has been remembered by historians mostly for its role in the Whistler-Ruskin libel trial of 1878 and its association with the Aesthetic Movement. It was at the gallery's inaugural exhibition in 1877 that Whistler's *Falling Rocket* ignited great controversy, both in the press and later in court. As John Siewert reveals in chapter 5, Whistler's Nocturnes proved a turning point not only in this artist's career, but also in the evolution of contemporary critical thought. The Grosvenor's association with the spread of Aestheticism and its "eccentric" adherents was brought to public attention in the pages of *Punch* in the late 1870s and 1880s and in the Gilbert and Sullivan operetta *Patience.* The memorable description in *Patience* of the "greenery-yallery-Grosvenor-gallery-foot-in-the-grave-young-man" alluded to the fad of supposedly pasty-faced, languid aesthetes who typically swooned before works of art at the Grosvenor Gallery.

The chapters in this book attempt to draw both a more detailed and a broader picture of the gallery's contexts and contributions. The functions of the gallery and the role of its co-founders, Sir Coutts Lindsay and Blanche, Lady Lindsay, are explored in considerable detail, contrasting their goals and accomplishments with prevailing exhibition practices and attitudes. In addition, several chapters explore the proximity of other galleries on New Bond Street—a hub of art dealers and gallery activity—to suggest intriguing possibilities of influence, competition, and cross-fertilization.

In chapter 1, on exhibition reforms at the Grosvenor, Colleen Denney outlines the ingenuity of the Lindsays in their careful positioning of the gallery in its aristocratic appearance, coding of spaces, amenities, and appeal to audiences. She further examines the legacy of the gallery in its activities that transcended the simple presentation of art on its walls, for it served as a locus of society events and created cultural activities and social spaces (like concerts and restaurants), which are integral to the organization and function of modern museums. Complementing Denney's essay, Paula Gillett's scrutiny of audiences at the Grosvenor (chapter 2) identifies those people who frequented the institution and contributed both patronage and a strong social cachet. While Denney highlights the role of Lady Lindsay in encouraging women artists and gallery-goers, Gillett offers different insights about the female "consumer" of art. In chapter 3, Allen Staley offers a survey of the winter exhibitions at the Grosvenor, thereby illuminating a little-known aspect of the gallery's activities such as its promotion of old-master paintings.

The Grosvenor Gallery's summer exhibitions were the principal site for commentary and commerce, especially for young artists unable to penetrate the more prestigious and long-established Royal Academy. In its early years, the gallery was the sole place to appreciate the works of Edward Burne-Jones and James McNeill Whistler, the two biggest "stars" of the entire enterprise. In chapter 4, Susan P. Casteras chronicles the history of the Pre-Raphaelite circle at the Grosvenor, from Dante Gabriel Rossetti's decision not to participate to Burne-Jones's spectacular success there and the effects of the reception of his work upon the so-called second-generation Pre-Raphaelites, notably Marie Spartali Stillman, John Melhuish Strudwick, John Roddam Spencer Stanhope, and Evelyn Pickering De Morgan. Not only did Burne-Jones gain critical acclaim for his powerfully mysterious canvases in his own country, but his fame at the Grosvenor also led directly to the expansion of his international reputation, particularly among the Symbolists in France and Belgium. Were it not for the Grosvenor, in fact, the fate of Pre-Raphaelitism might have been very different. The gallery's endorsement of women artists in this circle is also examined as part of a continuing concern with gender construction throughout this book.

In addition to attracting the young and the underrepresented, the Grosvenor featured works by established artists whose reputations were already solidly entrenched at the Royal Academy. To this category belonged Frederic Lord Leighton, Sir Lawrence Alma-Tadema, and George Frederic Watts, with the latter especially interested in experimenting with new forms of art and displaying the results at the unconventional Grosvenor. Watts, already considered a living "old master" by many when the Grosvenor opened, nonetheless did not receive the respect he deserved in the art world until he began to exhibit at the Grosvenor. As Barbara Bryant explains in chapter 6, Watts sent his most remarkable symbolical works not to the Academy but to the Grosvenor, where his portraits and allegorical pictures found a sympathetic reception that contributed to the flowering of his reputation abroad.

During the late 1880s the gallery became the site for experimental young artists who had worked on the Continent and embraced the tenets of Jules Bastien-Lepage, the French naturalist painter celebrated for his *plein air* landscapes. In chapter 7 Kenneth McConkey elucidates the tradition begun by Bastien-Lepage, making clear through his examination of Grosvenor Gallery exhibits that a strong thread of continuity existed between landscape and figurative artists who endorsed painting outdoors. The people who frequented the Grosvenor also bought art from other sources in contemporary London, and in chapter 8 Hilarie Faberman elucidates the history of The Fine Art Society, the Grosvenor's main commercial rival on New Bond Street. In discussing the society during the Grosvenor's existence, she provides new information on the exchange of ideas and artists between the two art institutions.

As the gallery opened its doors in 1877 with a commitment to excellence and innovation, it closed in 1890, arguably with the same ideals. Despite financial challenges and the defection of his key assistants at the end of the 1880s, Sir Coutts Lindsay remained dedicated to his original goals of providing new opportunities—as well as a new international visual forum—for young, often untried, artists. While much remains to be explored in other aspects of the gallery's rich history and impact, this book establishes a range of ideas and perspectives that help to transform our understanding of late Victorian culture.

Acknowledgments

THIS PROJECT, which originated in Colleen Denney's 1990 dissertation at the University of Minnesota, has gestated for the past six years. During this period the aid of numerous institutions and individuals proved invaluable, for which the co-editors offer thankful appreciation. Without the funding of the National Endowment for the Humanities in both planning and implementation grants, the exhibition could never have been realized.

At the Yale Center for British Art, former Director Duncan Robinson provided key support which was continued by Constance Clement in her role as Acting Director. We are especially grateful to Beth Miller, who assumed much of the responsibility for both the exhibition and the book at a crucial moment. She in turn relied on the editorial and research assistance of Diane Waggoner and administrative help from Kimberly Kneeland. We received unstinting support from colleagues at the Center: Mark Aronson, David Barquist, Jose Branco, Richard Caspole, Chic Cerillo, Gabriel Catone, Kathleen DeSanctis, Theresa Fairbanks, Elisabeth Fairman, Timothy Goodhue, Richard Johnson, Marilyn Hunt, Julie Lavorgna, Eric Lee, Anne-Marie Logan, David Mills, Patrick Noon, Maria Rossi, Sachiko Sugimoto, Lorelei Watson, Scott Wilcox, the late Gloria Cotter, and past staff members Betty Muirden and Barbara Mulligan. The handsome installation and accompanying brochure were the work of John Zelenik and the design team of Jeffrey Jerred and Yael Gen. The informative architectural drawings displayed in the exhibition are the work of Jeffrey Pond. At the Denver Art Museum, we appreciate the cooperation of Louis Sharp, Dan Jacobs, and Timothy Standring. From the outset the staff of the Laing Art Gallery, especially John Millard, has been enthusiastic about this project. Moreover, the volume editors are both extremely grateful to Kenneth McConkey for his guidance as a curatorial consultant in Great Britain.

We also thank all of the interdisciplinary scholars—especially Hilarie Faberman, Paula Gillett, Thomas Heyck, Caroline McCracken-Flescher, and Martin Weiner—who worked on this project in the planning stages and participated in meetings funded by a National Endowment for the Humanities planning grant.

Bernard Barryte provided help at an early stage, as did research assistants Marcene Lore and Romita Ray. Many curators, dealers, and scholars helped in locating objects for the exhibition, among them Gregory Hedberg of Hirschl & Adler; Rupert Maas, Jan Marsh, Pamela Gerrish Nunn, the Pyms Gallery, Peyton Skipwith, and colleagues at Christie's and Sotheby's in New York and London. In addition to those contributors to this book already mentioned, Barbara Bryant, John Siewert, and Allen Staley are due thanks for their diligent labor and scholarship. Furthermore, at Yale University Press, Judy Metro, as well as Mary Mayer, Noreen O'Connor-Abel, and Frank Tierney, have been a constant source of encouragement and help with the publication of the book.

Thanks are due to all the lenders who have generously agreed to make their beautiful objects available.

On a more personal note, the editors appreciate the encouragement of this project over the years by many scholars in the Victorian art community in North America and Britain. Susan P. Casteras is grateful to her family and friends for their support throughout this undertaking. Colleen Denney wishes to express her appreciation to Gabriel and Yvonne Weisberg for their unflagging support, and to Oliver Walter, Tom Buchanan, and Merrie McElreath at the University of Wyoming Office of the Dean of Arts and Sciences for their assistance at various stages. Mary Jane Edwards, Jean Owens Schaefer, and other colleagues in the University of Wyoming Art Department offered continual support in this endeavor. Colleen Denney also thanks her family, which grew in size along with the complexity and scope of this project.

The Grosvenor Gallery

Introduction

Colleen Denney

1. Thomas Buist, *Sir Coutts Lindsay and Lady Lindsay at Balcarres Castle*, 1864. Carte-de-visite photograph. Courtesy of the National Portrait Gallery, London (cat. 6)

THE GROSVENOR GALLERY was located on New Bond Street, London, from 1877 to 1890, at one of the most elite addresses for a gallery during the Victorian period. It was an exhibition site that embraced challenge and change at the end of the century, both in the artists it represented and in the ways their works were displayed within its spacious interior. It received immediate notoriety during its first summer exhibition of contemporary art when James McNeill Whistler affronted John Ruskin's sensibilities in showing his *Nocturne in Black and Gold: The Falling Rocket* (see fig. 48), which launched the infamous Whistler-Ruskin trial. Ruskin, whose power as a mainstay of English criticism was still fairly potent at this time, accused Whistler of "flinging a pot of paint in the public's face." Whistler sued for libel, stating that Ruskin was attempting to ruin his reputation. As a consequence, the trial escalated the dialogue about the complex relationship between artists and critics in England during the 1870s. Further, through the selection of artists and their worship of beauty in the form of fair women, as well as through Whistler's philosophy of art-for-art's-sake and his keen and thorough experiments in interior design, the gallery became synonymous with the Aesthetic Movement during its early years. It inspired Gilbert and Sullivan to remark, in *Patience; or, Bunthorne's Bride*, that its follower was a "greenery-yallery-Grosvenor-Gallery-foot-in-the-grave-young-man" because of the lovesickness this audience professed before the works of its previously undiscovered talents.

But that is just scratching the surface of the richness of talent and diversity of audience that this gallery embraced. Its owners, the aristocrats Sir Coutts Lindsay (1824–1913) and Blanche, Lady Lindsay (1844–1912), wanted to promote artists who were not receiving attention or proper recognition elsewhere, such as the group of Pre-Raphaelites led by Edward Burne-Jones who became its special focus through 1888. The gallery promoted contemporary artists within its summer exhibitions, although its winter exhibitions sometimes mixed living artists with old masters and recently deceased masters of British and foreign schools. Further, these winter exhibitions often consisted of major retrospectives of the works of living artists, which was seldom seen elsewhere. In addition, the gallery held fall exhibitions in its later years, mostly of pastels. The gallery assistants, Charles Hallé and Joseph Comyns Carr, under the guidance of Sir Coutts Lindsay and Lady Lindsay, invited contributions from men and women artists of the day for the summer exhibitions, which ran during the London season, from May through July. The Lindsays and their assistants wanted the public to recognize certain divergent tendencies; they wished to give attention to several young schools of contemporary art in Britain, setting them off against the established painters who also showed at the gallery, like Frederic Leighton and Edward Poynter. In addition, the Lindsays were interested, as amateur artists themselves, in providing space for their own works and those of their friends and acquaintances drawn from their wide social net.

In their exploration of exhibition reform on such a grand scale—its relationship to patronage patterns, audience, and class consciousness—the Lindsays brought a combination of class attitudes and talents to the gallery venture. Coutts Lindsay had become a baronet at age three upon the death of his grandfather and had inherited Balcarres, the ancestral home in Fife, Scotland. Thomas Buist's photograph, taken during the early years of the Lindsays' marriage, shows them on the grounds of Balcarres (fig. 1). As part of his aristocratic education, Lindsay's parents expected him to cultivate a devotional reverence for art and beauty. He spent a short stint in the Grenadier Guards, but his true love was art, a passion which led him to Italy. He had first been to Italy in 1838 in order to recover from an illness, afterward traveling with his cousin, Alexander, Lord Lindsay, who was an important scholar of early Italian art.[1] His admiration for his cousin's work inspired his own decision to become an artist. While in Italy studying, he became acquainted with Adelaide Sartoris, a leader of fashionable society in Rome, who had been a professional singer before she married Edward Sartoris in 1842. Adelaide was the daughter of actor Charles Kemble, sister of Fanny Kemble, and a niece of Sarah Siddons.

Her husband, like Lindsay, was an amateur painter. At their Italian gatherings as well as at their London home mingled painters, sculptors, and musicians who would later become intimates of the Grosvenor circle.[2]

At the time of this Italian stay, one of Lindsay's acquaintances described his personal and intellectual character: "His sensibility towards history and literature and his understanding of art and facility in drawing were impressive. He could discourse with authority, adding a mixture of sophistication and youthful ardour which, allied to a charming manner was very attractive."[3] The combination of these charms and talents with the good looks that he possessed prompted Whistler to call him "the handsomest man in London." Buist's photograph of him supports this opinion. These traits signaled the success Lindsay experienced as the spokesperson for modern art at the Grosvenor Gallery.

This Italian sojourn was cut short in 1855 by the death of Lindsay's father; practically speaking, Lindsay's inheritance required his residence at Balcarres, but he preferred London society, particularly that of Mr. and Mrs. Thoby Prinsep at Little Holland House who, along with the Sartoris circle, were important hosts when in London, as well as patrons of the arts. George Frederic Watts, portraitist and painter of mythological scenes, lived with the Prinseps until 1875. Here also Lindsay's future Grosvenor congregation gathered, which included the Pre-Raphaelite Brotherhood and their followers. This circle lauded the beauty of one or more "stunners" (Dante Gabriel Rossetti's term for a beautiful woman), as well as the talents of the most successful musicians, actresses, and singers of the period. This circle also admired Mrs. Prinsep herself, as well as Lady Somers, wife of Lindsay's cousin, and the famed photographer Julia Margaret Cameron.[4]

In 1863 at the Prinseps' home, Lindsay met his future wife, Caroline Blanche Elizabeth Fitzroy, daughter of Hannah Meyer Rothschild Fitzroy and Henry Fitzroy, M.P. Watts showed a portrait of her at the first Grosvenor summer exhibition in her favorite role as violinist (pl. 24), but she possessed many talents, including that of watercolorist and writer. After she had debuted in London society, she attracted the attention of John Everett Millais, William Holman Hunt, and several other artists and musicians.[5] Thus, she brought to the Grosvenor scheme not only the social graces of an elegant, capable hostess but also a love of the arts essential to the smooth running of an art gallery. Furthermore, through her family she provided important connections to potential patrons among the royalty and aristocracy.

Sir Coutts and Lady Lindsay were both amateur artists of some skill. For example, early in the 1860s Lindsay's brother-in-law, Robert Holford, chose him to decorate Dorchester House on Park Lane with frescoes (since destroyed) according to a technique that Lindsay developed himself.[6] This commission essentially made his reputation as a talented amateur artist devoted to the high arts. In addition, the Lindsays both submitted works to the Royal Academy in the 1860s and early 1870s, but they were not always successful in having their works accepted for its annual summer exhibitions. The Lindsays themselves partly wanted a space to show their own endeavors, Sir Coutts showing Greek mythological subjects as well as Italian literary scenes, whereas Blanche showed intimate watercolors of genre scenes as well as small portraits. Their reasons for opening the Grosvenor thus stemmed from their personal backgrounds as artists and as members of the upper echelons of society.

The exhibition space alone inspired comment because of its opulence, intended to emulate the palaces of Renaissance patrons. This was on purpose, Lindsay often being referred to as a modern-day Medici in terms of his aid to artists. The interior, which matched the exterior for elegance, spaciousness, and taste, consisted of a marbled foyer leading to a flight of stairs, which, after one had ascended, led into the galleries themselves. The two main galleries for paintings and sculpture and sometimes watercolors were long halls with skylights. The Lindsays reserved two specially lit smaller rooms for watercolors and smaller sculptures placed on pedestals.

The gallery's true reason for existence was its summer exhibitions of contemporary art, when the Lindsays could showcase all new young talent. These exhibits varied in how many works were shown, but the number of artists grew from year to year. In 1877 there were only sixty-four artists, which steadily increased to more than two hundred artists in the 1880 exhibits. The Lindsays always strove for a careful selection of artists within each exhibit, a marked original feature of this venue, so that the artists' works could be easily seen and appreciated without the fear of competing with a neighbor's work. For this reason, the number of works each year was relatively small: 199 works in the first exhibition—142 paintings, 46 watercolors, and 11 sculptures. By the mid-1880s these numbers had increased considerably to around 400 works in each summer show, with a similar distribution across media, but these numbers were still considerably lower than those of the gallery's official rival, the Royal Academy.

The Lindsays were eager to show not only underrepresented artists, but also underrepresented media, especially watercolor, which was favored by women artists. It is evident that Blanche Lindsay used her influence as co-owner of the gallery to bring in female artists of distinction from her own aristocratic circles, including Louisa Stuart, Lady Waterford, and Princess Louise (the rebellious daughter of Queen Victoria), and from other quarters as well, such as her good friend Louise Jopling. The Grosvenor became a prestigious and highly visible site for women artists, and the Lindsays reserved the watercolor room for their contributions (women having been encouraged in this medium because oils were considered too messy and undignified). Women consistently did not receive the same art training as men during this period and were kept from studying the human figure in formal classes until at least 1893. Some women artists openly defied these unwritten rules. Evelyn Pickering De Morgan, an important Grosvenor exhibitor and part of the Pre-Raphaelite circle, was chief among these iconoclasts as an artist determined to paint in oils, working secretly at odd hours to avoid the criticism of her mother. Despite these unwritten rules concerning "lady painters," as they were called, at the Grosvenor Gallery women were given equal opportunity as exhibitors. Women's exhibition records and numbers at the Grosvenor appear much more favorable when compared with those of other institutions, especially the Royal Academy.[7] Indeed, even the Paris Salons could not compete with the Grosvenor Gallery in terms of representation of women artists. Moreover, Lady Lindsay supported female artists in both financial and moral terms.

Just as the Lindsays were able to help women in their careers, their interests were also partly focused on helping the medium of watercolor, to which women contributed significantly during the Victorian period, Blanche Lindsay herself having a great deal of experience trying to win favor for this medium on the London art scene.[8] Not only did watercolorists have their own room at the Grosvenor, but their larger pieces were also shown in the two main galleries alongside oils without being overpowered by them, according to eyewitness reports. This type of hanging practice was very unusual and helped to mark the Grosvenor as a distinctive exhibition site.

Although the gallery had quite a heady success during its early years, by the period 1880 to 1884 personal problems and business difficulties beset Sir Coutts, forcing him to reassess his aims. These decisions were largely due to the loss of Lady Lindsay; they separated in 1882 and with her departure Sir Coutts lost key moral and considerable financial support. She had acted as hostess for all private and public openings, being especially praised for her at-homes held in the elegant restaurant and dining room, where she would bring together the artists and her aristocratic circle, as well as royalty. While Lady Lindsay occasionally exhibited her watercolors here after their separation, she removed herself completely from the social activities of the gallery. Sir Coutts was forced to become more business-minded, and during these years he created some vital innovations at his gallery that helped secure its unique reputation. During the 1880s he opened a circulating library on the premises and introduced electricity to his galleries. Later in the 1880s Lindsay even established a gentlemen's club on the premises (followed by a ladies' club close by). Although Lady Lindsay had been especially

attentive to the comforts of the audience, both at public and private events, Lindsay continued this attentiveness through these added amenities.

What artists fueled this venture? This exhibition concentrates on certain movements because these groups represent the overall spirit of the enterprise as a stronghold for unusual, untried, and progressive talent. In addition, the groups we have chosen from the vast numbers of artists who exhibited at the gallery were the stars. They received consistent critical reaction and were responsible for creating a visual and verbal dialogue between artists and critics during the late Victorian period. The groups are the second-generation Pre-Raphaelites; the Aesthetic circle around Whistler; the society portraitists such as James Tissot and, in his later years while showing at the Grosvenor, John Everett Millais; the Victorian Olympians, such as George Frederic Watts, who made use of stories of ancient Greece; Jules Bastien-Lepage, the young French artist who inspired the young Rustic Naturalists, as well as their companions, the Newlyn School; and Irish and London Impressionists, as well as the Glasgow Boys.

In the formation of his gallery and in general, Lindsay was always preoccupied with mural decoration and with works of art that decorated interiors, from his start as an artist-decorator at Dorchester House. As a result, he was keen to represent current trends in decorative art at his own gallery. Partly for this reason, the guiding light of the Grosvenor has always been recognized as Edward Burne-Jones and the Pre-Raphaelite artists who surrounded him. The first-generation Pre-Raphaelites (with the exception of Dante Gabriel Rossetti) showed at the Grosvenor alongside their younger cohorts, but the elder artists' work was very different, tending toward portraits and more conservative figurative subjects. Burne-Jones celebrated a languorous female type in loose-fitting clothes and with melancholic expression, as in *Laus Veneris* (pl. 3). His art and that of his circle— John Roddam Spencer Stanhope, Evelyn Pickering De Morgan, Marie Spartali Stillman, John Melhuish Strudwick, among others— embraced medieval, Greek, and Arthurian legends of love, life, and loss. Because of their worship of the beauty of human form, they became central to the mission of the Aesthetic Movement.

Artists of this decorative circle working in the same medievalizing style as Burne-Jones included Charles Fairfax Murray, William Edward Frank Britten, Edward Matthew Hale, George Percy Jacomb Hood, and T. M. Rooke. Others who were producing decorative pieces for interiors, working in a largely neoclassical style, included (in some cases) Royal Academicians: Frederic Leighton; Walter Crane, who worked in two styles, one close to the Burne-Jones school, the other a classical style; William Blake Richmond, who showed very large decorative panels; Lawrence Alma-Tadema, Sir Edward John Poynter, and Thomas Armstrong. Their works consisted of decorative figure panels, as well as portraits and studies of pure landscape. The decorative pieces were usually genre scenes set in ancient Greece and Rome, mythological stories, or symbolic representations of women as the seasons.

The Royal Academicians used this exposure as an alternative to the Royal Academy. The Grosvenor was criticized by Leighton, the president of this august rival, who felt it would drain the best contributors and paintings from its own pool of art. Not surprisingly, there was considerable discussion throughout the lifespan of the Grosvenor of how it differed from the Royal Academy, whose jury—forty senior artists of the Academy with full membership who were rarely the most forward-looking group—excluded many of the gallery's artists. The continual comparison often focused on Lindsay's hanging practices and choice of artists. However, in order to appease the Academy, Lindsay orchestrated a compromise, deciding to invite a certain number of Academicians, including Watts and Alma-Tadema.

Alongside this group could be seen the evocative, misty, suggestive landscapes and figurative works of James McNeill Whistler, who openly proclaimed that his works were first and foremost about the arrangement of line and color before they were anything else—a direct affront to a culture that sought out moralizing narratives of proper behavior. To promote a worship of beauty, as these artists were doing, was considered almost sacrilegious. With Whistler, Albert Moore and Watts were equally suggestive in their figurative works of the love of beauty for its own sake.

These artists inspired the works of the young French artist James Tissot, who took refuge in London during the Franco-Prussian war (1870–71) and stayed there until the early 1880s. He showed at the Grosvenor between 1877 and 1879, producing works that were partly indebted to Whistler's examination and adaptation of Japanese prints that depicted single figures of beautiful women much like the Japanese examples that inspired them. They both created works that were long and narrow in format, perfect panel sizes for interiors. Tissot was also well known for his portrayals of London high society, the very people who patronized the Grosvenor artists and who made the Grosvenor their social setting.

The realists were also a presence in Grosvenor exhibitions. During the gallery's early years, the French realist artist Alphonse Legros also showed there, exhibiting sculpture in addition to humble genre scenes. Among the realists who showed there was Hubert von Herkomer, who continually showed portraits, as well as peasant scenes from his native Bavaria, in both oils and watercolors. Frank Holl, best known now for his social realist paintings, was also in this circle but showed exclusively portraits at the Grosvenor.

The Lindsays had a deep and abiding love of Italy, reflected in part in Lady Lindsay's book of poems about Venice, *From a Venetian Balcony,* which was sold there as a guidebook. Through their sojourns of Italy they came into close contact with groups of English artists who worked there, including the three Montalba sisters, Clara, Henrietta, and Hilda, the latter two being sculptors, while Clara was an important landscapist working mostly in watercolors. Clara's views of Venice, which appeared at the Grosvenor almost annually, could have been illustrations to Blanche's poems. In addition, the Lindsays promoted the English circle of artists known as the Etruscans, a group devoted to pure landscape painting, which included their close friend George Howard, an artist who, like

Lindsay himself, was a dedicated amateur. The Etruscan group (actually comprised of English artists Matthew Ridley Corbett, William Blake Richmond, and Kate Perugini, daughter of Charles Dickens) worked in Italy, with Giovanni Costa at their head. Their Italian vistas gave general impressions of grand views rather than the minute details of a Pre-Raphaelite rendition.

Other landscapists whom the Lindsays showcased at the Grosvenor in its early years included one of Lindsay's special discoveries, Cecil Gordon Lawson, who created incredibly evocative English landscapes, mostly of dawn or dusk. After Lawson's untimely death in 1882 at the age of thirty-one, Sir Coutts along with his assistants arranged a retrospective of his works during the winter of 1884.

During the 1880s, as Aestheticism waned, Sir Coutts and his assistants brought in new blood to the gallery venture, adding to the list of stars Jules Bastien-Lepage, an indication of the gallery's support of new Continental talent. Furthermore, Sir Coutts insisted on showing young English artists who had received the majority of their training in Europe and who were also followers of this French artist. This group included the English Rustic Naturalists such as George Clausen, the Newlyn School (so named because they settled in the fishing town of Newlyn in Cornwall), including Henry Scott Tuke, Elizabeth Armstrong Forbes, and Stanhope Forbes, and the Irish and London Impressionists, who included Frank O'Meara and Philip Wilson Steer, respectively. Each of these groups benefited from French training, which was much more open to stylistic experiments in form and manner than English training (the Royal Academy having come under increasing attack by such young artists for this reason). They also used French stylistic innovations introduced by Bastien-Lepage, notably a broad, dragging brushstroke in large square patterns and painting *en plein air* (outdoors and directly from nature). While the first-generation Pre-Raphaelites had been the first to paint outdoors, they finished their works in the studio. The 1880s artists were the first English painters to exhibit works in England that they had executed completely outdoors. Part of their inspiration came from Bastien-

Lepage himself. While maintaining the freshness of plein air scenes manifest in the contemporaneous works of the Impressionists, his outdoor scenes were always acceptable because of their fine finish, so unlike the "tongue-lickings" (according to one critic) of the Impressionists' "daubs." They also learned to admire his wide thematic range because he established a fresh, vibrant approach to contemporary portraiture, as well as to contemporary genre subject matter, as in *Les Foins* (pl. 9), turning to scenes of peasants in the fields inspired by his native Damvilliers in eastern France.

Other British artists were buoyed up by these examples and showed their own rustic scenes of fisherfolk, peasants, and rural laborers at the Grosvenor in the 1880s; they included John Robertson Reid and his sisters, Flora and Lizzie. During the 1880s one could also see at the Grosvenor similar genre scenes by G. H. Boughton and R. W. Macbeth and works by the landscapists James Orrock and David Murray.

During the early 1880s other Continental artists appeared at the Grosvenor, including John Singer Sargent, an American expatriate living and working on the Continent, who showed views of his Venetian interiors. Perhaps more surprising was the inclusion in 1882 of *Bronze Mask* by Auguste Rodin, as well as his portrait in bronze of Alphonse Legros, by this time professor at the Slade School and a Grosvenor exhibitor himself. Henri Fantin-Latour, along with Victoria Dubourg, showed exquisitely painted still lifes and figurative pieces. With the continued stronghold of Pre-Raphaelite works and the further presence of the neoclassical school, as well as the challenging experiments of Whistler and the realist-naturalist school, the Grosvenor's introduction of these Continental artists communicated the fact that English art could no longer be considered insular. A visual dialogue which Lindsay had begun in 1877, when he brought in Gustave Moreau's *L'Apparition* to explore the symbolistic content of Pre-Raphaelite art, remained a priority for him.

The last addition to the Grosvenor exhibits came with the introduction of the Glasgow Boys, who joined the gallery enterprise in 1889 and

1890, at the same time that some other groups changed their allegiance to the New Gallery on Regent Street, run by Lindsay's former assistants. Through a business falling-out with Lindsay, Hallé and Carr decided to open their own gallery and took Lindsay's chief artist, Burne-Jones, with them. Most of the Academicians followed, leaving Lindsay with space that he filled well with this stimulating young Scottish group who had not been seen in London previously. The primary artists in this group were Ernest Hornel, George Henry, Arthur Melville, and John Lavery. The Glasgow Boys synthesized Bastien-Lepage's concern for fresh outdoor observation with Whistler's interest in harmonious patterns on a surface. The new elements that these artists brought to late-century works of art included a bold color scheme and spatial arrangement, as well as unusual subject matter such as that in Henry and Hornel's *The Druids: Bringing in the Mistletoe* (pl. 16).

The 1890 showing of the Glasgow Boys was the Grosvenor's last hurrah; due to financial difficulties Lindsay was forced to close the gallery in December of that year. The final show was of the new Society of British Pastellists that he had founded. As with all of his previous experiments, Lindsay's decision to create such a society marked the Grosvenor Gallery as a site for artistic and social change, as well as the locale of debate about the changing role of the artist in relation to the exhibition scene.

1

The Grosvenor Gallery
as Palace of Art
An Exhibition Model

Colleen Denney

2. "Intended Façade of the Grosvenor Gallery,"
The Builder, May 5, 1877

WHEN SIR COUTTS LINDSAY and Blanche, Lady Lindsay, opened the Grosvenor Gallery, located at 135–137 New Bond Street, London, as a gallery of fine art in 1877, it was one of the most significant alternate venues to the official arena of the Royal Academy. The Lindsays sought to accommodate artists who were not receiving recognition from the conservative official bodies and who desired new outlets for exhibiting their works and attracting patrons. The Lindsays' groundbreaking approach to the staging and advancement of fine art, in particular their polemical exhibition practices, threatened the authority of the Royal Academy and aided the Grosvenor in its evolving role as an exhibition model for other sites. In this sense, the Grosvenor extended the circle of artists available to the public, and, with motives removed from notions of trade, it created aesthetic hanging practices and instigated new forms of institutional support. William Thomas Sams designed this new building under Sir Coutts's guidance, to emulate the spatial flow, opulence, and elegant (though vast) scale of an aristocrat's palatial home (fig. 2).

In this context, the Grosvenor Gallery was first called a "palace of art" in the London press just two months after it opened for its first summer exhibition on May 1, 1877. The *Punch* poem "The Palace of Art (New Version), Part I," read in part:

I built myself a lordly picture-palace
  Wherein to play a Leo's part.
I said, "Let others cricket, row or race,
  I will go in for Art!"

Full of great rooms and small my palace stood,
  With porphyry columns faced,
Hung round with pictures such as I thought good,
  Being a man of taste.

The pictures—for the most part they were such
  As more behold than buy—
The quaint, the queer, the mystic over-much,
  The dismal, and the dry.[1]

This poem was a "new version" of Tennyson's allegory by the same title, in which a person is cloistered in a palace living for art alone. After seeing the weakness of such an existence, the protagonist begs for the light of the natural world once more.[2] While the *Punch* poem alludes to Lindsay's dedication to art, it also exalts his role as arbiter of taste in creating a structure so elaborate and built on such a scale that it was immediately perceived as a space set apart from the average exhibition hall by the "palace" in the title.

This chapter focuses on Sir Coutts Lindsay's contributions to exhibition reform in Victorian England, specifically, his philosophy on gallery displays and management in relation to his architectural sources, his new approaches to the arrangement and presentation of contemporary art, his promotion of neglected artists and art forms, and the additional gallery activities he and Lady Lindsay organized for that select group and their patrons.[3] This consideration of the full range of the gallery's contributions situates the gallery in the history of the reception and consumption of modern art and examines Lindsay's role as a forerunner of the contemporary museum director in balancing the needs of the gallery audience and a commitment to advanced artistic circles and specialized groups.

THE LINDSAYS

In their exploration of exhibition reform on such a grand scale—its relationship to patronage patterns, audience, and class consciousness—the Lindsays brought a combination of class attitudes and talents to the gallery venture. Their reasons for opening this gallery stemmed from their personal backgrounds as artists and as members of the upper echelons of society. For example, early in the 1860s Lindsay's brother-in-law, Robert Holford, chose him to decorate Dorchester House on Park Lane with frescoes (since destroyed) according to a technique that Sir Coutts developed himself.[4] This commission essentially made his reputation as a talented amateur artist devoted to the high arts. In addition, the Lindsays both submitted works to the Royal Academy in the 1860s and early 1870s, but their works were not always accepted for its annual summer exhibitions. In order to have one's work shown there, one had to go through a jury which, by the 1870s, was gaining a reputation for its conservative nature. Grosvenor artist Walter Crane

remembered: "Lindsay . . . felt that many most distinguished artists were either very inadequately represented at the exhibitions of the Royal Academy, being either entirely ignored or indifferently treated by them, while there were others who never submitted their work to that body at all. Among these were painters of such distinction as Edward Burne-Jones, Alphonse Legros, James McNeill Whistler, John Roddam Spencer Stanhope, Cecil Gordon Lawson, William Holman Hunt, and many less known younger artists."[5] Hence, the Lindsays had firsthand knowledge of the Academy's exhibition practices, which helped them in reaching decisions about their own gallery. In 1863, Lindsay was listed as "the distinguished representative of high art as practised by non-professional painters" in a commission report.[6] In defining "high art" at the time, such reports would emphasize an artist's close study of Renaissance masters, as well as a strong commitment to serious subjects taken from Greek and Roman mythology, classical literature, and Shakespeare. "High" refers to the fact that only educated people of the upper classes would understand the subjects and the references to the works of old masters. The French sociologist Pierre Bourdieu argues that such aesthetic distinctions determined through this visual language of intellectual subjects reinforces the social hierarchy of classes in relation to taste. John Codd interprets his views as follows: "The opposition between heavy and light (as in heavy music/light music) [corresponding here to high and low art] serves to distinguish bourgeois from popular tastes. Likewise, the oppositions between high (sublime, elevated, pure) and low (vulgar, low, modest), fine (refined, elegant) and coarse (heavy, fat, crude, brutal), light and heavy, free and forced . . . are homologous, Bourdieu suggests, to the oppositions constituting the field of social classes."[7] Thus, there is an important correlation among class, the language of that class, and the attitudes of that class toward what Bourdieu calls "cultural capital," which involved the cognizance of good taste in aesthetic decisions such as that of "high art," on Sir Coutts's part.[8] In 1863 Sir Coutts had already determined not only his own position in relation to the arts, but also the position he would take when he and Lady Lindsay opened the Grosvenor Gallery in 1877. Their establishment would be different and exclusive, just as the artists it served would represent such attitudes.

These distinctions, which the Lindsays began to recognize as a result of the exclusion of their own work and that of their fellow artists from the Academy exhibits, led them to think about alternate exhibition arenas. In the autumn of 1875, Charles Hallé visited with the Lindsays at Balcarres Castle in order to formulate plans for a new gallery. An amateur painter and the son of the famed pianist and conductor Sir Charles Hallé, he had studied in France with Victor Mottez, a pupil of Ingres, before his own travels in Italy.[9] Joseph Comyns Carr and his wife, Alice Strettel Comyns Carr, were also present at Balcarres for this planning session. Carr had come to Lindsay's attention because he had written favorably about Edward Burne-Jones and Dante Gabriel Rossetti in contemporary journals. He had started his career in law but found his true passion lay in journalism (and writing the occasional play). He became the press representative in residence at the gallery, hired to promote the gallery's cause in various journals, including the French journal *L'Art*, as well as the *Pall Mall Gazette* and the *Manchester Guardian*. He also became co-assistant of the gallery, along with Hallé.[10] Alice Carr, equally passionate about the arts, developed a reputation as an important costume designer.

In their discussions with Hallé and Carr about a gallery, the Lindsays at first wanted to organize a temporary exhibition in an existing building with the aid of some of the artists who were unable to show their works in public arenas. When those artists could not promise financial support, the Lindsays then took upon themselves the financial responsibility of building and opening their own gallery at an estimated total cost of £100,000 to £150,000. The Lindsays split the financial burden, making them equal partners in the scheme. This financial plunge declared the Lindsays' deep belief in these artists, this new direction representing for them a mission as majestic guardians of a new artistic circle.

EXHIBITION POLICIES

The Lindsays' decision to provide an independent exhibition space came at a significant juncture in Victorian exhibition history. During its time the art public considered the Grosvenor Gallery a site of change, coinciding with a crucial shift in artistic opinion about the direction of British art in the 1870s, and this was arguably largely due to the specific innovations Sir Coutts introduced into the realms of theory, criticism, and the art marketplace. The originality of this occurrence will become clear with an examination of the exhibition offerings up until the Grosvenor's foundation.

Since 1800 England had offered many exhibition opportunities for the aspiring artist, from private galleries and prestigious institutions with exclusive membership like the Royal Academy, to the commercial galleries of art dealers.[11] Numerous chartered bodies which formed at the beginning of the century—the Old Water-Colour Society (1804 to the present), the British Institution (1806–1867), and the Society of British Artists (1824 to the present, under various names)—were founded in response to the abuses of the Royal Academy.[12] Many artists, writers, and critics had attacked the Royal Academy, from its foundation in 1769 onward, for the bias of its forty artist members, who determined the taste of the times and were, more often than not, totally self-serving in their artistic interests.

All of these chartered institutions, although they provided alternate exhibitions, closely followed the Royal Academy in their rules and exhibition practices and were equally exclusive, each with its own set of members and a hand-selected hanging committee. Because the emphasis was on sales and the promise of patronage, as it was at the Royal Academy, the more works an artist could show the better, an attitude which resulted in crowded exhibiting conditions.

New Bond Street, the location of the Grosvenor Gallery (fig. 3), was also the site of many art dealers, but their spaces could not compete with that of the Grosvenor, which took up not one but two shopfronts. Most of the other galleries were small spaces, the width of one shopfront, with just one principal room for showing works of art, usually on the ground

3. *New Bond Street*,
c. 1885. Photograph.
Guildhall Library,
Corporation of London

4. *Monsieur Jean
Baptiste Isabey's Gallery,
Exhibition Room, 61 Pall
Mall, 1820.* Aquatint.
Guildhall Library,
Corporation of London

floor, as illustrated in the engraving of Isabey's Gallery in Pall Mall (fig. 4). Hence, these galleries could not compete with the Grosvenor in terms of its palatial scale.

The organizers of the Dudley Gallery (1865–1918?), the New British Institution (1870–1876), and the Supplementary Exhibition (1869–1871) intended their institutions to be rivals to the Royal Academy but, unlike the Grosvenor Gallery, they still followed its crowded hanging standards.[13] The Dudley Gallery's variety of exhibitions included a spring watercolor show, a winter oil exhibition, and an exhibition devoted to prints and drawings. The gallery consisted of one small room inside the larger Egyptian Hall, which housed numerous events and popular spectacles.[14] The New British Institution maintained a practice which Lindsay would later emphasize at the Grosvenor—special attention to non-Academicians, who included Alphonse Legros and John Roddam Spencer Stanhope, a later special feature of the Grosvenor. Despite these promising alternatives, this showcase was short-lived.[15] The Supplementary Exhibition had attempted to organize a new society of artists, but it featured mainly works that the Royal Academy had rejected.[16] These three sites catered to the same group of artists, the organizers understanding the artists' need to seek every available outlet for showing their works.[17]

The Royal Academy, the main arena in which a British artist could achieve a reputation, was in a steady decline in the 1870s even before the Grosvenor opened, its deterioration partly if not wholly due to the types of art it promoted as "a matter of sentiment and anecdote."[18] The middle-class public which frequented the Academy's exhibitions wanted works which told narratives about their own Victorian lives in great detail, appropriately called "subject pictures," and the Academicians readily complied. These images tugged at the heartstrings of the Victorian viewing public, informing or educating them about the tragedies and triumphs of life. Dennis Cooper states of the Academic scene: "Pictures were judged by their subject matter; few artists were interested in painting natural scenes; and no attempt was made to exploit the suggestive or sensuous properties of oil-paint. Every painter, it seems, subscribed only too gladly to Wilkie's cynical formula that 'to know the taste of the public, to learn what will best please the employer, is to the artists the most valuable of knowledge.'"[19]

Great masters were also on the wane. By the 1870s the two great landscapists, J. M. W. Turner and John Constable, were dead and had left no followers, and the Pre-Raphaelite Brotherhood, the other English stronghold of talent, had split as a group, losing its impact in the process. John Everett Millais, who had shown such great early promise in his Pre-Raphaelite experiments, had become an Academician and had begun to produce works ripe with Victorian sentimentality. Few people could see Dante Gabriel Rossetti's Pre-Raphaelite imagery, as he relied on private patrons and never showed his works. William Holman Hunt rejected the Academy as a venue altogether, using independent galleries to show his religious paintings; he later became a Grosvenor Gallery exhibitor. Even after the Grosvenor had opened and introduced its principal figures, such as Burne-Jones, who was the important link to the first-generation Pre-Raphaelites and the one who resurrected the idea of a British school of painting, the middle-class public's desire for melodramatic subject pictures prevailed over both the interest in old masters and in the Pre-Raphaelites' imagery. Gerald Reitlinger, in his examination of picture prices and changing taste during this period, has observed: "As the 1880s opened, the Royal Academy subject-picture dominated the salerooms, rivalling the Turner cult and almost extinguishing the Old Masters. . . . Yet to the more sensitive sort of patron the pictures were distressing. But unless he moved in a very sophisticated circle, escape was not easy for him. To travel in the company of Burne-Jones and Rossetti into the world of Dante . . . was to invite the reproach of being artistic, the greatest insult which could be hurled at a middle-class family in the classic age of the British matron, when to admire Botticelli was to be thought a cissy."[20] Sir Coutts's gallery provided an opportunity for careful contemplation of individual artists and individual objects that was not the experience of the Royal Academy visitor, bombarded as he or she would be by the floor-to-ceiling arrangement of safe, happy family pictures. Further, unlike Wilkie's edict for Royal Academicians, which emphasized acknowledgement of the taste of the public over the personal interests of the artist, Lindsay's artists were concerned first and foremost with their own expression unhindered by any barriers of delicacy imposed by a largely moral middle-class public. This attitude signaled a revolution in the role of the artist during the late Victorian period, at least through Lindsay's vision. The *Daily News* critic discusses this conflict of artistic interests in the first summer exhibition at the Grosvenor Gallery: "The pictures may please the learned, but they are not what the public is accustomed to. The spectator feels inclined to cry anxiously, 'Where is the baby?' for babies and cradles are but inadequately represented in the Grosvenor Gallery.

This is not as it should be; this is not in accordance with the practice of the Royal Academy and with the traditions of British art."[21]

Many artists who exhibited at the Grosvenor Gallery challenged the middle-class consumers who frequented the Academy with an art that no longer reflected such safe, carefully constructed, devout lives. Through their dedication to "high art," these artists' iconography and subjects were often obscure if not altogether unknown to the average viewer (especially myth and legends). Such seemingly mysterious and self-absorbed choices alienated them from a Victorian audience brought up on sentimental tales and moralizing anecdotal paintings. Other Grosvenor artists challenged the status quo in formalistic concerns through their exploitation of painting in and of itself. Artists who exhibited at the Grosvenor from

5. Linley Sambourne, "Welcome, Little Stranger!" *Punch*, May 12, 1877. Wood engraving.
Yale Center for British Art, Gift of Henry S. Morgan

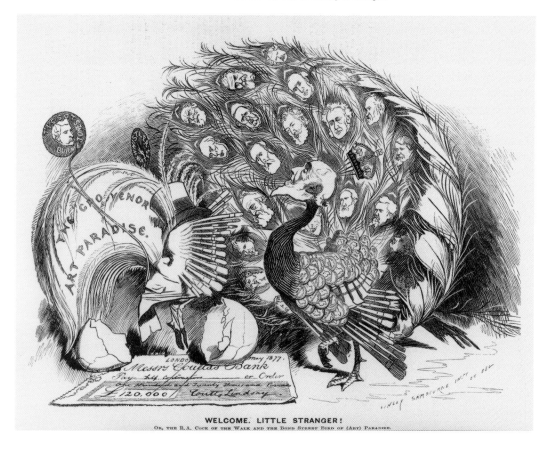

WELCOME. LITTLE STRANGER!
Or, the R.A. Cock of the Walk and the Bond Street Bird of (Art) Paradise.

1880 onward tended to have received their artistic training abroad rather than in the declining English art schools and thus turned to natural landscape and outdoor lighting. These efforts repelled the average Victorian patron, who perceived their works as foreign and imitative of French examples. Hence, these artists had to find new patronage through Lindsay's support.[22]

While Hallé, one of Lindsay's gallery assistants, later insisted that Lindsay did not found the Grosvenor in opposition to the Royal Academy, the Academicians were nonetheless uncomfortable with its presence.[23] For example, Hallé recorded the annoyance of one particularly important Academician, Frederic Leighton, over the plans for the Grosvenor: "He told Sir Coutts that it was a pity to draw off so much good work from the Academy, and finally added that he considered his conduct unpatriotic. . . . After a time they calmed down and eventually Leighton promised some of his works to our first exhibition."[24]

Linley Sambourne's *Punch* cartoon "Welcome, Little Stranger!" (fig. 5) indicated that the Academy and the Grosvenor were on pleasant terms of rivalry. During the early years of the Grosvenor Gallery's history the critics were concerned with how the Grosvenor compared with the Royal Academy rather that with any other existing institution. Despite Lindsay's goal to sponsor artists who, for the most part, found themselves excluded from the Academy, his endeavor was seen as a threat.

By the time William Thomas Sams was building the Grosvenor in 1876, the chartered institutions remained, although they limited their members, and the independent efforts (except for the Dudley Gallery) had all closed. The Dudley could hardly compete in scale or scope with the new Grosvenor Gallery, however. At the same time, the Royal Academy and its schools were slipping into decline. In terms of artistic developments and exhibition opportunities, Sir Coutts Lindsay and his "palace of art" arrived on the scene at a timely moment.

The first summer exhibition opened on May 1, 1877, and closed on July 31. These summer exhibitions were the most essential in determining the contemporary artists of merit, and they included experiments in painting, sculpture, and watercolor (and sometimes prints). These shows also coincided with the summer exhibitions of the Royal Academy. While Lindsay and his assistants promoted contemporary artists within the summer exhibitions, their winter exhibitions sometimes mixed living artists with old masters and recently deceased masters of British and foreign schools. The gallery also held fall exhibitions in its last three years of existence, mostly dedicated to pastels.

In his formulation of a gallery, Lindsay's exhibition policies were unlike those of any other establishment in England.[25] His dual purpose in opening the gallery was to bring about artistic reform and exhibition reform, both in the young and neglected artists he chose to present, including women artists, watercolorists (of which the women formed a chief part), and decorative works, but also in how he organized their works on the walls of a gallery which itself was a work of art. He wanted to provide a kingly residence that would signal the magnificence within which one should contemplate individual objects and individual talents.

Similarly revolutionary were his tactics in terms of gathering these artists. He admitted artists by invitation only, rather than through the juried systems which discouraged young talent at other venues. Further, he made no restrictions on the number of works an artist could show and he allowed them to choose which works they wanted to exhibit.[26] In this context, Lindsay emphasized his support of artists who were "either unable or unwilling to exhibit elsewhere," and he stressed that "there are several thoughtful men in London whose ideas and method of embodying them are strange to us; but I do not think strangeness, or even eccentricity of method, a sufficient excuse for ignoring the works of men otherwise notable."[27] Lindsay was promoting a gallery suitable for an avant-garde group who would be unacceptable to the uninitiated. Lindsay's commitment to an elite group is expressed most succinctly in his comments in the *Times* in March 1877, where he claimed that his artists would be too "ascetic" to find a place on the Academy walls and that these painters of a "sensitive fiber" had to be treated with "indul-

"THE LAST STRAW!"

Polite Stranger (to Smorlt, as he is removing his rejected Picture from the Cellars of Burlington House). "PRAY, SIR, CAN YOU KINDLY INFORM ME WHEN THE—AH—ROYAL ACADEMY EXHIBITION OF PICTURES OPENS TO THE PUBLIC ? ! !"

6. Charles Keene, "The Last Straw!" *Punch*, May 12, 1877.
Wood engraving. Yale Center for British Art, Gift of Henry S. Morgan

gence and consideration," if Lindsay's efforts on their behalf were to succeed.[28] Thus, his artists became his own set of royalty, pampered and sheltered in an exclusive palace suited to their delicate tastes and sense of refinement.

The Grosvenor's innovations separated it from the venerable Academy in terms of both its attitude toward its artists and its exhibition practices. Whereas the Academy had works brought to them to be judged by the forty-member selection committee, at the Grosvenor, after Lindsay and his assistants sent out invitations, Hallé and Carr would go from studio to studio to pick up the canvases.[29] This system was more practical for the artists and less costly than the Royal Academy arrangements. Charles Keene's *Punch* illustration "The Last Straw!" (fig. 6) satirizes the inconvenience, not to mention the embarrassment, of the Academy's

scheme. Here the Academicians have rejected the poor artist, who has had to retrieve his work. It is no coincidence that this image dates from May 1877, the very time when the Grosvenor opened to the public and, hence, a time when the contrast between the two venues would have been most acute. However, the system of invitations was not always ideal. Lindsay had many applications from artists, just as modern-day galleries receive applications from aspiring artists, but he also had to accept the requests of one of the gallery's main patrons, the Prince of Wales, so that some individuals forced his hand on occasion.[30] Despite such occasional compromises, Lindsay's system of inviting specific artists to show in his gallery resembles the acquisition methods of the modern-day museum director, who handpicks artists for the collection.

Further, at the Royal Academy, there was no system such as special memberships to honor patrons, though there was a system to honor artists. The main body of Academicians elected artist members (designated first as Associate Member, then as Full Member, depending on their success). At the Grosvenor there was no such practice to create competition for prestige among artists. There was, however, a system of supporting members, initiated in 1877, who were entitled to a special seasonal ticket for admission at any time, including Sundays, and the number of such members was limited to five hundred. Subsequently lists of prospective supporting members were given to this group of original members, who then voted. This system acknowledged the support of a select public and invited them to participate, as art galleries and museums still do today, in sustaining the efforts of gallery patronage.[31]

Lindsay did not organize his gallery for commercial profit, an approach that was very different from the emphasis on sales which prevailed at art dealers' establishments and at the Academy. Admission to the gallery (one shilling) and season tickets (five shillings), along with the sale of catalogues, was, at least initially, the sole means through which the Lindsays regained their financial outlay on the building campaign and kept the gallery running.[32] In addition, Lindsay charged only a 5 percent commission on any sale made. He did not take out copyrights on artists' works, nor did he charge artists to use the space, as was the case at other institutions of the period.[33] Pictures marked as being the property of the artist were generally for sale, and they were advertised this way in the gallery catalogues. Artists gave sale prices to the secretary of the gallery, from whom a potential buyer could request the sum. In addition, works loaned from private collections were shown alongside works which were for sale. Lindsay instituted this practice to give a broader representation of an artist's works from year to year. The act of displaying works from private collections reflected the gallery's role as a site for the recognition of these class tastes. The works represented "pictures to see," for the most part, rather than "pictures to sell" (an attitude revealed in the passage that "more behold than buy" in the *Punch* poem), much like the pre-Revolutionary French Salon.[34] In this sense the Grosvenor practices emulated the original exclusivity of the French Salon, where artists "consented to show to a limited public some pictures commissioned in advance for a specific destination."[35] Although Lindsay located the Grosvenor Gallery within the art marketplace district, its aristocratic air and its inclusion of works from private collections set it apart. Similarly, in speaking of the differences in audience for the French Salon and the Triennale exhibitions in Paris in the 1880s, Mainardi has recognized this same distinction: "The more frequent would be inclusive [regular Salon], the less frequent one [Triennale] would be exclusive. . . . In the politico-aesthetic language of the nineteenth century, the first would serve the 'democracy' of art, the other would serve its 'aristocracy.'"[36] As Bourdieu has observed of this process, the elite is likely to abandon any institution if it becomes too democratic—by doing so, it negates the privileged position of that elite class.[37] This was one reason why critics immediately associated the Grosvenor with upper-class tastes, a discernment reinforced by this pattern of selecting works from private palaces to place on view.

THE PALACE

The term "palace of art" was first used to describe the Manchester Art Treasures Exhibition held in 1857, and, as a result, "the idea of the 'Palace of Art,' with its connotations of wealth and splendour and its implication that paintings should be shown in buildings of a special character, with their function externally identifiable and their interiors appropriately lit, planned and decorated, remained an expectation of patrons and public in this country from the late eighteenth century until at least the First World War."[38] Although it remained an expectation and was not always a reality, it was the reality at the Grosvenor. Just how this grandiosity was conveyed to the Grosvenor audiences is, in part, symbolized in the entrance doorway by Palladio (fig. 7), formerly belonging to the Church of Santa Lucia at Venice, which harmonized with the Italian Renaissance style of the façade. This entrance revealed Lindsay's concerns to pro-

7. Horace Harral,
"The Grosvenor Gallery, New Bond Street—The Entrance,"
The Graphic, May 19, 1877. Wood engraving (cat. 22)

mote himself as a modern-day Maecenas or Renaissance patron (in fact, Walter Crane called him the "modern day Lorenzo" in honor of the Medici role that he took on, and the *Punch* poem assigned him "a Leo's part").[39] An early engraving shows the façade elevation of the gallery (see fig. 2); a contemporary photograph shows minor changes in the completed version (fig. 8) with the later doorway added in 1925.

The interior, indicated in this ground-floor plan (fig. 9), was in complete aesthetic agreement with the façade, lending a further air of upper-class extravagance to the building. The entrance hall (laid out in the plan) was flanked with green Genoan marble columns and Ionic pilasters, which led to a flight of steps fifteen feet wide (fig. 10), with pedestals for statues on both sides.[40] In addition, Lindsay located a large dining-room directly beneath the main gallery,

8. *The Grosvenor Gallery Façade, with 1925 Doorway*, 1993. Photograph. Courtesy of the Paul Mellon Centre, London

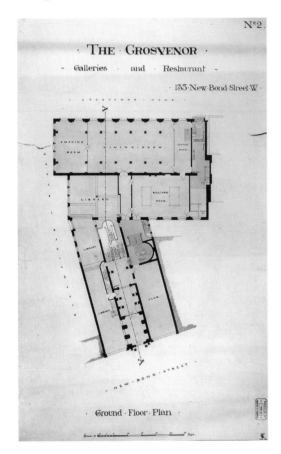

9. *Ground Floor Plan, the Grosvenor Galleries and Restaurant, 1889.* Corporation of London, Greater London Record Office

10. *Stairway, Aeolian Hall Interior (formerly the Grosvenor Gallery)*, 1904. Photograph. Guildhall Library, Corporation of London

also on the ground floor. In keeping with the ornateness of the entrance, Sams divided it into a nave with aisles by two rows of Scagiola columns with gilt capitals, eight on each side.

The elaborate staircase, which one took upstairs after visiting the dining room, leads in to the galleries themselves. The West Gallery, measuring 104 by 35 feet, seen in the first-floor plan (fig. 11) and in an interior view (fig. 12), was the principal space. Natural light flooded in from the skylight during the day, and gas jets (later, electricity) lighted it during the evening. Sams divided the ceiling, which James McNeill Whistler may have decorated, into bays painted in a deep blue, each bay or panel representing a phase of the moon accompanied by gold stars.[41] The frieze, designed by Lindsay, consisted of cherubs holding fruits and flowers. Sams di-

vided the walls with sixteen Ionic pilasters of richly gilt oak, which Lindsay had salvaged from the foyer of the old Italian Opera House in Paris. As a background for the paintings, Lindsay covered the walls with a Lyons silk damask in deep scarlet, which was richly embossed with infoliated patterns. There was a hanging area of seventeen and a half feet between the dado and frieze. The engraving renders quite accurately the effect of the damask, which shows the tasteful, uncrowded arrangements of the works between the pilasters. Lindsay left some breathing room between pictures (at least six but preferably twelve inches). For the dado below the pictures, Lindsay called for a stamped deep green velvet. In addition, the Lindsays hung portières of a white print on a dark blue ground at the entrances to the gallery.

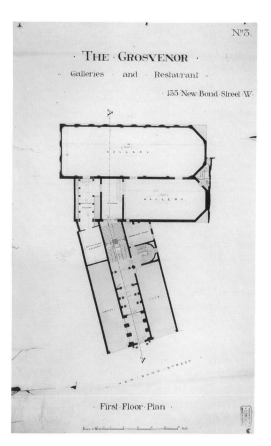

11. *First Floor Plan, the Grosvenor Galleries and Restaurant, 1889.* Corporation of London, Greater London Record Office

12. "The Grosvenor Gallery of Fine Art, New Bond Street," *Illustrated London News*, May 5, 1877. Wood engraving. Yale Center for British Art, Paul Mellon Collection

The East gallery on the first floor was the smaller of the two main spaces, measuring sixty by twenty-eight feet. A velarium controlled the light from the exterior of the building, something seldom before tried in a picture gallery of this scale in London. Velaria, tentlike drapings used to tone down the light, could be seen in smaller London galleries, such as in Isabey's Gallery, Pall Mall, and Benjamin West's galleries from the late eighteenth century, but there the velaria were hung on the inside, which created an oppressive atmosphere. The East Gallery was similar in its decoration to the West Gallery, its doorways also draped with portières of a white print on dark blue ground. Although in its first year the Lindsays papered this gallery in crimson silk damask, due to the protests from such artists as Burne-Jones, they subsequently redid it in olive green.[42]

Walking across the first-floor vestibule, where works were sometimes hung, one entered the sculpture gallery, a small room thirty-five by eighteen feet. This gallery possessed top-lighted recesses for the display of statuary in the alcoves, with yellow marble columns supporting a cornice and a barrel-vaulted ceiling, the walls lined with olive-green. Adjacent was an intimate room of twenty-four by fifteen feet, softly lit, for showing watercolors.

The basement plan (fig. 13) shows one of the gallery's main attractions, the restaurant, which did a good business and also served as a site for the mingling of important patrons, society, and artists. In addition, the basement and the first floor housed special amenities for the visitor, which included buffet bars, billiard rooms, smoking rooms for the gentlemen, a circulating library (added in 1880), and a gentlemen's club (added in 1885 as the Clergy Club but later called the Grosvenor Club), and, in its later years, a ladies' club.[43]

HANGING AND DISPLAY
Complementary to this tasteful decoration, Lindsay's hanging practices gave special attention to each artistic talent. One of the chief problems with the annual summer exhibitions of both the Royal Academy (fig. 14) and the French Salon was lack of sufficient space to

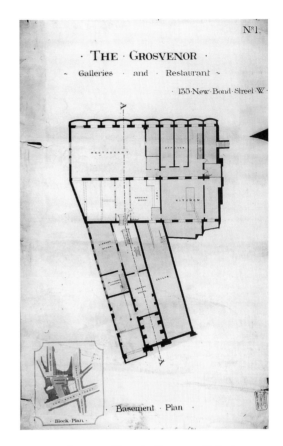

13. *Basement Plan, the Grosvenor Galleries and Restaurant, 1889.* Corporation of London, Greater London Record Office

show works adequately. The "ceilinged" arrangements at these institutions had prevailed for over one hundred years and were often disastrous for the works of art on view; no space remained between paintings, and unfavorable or even controversial works, when accepted for exhibit at all, were hung close to the ceiling so as not to be seen. Critics continually ridiculed the Royal Academy throughout the nineteenth century for this reason. Lord Henry Wotton tells artist Basil Hallward in Oscar Wilde's *Picture of Dorian Gray*: "It is your best work, Basil, the best thing you have ever done. You must certainly send it next year to the Grosvenor. The Academy is too large and too vulgar. Whenever I have gone there, there have been either so many people that I have not been able to see the pictures, which was dreadful, or so many pictures that I have not been able to see the people,

14. George B. O'Neill, *Public Opinion*, c. 1863.
Oil on canvas. Leeds City Art Galleries

which was worse. The Grosvenor is really the only place."[44] Wilde encapsulates the cultural importance Lindsay attributed to art as a distinctly upper-class experience, as well as the important role of innovative hanging practices in creating the kind of atmosphere in which such a class was most comfortable. In this passage Wilde suggests that the Grosvenor Gallery was superior to the Royal Academy because of its rejection of the vulgar, coarse, and popular. Wilde's view reflects Bourdieu's studies of "the sacred sphere of culture," that is, the upper classes, which denies such "lower, coarse, vulgar, venal, servile—in a word, natural—enjoyment." In fact, for Bourdieu this denial marks the superiority of those who seek beyond the popular, such as Wilde himself (here representing the most devoted Grosvenor worshiper), who search instead for "the sublimated, refined, disinterested, gratuitous, distinguished pleasures forever closed to the profane." This paradigm is precisely what Lindsay set up at the Grosvenor at the outset, and this claim of supe-

riority is what defines the gallery's mission. According to Bourdieu, "art and cultural consumption are predisposed, consciously and deliberately or not, to fulfill a social function of legitimating social differences."[45] In this regard, not only the appearance of the gallery but also its method of display held class codes for the viewer.

Hence, the Grosvenor, in its efforts to achieve the "sublimated" and "refined" importance of art and culture, created a select hanging practice, one which did away with the controversial "line" of the Salon and Academy, the line being the area roughly at eye level which was meant to be the most advantageous height at which to have one's work positioned. Lindsay's hanging concept was more than just an aesthetic decision; he developed an arrangement which commanded power and authority by transforming the gridlock of floor-to-ceiling pictures at the Academy and other institutions (that is, the idea of the art object as just simply another commodity, tied to the middle-class attitudes of the Royal Academy audience) into one devoted to an individual object.[46] Lindsay's system was the first in London to achieve some breathing room between pictures.

In this kind of arrangement, Lindsay gave over the authority to the artist by placing an artist's works together on one wall, a practice which was seldom carried out at other venues of the period.[47] He hung an artist's works all together or in one or two separate groups. The interior (see fig. 12) shows, for example, pilasters lining the walls as a way of dividing each artist's works. Such organization resulted, for the first time, in the realization of artist as creator, a concept strengthened by the fact that an artist could show his or her works in miniretrospective fashion from year to year.[48] Contemporary accounts testify to this recognition of individual "creators," such as that of Mary S. Watts, George Frederic Watts's second wife (Watts had been a regular Royal Academy exhibitor prior to the Grosvenor Gallery opening):

Afterwards came the consciousness that the work of some English painters of the day was being revealed to the public for the first time . . . in the setting of this well-conceived building each was being allowed to deliver his message consecutively, and *the visitor was not called upon to listen to him between other and conflicting voices, or to hear from him nothing but a broken sentence.* The works of each artist, grouped together and divided by blank spaces, allowed the spectator's eye and mind to be absorbed entirely by what that painter had to give them. . . . Those who had cared to search the Academy walls, season after season, for the work of George Frederic Watts . . . stood before the end of the West Gallery wall, and hailed their master. . . . It was not too much to say that now to a larger public, beyond the circle of his friends, the mind of the painter was speaking for the first time.[49] (emphasis added)

Thus, through this aesthetic decision-making practice, Lindsay's gallery became the first location to recognize the artist as individual genius. The audience could study a body of work in chronological fashion, both in individual exhibits and by following that artist from year to year on the walls of this gallery. Gordon Fyfe emphasizes the great impact of such display tactics in manipulating the audience,

stating that "the relationship of the artist to exhibition consumer/visitor is one of power and persuasion for it is associated with a growing pre-occupation with the requisite strategies (gallery arrangement, decor, lighting, etc.) for determining the encounter between pictures and the public gaze. The visitor's eye is now constituted in relation to the authority of the artist," rather than the authority of the institution, as was the case with the Salon and Academy.[50] In this process, Lindsay, working together with Blanche and his assistants, determined the layout of the exhibits from year to year. In some cases they used models of the galleries, placing miniature versions of the artwork within those spaces to achieve the desired distribution.

To lend further visual credence to these galleries in terms of such power and authority, Lindsay constructed and lighted them according to the system adopted by Captain Francis Fowke for the Exhibition Building at the 1862 International Exhibition at South Kensington (fig. 15).[51] The architectural community considered Fowke's building retardataire in its engineering (unforgivable in a building at a World's Fair); its scale was its only saving grace.[52] In his search for an atmosphere that would allow artists to command a presence, Lindsay exploited the scale of Fowke's building. The Grosvenor's system further mirrored Fowke's gallery in its discerning proportion of wall space to frieze to skylight. However, in Fowke's building, the gridlock hanging method remained. Whereas one is overwhelmed by pictures in Fowke's gallery, in Lindsay's gallery one has space to admire individual talents.

Although Lindsay's experiments in display aesthetics were singular, another possible source for his new approach to exhibition strategies may have been the National Gallery in Trafalgar Square, founded in 1824. Sir Charles Eastlake, one of the museum's directors, lamented the crowded hanging arrangements of his galleries and worked continually to improve these conditions, due in part, ironically enough, to the fact that the Royal Academy occupied one half of the building during his directorship.[53] The E. M. Barry block of the National Gallery, finished in 1876, reflects

15. Captain F. Fowke,
*Exhibition Building in
1862: Picture Gallery,
interior in 1862.*
Photograph. Courtesy
of the Board of Trustees
of the Victoria &
Albert Museum

Eastlake's legacy (fig. 16). Its elegant selection of maroon hangings, with its palatial scale, works hung at or near eye level, and skylighting paralleled the system Lindsay installed at the Grosvenor.[54] That his gallery is closer in its appearance to a museum than to an art gallery indicates how Lindsay sought to honor artists as significant contributors both to the history of art and to artistic dialogues, just as the museum does.

Similarly inspirational for Lindsay's design aesthetics was the South Kensington Museum, where Richard Redgrave planned the National Competition Gallery in 1865. In Redgrave's scheme there was no dado; however, the division of the room into distinct bays separated by pilasters, surmounted by decorative painted friezes in arches above, closely paralleled the sumptuous and tasteful organization of Lindsay's gallery.[55] In his promotion of a new system of aesthetic presentation, Lindsay was breaking with a tradition that was at least one hundred years old and, in so doing, he created a kind of space and arrangement which museums still use today, one in which the followers of a particular artist can appreciate his or her achievements.

ARISTOCRATIC RITUALS AND SITES
The building's location, personally selected by Lindsay, contributed to its ability to draw patrons as well as to its reputation as a palace of art. The Bond Street area was a tasteful combination of fashion and commerce—a strategic location for a gallery whose owner wished to encourage the fine arts and gain exposure and patronage for artists who were largely unseen in official arenas. London was the most exciting place to be during the "season," a time of year when debonair escorts took debutantes to balls and dinners and leading hostesses vied for the most spectacular guest lists. A tourist guide from 1879 attests: "London should be seen in May, June, and July; three months which include what is called 'the Season.' In May, the Royal Academy Exhibition opens.—The Court is in residence.—The Queen or Prince of Wales holds Drawing-rooms or Levees.—The Parliament is sitting.—The Opera in mid-season. —Concerts and other public entertainments daily.—the town is full." This handbook also lists "objects of interest," including the Grosvenor Gallery, and recommends when to attend—before eleven in the morning. This was good advice, considering that during its first season, the Grosvenor's daily attendance was

16. Giuseppe Gabrielli,
*Room 32 in the National
Gallery*, 1886. Oil on
canvas. Government Art
Collection, London

about 1,100. If one wanted to see the pictures rather than the people, one went early.[56]

There was a new mixture of classes in the seasonal invasion of London as a result of a decided change in the composition of London society itself in the 1870s. For example, prior to the 1870s, class codes made it impossible to admit businesspeople and manufacturers of the plutocracy (the parvenus, or new upper classes) into "society." This attitude changed in the 1870s because "the economic base of the landed aristocracy itself began to give way under the effects of the agricultural depression. The amount of wealth became as important a criterion of entry to Society as its source."[57] Historian of Victorian intellectual circles Thomas Heyck explains that both the landed aristocracy and the plutocracy "had something to gain by openly displaying refined aesthetic sensitivities: the landed people could reassure themselves of their importance in a time when economic and political considerations were teaching them otherwise; and the wealthy commercial people could assert a claim to genuine aristocratic standing."[58] Families who benefited from this shift of emphasis included Lady Lindsay's Rothschild relatives as well as other Jewish banking magnates. Lady Lindsay's marriage to Sir Coutts represented one of the earliest examples of this

mixed-marriage trend in Victorian culture.[59] Such an intermarriage was also a sign of the economic situation of the times, for while Lindsay was not suffering financially, he may have joined with Blanche in part because of growing insecurities about his land-based wealth. Many members of the aristocracy joined with banking families and the new industrialists for the support those associations provided.[60] Bourdieu argues that the parvenus, such as Lady Lindsay, as opposed to those who were born to the upper class, such as Sir Coutts, had to make an extra effort to achieve the graces of "cultural capital." The Lindsays' awareness of class shifts and their own rather controversial position may have forced them, in opening their gallery, to prove their equal cultural heritage and appreciation of the arts. In their public personas as gallery owners they could promote the value of their own class intermarriage and the validity of its tastes.[61]

In this context, the gallery was located in an area of London, as shown in the bird's-eye view of St. James's Street and Old and New Bond streets (fig. 17), which encapsulated the fashionable invasion for this London season, meaning the gallery would have high visibility. Bond Street was recognized as the center of the fashionable district of London even in the

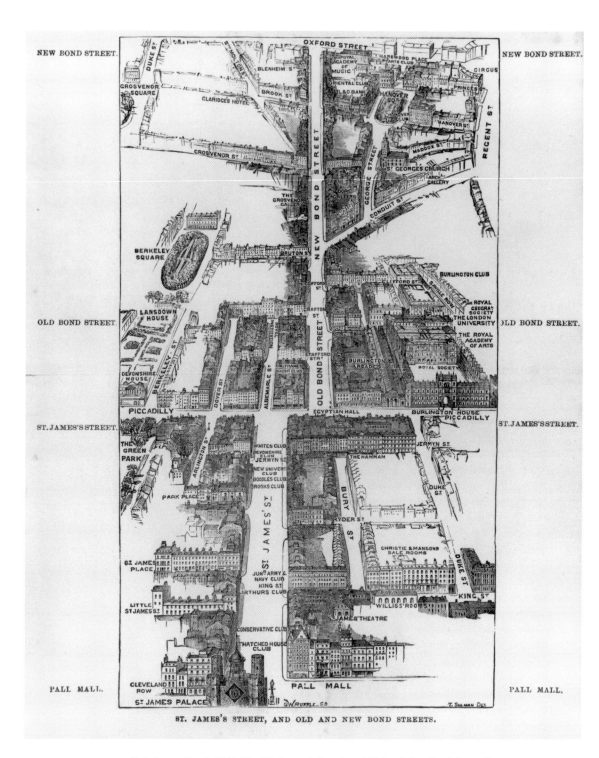

17. T. Sulman after G. W. Ruffle, "St. James's Street, and Old and New Bond Street,"
1889, from Herbert Fry, *London in 1889*. Wood engraving.
Yale Center for British Art, Paul Mellon Collection

eighteenth century; today many famous jew-
elers, designer clothing stores, picture galleries,
and auction houses still line the street and attract wealthy customers and celebrities. When
the Grosvenor Gallery opened, the Bond Street
area was a tasteful combination of fashion and
commerce—a strategic location for a gallery
whose owner wished to encourage the fine arts
and gain exposure and patronage for artists who
were largely unseen in official arenas.

Not only did private and public events take
place in this part of London, but also the upper
classes who made up this society lived in or
leased houses in this area for the season.[62] The
society which constituted the London season
wanted others to see them at the elegant
Grosvenor Gallery, and not to receive a private
invitation or have a special season ticket was
considered a great social disadvantage. The
gallery was such a success that it apparently
passed 7,000 people through its stiles on
opening day alone.[63]

In the formation of his palace, Lindsay was
trying to create a home away from home for
these classes who enjoyed the season—a kind of
aristocratic retreat or, as Fyfe phrases it, "aristocratic retrenchment."[64] Toward this end
Lindsay emulated the atmosphere of the aristocratic home. It was a palace of domestic
comforts, like the English country house, with
all of its associated rituals. A contemporary
account reveals the nature of this "aristocratic
retrenchment" at the Grosvenor: "Pottery and
china, and groups of plants are disposed about
the rooms, some to heighten the impression that
this is not a public picture exhibition, but rather
a patrician's private gallery shown by courtesy
of its owner; indeed so studiously are the business arrangements kept out of sight, that but for
the inevitable turnstiles and catalogue-keepers
the illusion would be complete."[65]

Thus Lindsay took on the role of aristocratic host, as if he were inviting friends in for a
long weekend in order to enjoy his private collection of pictures. Lindsay understood the
important connection between space and class,
and he attempted to duplicate the extravagant
features of the private palace of art in order to
draw these classes to the gallery and, consequently, keep out the lower classes.

Hallé reveals Lindsay's underlying inten-
tions in creating such a palace of art:

A picture is, or is supposed to be, a beautiful decorative object. In old days, when architects had finished
their work, painters were called in to enhance the
beauty of churches and palaces. Their works were not
regarded merely as specimens of certain schools or
manners of painting, to be ranged in museums or
picture-galleries, much as an entomologist might
arrange his butterflies in the drawers of his cabinet. It
was to maintain this decorative value of pictures that
Sir Coutts built and furnished his gallery in a sumptuous manner, and had the pictures arranged for
public exhibition as nearly as possible as though they
formed the decoration of the walls of the house he
lived in, and could live in with pleasure. Would any
sane person elect to spend twenty-four hours in an
ordinary exhibition-room of modern pictures, where
the works are plastered together from floor to ceiling
as tightly as the frames can be made to fit?[66]

In the West Gallery, the shapes, sizes, and
subjects of the art objects reflect the decorative
purpose, as the artists created many of them
specifically as wall panels to be inserted into
spaces of people's homes.[67]

That Lindsay had the aristocrat's personal
picture gallery in mind as he designed his
gallery is evident from several examples. These
private galleries conformed to a certain code, as
in Robert Huskisson's painting *Lord Northwick's
Picture Gallery at Thirlestaine House* (fig. 18)
and Grosvenor House (fig. 19), city home of the
Duke of Westminster. Such private galleries
usually consisted of a rectangular room; a skylight lit it from above, and the side walls of the
rectangle were longer than the end wall to allow
for adequate hanging space for the pictures.
Some owners, in emulation of their Renaissance
palace forebears, as in the case of Grosvenor
House, included a columned section at either
end to set off a particularly important work of
art.[68] Lindsay emulated this rectangular
arrangement, and Grosvenor House may have
been the source for the crimson damask he used
on his walls since both examples use this same
wall coloring. Both spaces included tasteful
furnishings. The Lindsays adorned their entire
building with a similarly rich array of Rococo
chairs, consoles, chairs of Italian design, and
Persian rugs. The floors were of parquetrie

work in dark colors and quiet patterns; these helped to create rooms of a striking effect, similar to aristocrats' private picture galleries. The Lindsays included these furnishings in part to encourage the private contemplation of art. Although the cramped spaces of other exhibition buildings in Britain did not always encourage such a frame of mind, Isabey's Gallery did earlier in the century; the tasteful spaces of the Grosvenor similarly encouraged such meditation. For example, the Lindsays placed movable furniture in the galleries so that visitors could arrange chairs to sit in front of individual pictures for close study.[69]

Architects designed large city estates such as Grosvenor House with grand entrances to accommodate hundreds of visitors during the season for elaborate receptions, teas, suppers, and balls. Giles Waterfield argues that, in reference to the Grosvenor's elaborate entrance and stairway up to the galleries, "the creation of processional routes or indeed the simulation of

18. Robert Huskisson, *Lord Northwick's Picture Gallery at Thirlestaine House*, c. 1846–47. Oil on canvas. Yale Center for British Art, Paul Mellon Collection (cat. 25)

19. Charles Robert Leslie, *The Grosvenor Family*, 1823. Oil on canvas. By kind permission of His Grace The Duke of Westminster DL

a sense of occasion in the arriving visitor were most satisfactorily worked out in such ambitious non-museum enterprises as the Grosvenor Gallery."[70] How better to mark the majestic entrance of his visitors than through such a symbolic palatial portal and path, much like the ceremonial path one would take to meet royalty in their private palace.

Another specific feature which Lindsay incorporated in imitation of the aristocratic home (and very unusual for a gallery) was the billiard room, on the ground floor opposite the library and adjacent to the dining room and smoking room. The billiard room became popular in private houses after 1815; by 1870 private country homeowners considered them a normal feature of their homes.[71] Increasingly gentlemen enjoyed the billiard room as a male preserve, although in the more progressive circles women enjoyed playing also.

The smoking room became popular at the same time as the billiard room, and it was yet another feature of the Grosvenor establishment. Smoking rooms were located on the ground floor next to the dining room and in the basement adjacent to the bar and the smoking room. This, too, was an unusual addition for an art gallery. Like the billiard room, it was a male preserve. Smoking was not entirely acceptable during the early Victorian period; gentlemen

who wanted to smoke (ladies never partook) had to go outdoors.[72] Prince Albert had a special smoking room built at Osborne in 1845, and by the 1850s, due to the male domination of both activities, billiards and smoking rooms were placed adjacent for the convenience of male guests (although at the Grosvenor Gallery they were separated on the ground floor by the dining room). Apparently, the Prince of Wales followed Albert's example—considering his love of a good cigar, he "did even more than his father to make smoking a fashionable upper-class vice."[73] By installing a billiard room and a smoking room (on two levels) Lindsay was appealing to an upper-class taste, including that of the Prince of Wales, who was one of his chief supporters.[74] Many aristocrats' smoking rooms were incredibly elaborate, employing a Moorish decor as if to imply they were a kind of opium den. This kind of display is evident in George Du Maurier's cartoon "La Chasse aux Lions" (fig. 20), in which Ponsonby de Tomkyns's smoking room has a dramatic appearance, including the large heraldic window. Although descriptions of the Grosvenor's billiard and smoking rooms have not survived, the rooms would have matched the opulence of the dining room and other areas of the gallery's facilities.

The circulating library was added in 1880, an innovative feature for a picture gallery and

20. George Du Maurier, "La Chasse aux Lions," *Punch*, July 12, 1879. Wood engraving. Yale Center for British Art, Gift of Henry S. Morgan

LA CHASSE AUX LIONS.

directly tied to its role as an institution of culture, reflecting Lindsay's desire to promote and erect a palace for all the arts, literature included. The library's storehouse was in the basement in two locations, with stairs leading up to the ground floor, where the library occupied the most space, covering the south side of the building. In addition, Lindsay also housed part of the library on the first floor, opposite the club added later.

Both in its location and in its circulating practices, the Grosvenor Gallery library belonged to a tradition in London which started as early as 1842 with the innovations made by Charles Edward Mudie, the owner of the famous "Select Circulating Library," to which thousands of families in the city and country subscribed.[75] Mudie was a powerful figure in the literary market, due to his ability to maintain strict censorship, as Richard Altick notes: "Mudie, a man of strong Evangelical views, could make or break an author's career by his acceptance or rejection of a new book. His favor could mean the sale of several hundred copies, a substantial part of an edition, to him alone; added to this would be a boost in retail sales if the size of Mudie's purchase were well publicized."[76] However, Altick testifies that the Grosvenor Gallery library, among others in the Bond Street area, managed "to prosper in the face of Mudie's aggressive methods."[77] Arthur Waugh, managing editor of Chapman and Hall in the early twentieth century, reported that Mudie's rivals included the Grosvenor's library, an institution which rejected the harsh censorship rules imposed by Mudie's monopolization of the circulating library industry, and allowed the readers more freedom of choice in reading materials.[78]

The Grosvenor library was successful in its lifetime partly because its offerings were extensive. At its opening in 1880, the services listed included English and foreign circulating collections, a reference collection, a holding of instrumental and vocal music, and such amenities as a reading room that provided reading and writing areas for ladies and gentlemen supplied with the most important newspapers and reviews from England, America, the colonies, and foreign countries. Lindsay also provided access to other areas of the gallery, including a ladies' drawing-room for afternoon tea, dining and luncheon rooms, and a smoking room. By placing a library within his gallery, with added attractions, Lindsay offered the gallery-goer a place to reflect and to examine the latest and newest reviews on the artists at his gallery. This system, like his other innovations, prefigured the modern museum's approach to its patrons and showed Lindsay in advance of his times as, at the same time, it connected him with the tradition of the country-house private library.[79]

A key innovation at the Grosvenor that aligned it with changes in the country estate was the introduction of electricity in 1882.[80] In 1880 private country estate owners began to use electricity; in fact, the first estate owner to have arc lamps installed was one of the Grosvenor patrons, Sir William Armstrong.[81]

By bringing modern lighting into his gallery, Lindsay was providing several benefits. First, he was helping to conserve the artworks. Although we do not know whether or not he used direct lighting, modern electricity would damage the works less than the smoke emanating from gas lamps. Second, this method guaranteed continued notoriety for the gallery, as people would flock to see a gallery lit by electricity. In addition, the new lighting techniques were in keeping with Lindsay's desire to show the works off to their best advantage. Lindsay made the evening hours a more popular time through the advent of electric light.[82]

F. M. L. Thompson's comment shows that the upper classes appreciated Lindsay's efforts to duplicate the comforts of their country homes. "The Victorian middle classes were the most home-centered group in British history; but they were easily surpassed as the most house-conscious group by the landed aristocracy, for whom the country house was not only the essential emblem of status but also the grand theater in which rituals of display and hospitality were enacted. So important were country houses to social and political position, indeed, that membership of the ruling class can be measured through ownership of country houses of specified size."[83]

The responsibility of a private country house brought with it the need to institute certain society rituals, which Lady Lindsay duplicated at the Grosvenor Gallery (at least up until 1882 when she separated from Lindsay, when the tasks were taken up by Lindsay's assistants and a new business manager). And indeed, the public recognized the Grosvenor, under Lady Lindsay's graceful hand, as a social setting for wealthy types and "the place" to be seen. Fyfe has determined that the Grosvenor sought "differentiating rituals," that is, he sees the Grosvenor exhibitions as having a role as a ritual in and of themselves, one that reproduced "the cohesion and separation of an elite culture."[84] For example, at the opening of each summer season Lady Lindsay orchestrated three separate gatherings at the gallery: a private view for intimate friends on Sunday afternoons; a private grand dinner party held in the dining room in the evening, which was followed by a personal tour of the show; and the public opening. Coinciding with one of these events would be a special press preview.[85] As Leonore Davidoff explains, not to receive a ticket to Lady Lindsay's carefully arranged private views and "at homes" was considered "a social death."[86] As with the amenities provided for visitors to the gallery, these parties mirrored the typical country house party, and also forecasted the elaborate opening galas at modern-day museums.

The banquet for the first Grosvenor opening was given on May 9, 1877, and was attended by the Prince and Princess of Wales, William Gladstone and his wife, Whistler, Albert Moore, John and Effie Millais, and more than one hundred other guests including royalty, dignitaries, and artists.[87] Like other events of the London season, the hosts carefully directed this banquet. Lord Henry Somerset wrote to his mother-in-law, recording the events of the first banquet: "The Grosvenor Gallery dinner was a great success last night. Everything was wonderfully well done. There was I should think about a hundred and fifty at dinner, which was at several large tables with Sir Coutts and some of the Royalties and particular swells at the top end and Lady Lindsay and some more Royalties at the bottom. The dinner itself was very good,

really wonderful considering the number that had to be fed, and altogether it was in every way very *well* done."[88]

Louise Jopling, a successful Grosvenor artist and Lady Lindsay's best friend, addressed how social connections benefited artists at the gallery through these elite gatherings: "We went to the Grosvenor Gallery, where we found a congregation of swells to meet the Prince and Princess. The Prince introduced me to the Princess, and she was very nice, and liked my picture so much. I was introduced to Prince Leopold too, and Alec Yorke is going to bring him some day to see our Studio. I went in to tea with Prince Leopold, and the Prince of Wales cut me some cake right before the eyes of Mrs. Millais. . . . Lylie Lindsay told me that Col. Lloyd [sic] Lindsay intended buying the portrait in armour that I did of Col. Charles. . . . Prince Leopold told me that he had told Mrs. Langtry that I ought to paint her portrait, so now I think I may venture to ask her to sit."[89] This account is a good example of the means of patronage at an artist's disposal, as well as an example of how Lady Lindsay created an elite circle of admirers for her artists.

Also mirroring activities that took place in the country estate, the Lindsays originally intended to have auditoriums for concerts and other gatherings within the Grosvenor building. Although this project did not materialize, the public could hear musical concerts in the galleries during the 1880s. First these efforts were the work of Sir Charles Hallé, with the assistance of his son, and later the concerts were organized by another of Lindsay's assistants, Fairfax B. Wade.[90] The musical concerts under the senior Hallé's direction were much more successful than those under Wade's direction, and they included such stars as Franz Liszt in 1885.[91] These musical events also echoed the practices of London society hostesses, who would compete to have the best musicians present in their homes to ensure the success of their dinner parties during the season.

While all of these features align the Lindsays' work at the Grosvenor Gallery with the ambiance, status, and wealth of the upper echelons and hence gave the site its "palace" title, Sir Coutts should also be viewed as the precursor to

"MR. FIELDING, WHAT DO YOU THINK OF THESE PICTURES? THIS IS ART."

21. George Du Maurier, "Prudence at the Grosvenor," *Prudence: A Story of Aesthetic London*, by Lucy C. Lillie (New York: Harper and Brothers, 1882). Wood engraving

modern-day museum directors in terms of these same amenities, public programs, and events that he (and his wife until 1882) provided for visitors at the gallery. In fact, many modern-day museums' programming practices and activities and attention to the comforts of the public within an exhibition space owe a debt of gratitude to Lindsay's legacy at the Grosvenor. No other exhibition setting could boast the kind of programs that the Lindsays organized.

AESTHETICISM AT THE GROSVENOR GALLERY
While Lindsay duplicated, in appearance and accommodations, the private "palace of art," critics also dubbed his gallery "the Palace of the Aesthetes" because many of Lindsay's ideas mirrored those of the newly moneyed classes involved in the Aesthetic Movement. Many of these people not only owned elegant city homes, but also country estates, which were decorated by the Aesthetic circle. One example is Clouds, an estate owned by the Wyndham family, who were important patrons of many of the Grosvenor artists. Lindsay's circle of friends—writers and painters—were at the center of the Aesthetic Movement; they included Walter Pater, Dante Gabriel Rossetti, Wilde, Algernon Swinburne, and Whistler. As a group, they wanted life to imitate art. The movement affected all aspects of the arts and helped to create this new concern for taste and beauty in painting, music, theater, architecture, and home furnishings.

The Aesthetes made the Grosvenor their private palace, as illustrated in George Du Maurier's drawing from Lucy C. Lillie's 1882 novel, *Prudence: A Story of Aesthetic London* (fig. 21). The engraving shows Prudence, the young beauty engulfed by Aestheticism, at the center of a throng of young admirers in the West Gallery during a private view. The women in the far left of the picture are the wan limp models of Edward Burne-Jones's paintings, attired in the loose clothing worn by Aesthetic women.

The fact that Lindsay's gallery became the residence of Aestheticism suggests the strong possibility of other sources for it among Aesthetic Movement experiments. It is no coincidence that a woman hostess is at the center of Du Maurier's cartoon "Music and Aesthetics" (fig. 22), as critics largely credited women with the rising power of the interior design movement in the 1870s. Here, Du Maurier parodies Aestheticism and its total devotion to domestic appearances and the coveting of exquisite objects, such as the Italian mirror in the cartoon. Such influential women in the domestic design circles included the cousins Rhoda and Agnes Garrett, who made their names as designers of the Queen Anne style, a movement seen by many as a middle road be-

22. George Du Maurier, "Music and Aesthetics," *Punch*, February 16, 1878. Wood engraving. Yale Center for British Art, Gift of Henry S. Morgan

MUSIC AND ÆSTHETICS.

The Lovely and Accomplished (but extremely Short-Sighted) Madame Gelasma, yielding to the importunity of her many Admirers, bends gracefully over the Piano, and, after striking a few Chords, warbles one of Schumann's saddest Melodies in her own inimitable Manner. Unfortunately, her Host is "Æsthetic," and, more mindful of mural Decoration than beautiful Music, has fixed one of those delightful old-fashioned round Mirrors just over the Piano.—

tween the Classical style and Gothic style.[92] Coinciding with the need for advice on interior decoration, the newly moneyed middle classes desired homes in the Queen Anne style. European domestic architecture largely inspired the exteriors of these Queen Anne houses—E. W. Godwin and Richard Norman Shaw were its chief architects—but the new interest in Japanese art (brought about by the Aesthetic Movement and specifically celebrated by Rossetti and Whistler) influenced the appearance of the interiors. This was one way the Aesthetic Movement became closely allied to Lindsay's experiments at the Grosvenor, for while Lindsay's interior was decidedly not oriental in inspiration, the art of his stars (namely, Whistler, Moore, and Burne-Jones especially) was.

Through his associations and conversations with these artists, Lindsay would have been aware of the Garretts' ideas on interior decoration, which they shared with a wide audience through their publication *Suggestions for House Decoration in Painting, Woodwork, and Furniture*.[93] The Garretts' requirements for an interior included: a painted or plain frieze at the top of the room to counteract the overimpressive height of most ceilings (like Lindsay's frieze in the West Gallery); and a single color on the walls as the best background for pictures, for "the walls of the room are, after all, only the

framework of the picture, and if these are brought into too great prominence by being overloaded with ornament, however good, the harmony of the picture will be destroyed."[94] The Garretts' concerns were in part a reaction to cluttered Victorian homes, which themselves reflected the compact hanging practices of the Academy; the Victorians crammed pictures, furniture, and other objects into the spaces of dining rooms and drawing rooms and filled the walls from floor to ceiling.

Lindsay would also have known the works of another prominent figure in this interior design movement, Mary Eliza Haweis (Mrs. H. R. Haweis), who popularized the ideal aesthetic interior through her series of books, which included *The Art of Beauty* (1878), *The Art of Decoration* (1881), and *Beautiful Houses* (1882). In *The Art of Decoration* she gives a vivid description of what an interior should entail: "A room is like a picture; it must be composed with equal skill and forethought; but unlike a picture, the arrangement must revolve around to a point which is never stationary, always in motion; therefore the 'keeping' becomes a problem far harder than the colour."[95]

Lindsay was familiar with the philosophies of the forerunner of this interior design movement, William Morris. Burne-Jones, one of his chief artists, was a shareholder in Morris's company which, like the efforts of the Garretts, sought to refine Victorian tastes in the home environment. These new designs are best revealed in the London home of one of the chief patrons of Grosvenor artists, Constantine Alexander Ionides.[96] Ionides's home at Addison Gardens included works of art by Burne-Jones, surrounded by Morris wallpapers and Morris furnishings, all coordinated in a unifying style. Lindsay worked by these same principles of coordination in the arrangement of his gallery, implying that he based his ideas, at least in part, on recent innovations in interior decoration, certainly those of the Aesthetic Movement.

This system of decoration was central to the Grosvenor philosophy; by 1877, the year that the Grosvenor Gallery opened, establishments that specialized in decorative work for interiors had begun to increase, but these firms seldom found a space to show their work in public because the Academy did not consider work of this kind. Thus, the Grosvenor became the showplace for these decorative artists excluded by the Academy. Before the 1860s critics would not have applied the term "decorative" to easel paintings; however, by the 1880s it was a much more common description, witnessed in part by the frequency of its use in the Grosvenor Gallery catalogues.[97] Helen Smith explains how this tendency evolved:

The intervening years show the transition from a strict polarity between easel painting (anecdotal, historical, portraits, landscapes, etc.) and painted decoration on walls (including figurative work in some cases), towards a fashion for portable works of art that were nevertheless wholly "decorative" in intention. Painters of easel paintings in these years found their work increasingly criticized in terms of its suitability for mural painting and its general decorative tendencies. "Decorative painting" as a term rapidly changed meaning from diapers and arabesques, through pictorial and figurative mural decoration, to any kind of painting aimed at satisfying the eye (rather than the intellect) when in combination with other objects and features of room decoration.[98]

Lindsay had these ideas in mind when he handpicked his artists for exhibitions, for many of the selected artists had previous experience with mural decoration, and they showed examples of this work at the Grosvenor. Among this school of decorative painters at the Grosvenor were Burne-Jones, Watts, Moore, and Whistler, as well as neoclassical artists Sir Edward Poynter and Walter Crane, as well as Spencer Stanhope, William Blake Richmond, Thomas Armstrong, Charles Fairfax Murray, and W. E. F. Britten.

FINANCIAL DIFFICULTIES

Although the Grosvenor experienced a great success through its promotion of a select group of artists and through its innovative gallery philosophy, the path to success was not always smooth, and Lindsay's commitment to artists led to struggles with the financial side of running the gallery. The Lindsays had decided to include an elegant restaurant, dining room, and buffet bars in the scheme, in part to help cover the costs of the large financial outlay. The Grosvenor's only forerunner in these efforts was the South Kensington Museum, where designers created a refreshment room in 1866–75; such facilities did not exist at the Royal Academy until 1885 and were not added at the National Gallery until 1947.[99] The restaurant was one of the most unusual and innovative features of the Grosvenor Gallery; Lindsay housed it in the basement, where it had its own separate entrance.[100] Before 1850, the public considered such eating places dark and unattractive, and most people who wanted to eat out were served simple English fare.[101] By the time Lindsay opened the Grosvenor Gallery restaurant, there were a few select and successful eating establishments (one was the Criterion Restaurant, with its huge suite of rooms, founded in 1873). Public establishments no longer segregated women by the 1880s—it was becoming acceptable for them to eat in public (although a respectable upper-class woman would not want others to see her eating in public). Lady Lindsay remedied this situation at the Grosvenor through the advent of private dinners. Most of the advances in hotels and restaurants did not occur until the 1890s, after the close of the Grosvenor; hence, Lindsay's extensive efforts in organizing the restaurant belonged to the beginning of restaurant history.

The Grosvenor Gallery restaurant was well-established and doing a good business just two years after its opening, as evidenced in

Charles Dickens's account in his *Dictionary of London, 1879,* where he groups the Grosvenor Restaurant with the Criterion Restaurant, second in terms of importance only to Verrey's in Regent Street, the oldest London eating establishment, and Nicols's Café Royale. At the Grosvenor restaurant, Dickens reports, one could expect to have an excellent *table d'hôte* meal served between 5:30 and 8:30 P.M. for five shillings.[102] In another guide to London for 1879, the tour writer mentions the Grosvenor Gallery restaurant along with other "Dining and Luncheon Rooms.—Westward of Temple Bar," where one could find, in addition to the evening *table d'hôte,* "luncheon off the joint 2s. 6d., 12 to 4 daily."[103] In 1883, as advertised in the gallery's catalogues, select wines and fine delicacies were offered at the restaurant, suggesting the kinds of services available in modern art galleries, as well as museums.

By including such comforts as buffet bars and the restaurant, Lindsay made a commitment to women as consumers. For example, journalists reported that thousands of upper-class women relied on it for its refreshment,[104] since the gallery had obtained a liquor license through the auspices of its powerful aristocratic landlord, the Duke of Westminster. It would have been unacceptable for any lady to enter a common pub, but the upper-class ambiance and sophistication of the Grosvenor provided a respectable site for women to partake of sherry as well as view the exhibitions.

Although Lindsay's inclusion of such amenities was a business decision, calculated to bring in capital, what was the broader significance of such aspects of his gallery? Lindsay was certainly thinking about the best way to attract wealthy patrons who, instead of planning an elegant supper at their London homes during the season, could invite guests to join them at the Grosvenor Restaurant.

However, other business changes became necessary later in the gallery's history in order to keep it afloat financially. Beginning in 1884, Lindsay hired a business manager, the jeweler Joseph Pyke, who owned shops at the corner of Bond Street and Grosvenor Mews, just north of the Grosvenor. Lindsay brought in Pyke for his business acumen, thinking that he could ex-

plore creative suggestions about how to make money at the gallery through different events, public dinners, and so on. Hallé was bitter about the new management both as an artist and as co-assistant with Carr; he felt that Lindsay was becoming preoccupied with commercial gain at the expense of the artists.[105]

Part of the reason for financial difficulties was Lindsay's domestic situation; he separated from Lady Lindsay in 1882, apparently owing to his philandering.[106] Blanche did not exhibit at the gallery very often after 1882; she lived with her daughters, completely removed from the spotlight of the Grosvenor's social circle. She also withdrew her significant monetary investment in the gallery.[107] Many writers have stated that Blanche Lindsay brought the entire fortune to the marriage, but Lindsay was a first-born son and had inherited his father's fortune.

Lindsay certainly suffered a financial burden at Blanche's departure from the gallery, but, in the absence of detailed business accounts, it is difficult to say how much money she had personally invested in the gallery. We do know that Lindsay's younger brother, Lord Wantage, came to his financial rescue in 1884, which allowed him to continue with the gallery. When it closed in 1890, it was due to financial troubles—not surprising in view of Lindsay's extravagance.[108]

Hallé, perhaps overdramatically, described the situation:

The departure of Lady Lindsay sounded the death-knell of the Grosvenor Gallery. Lady Lindsay, whether in Scotland, Cromwell Place, or the Grosvenor, was an ideal hostess; her personal influence and tact, both on the artistic and social side, were inestimable, and when that was removed our difficulties were enormously increased. It was not to be expected that a high-spirited woman would accept a condition of things repugnant to her feelings in the interests of a picture-gallery; nor, on the other hand, was Sir Coutts prepared to make a sacrifice of his personal inclinations for a similar cause. When everything was settled he wrote me a letter in which he said that under no circumstances would he withdraw from the duties that had grown out of the Grosvenor Gallery, and that he considered himself pledged in honour to those who had given him their support in the undertaking. He added that, as a matter of fact, no change whatever would take place at the Grosvenor, nor would it be diverted to any other use, in spite of the unhappy differences which existed between himself and Lady Lindsay. Under these circumstances, Carr and I considered that, on a personal matter which in no way concerned us, we could not possibly take any other course than to continue to do our duty by the Gallery. This was also the feeling amongst the majority of the exhibitors; they felt that they could only ignore what was kept as a private matter, and that any other action might be resented by Lady Lindsay as much as by Sir Coutts.[109]

This passage attests to Lindsay's commitment to the gallery and his attempt to stave off disruptive changes to the management (he did not hire Pyke until 1884). It also reveals the important presence Lady Lindsay had won for herself prior to this separation, at the center of the social circle of the gallery. It would, indeed, be difficult to fill her shoes, but the myth of the gallery's "death" in 1882, which Hallé began with this passage, is largely inaccurate—there is no evidence to prove that Lindsay discontinued the social gatherings at the gallery. Newspaper reports reveal that the special openings did continue even after her departure.[110] This passage further shows that the artists continued to support Lindsay's endeavors after 1882. In addition, Joseph Jopling's 1883 portrait of Lindsay standing outside the gallery (fig. 23) attests to the Grosvenor's continued success. The year Jopling did this portrait was the year after Blanche had left the enterprise. This watercolor was published in *Vanity Fair*, considered and understood not only as *the* society newspaper reflecting the attitudes of England's upper classes, but also seen as a journal that recorded "the wishes of those who desired to maintain the *status quo* and as a collection of images of those who envisioned themselves at the apex of the English class system."[111] While having his image in *Vanity Fair* may have represented an effort to resurrect his gallery after Blanche's departure, it seems more likely that it was a reaffirmation of his important position as an art patron.

Lindsay's correspondence with his two assistants, who abandoned the gallery in late 1887, suggests that from 1882 there was more of a commercial taint to the enterprise than previously. Burne-Jones was the first to complain of "club rooms, concert rooms, and the rest" which "were not in the plan and must and will degrade it. . . . Clubs, feasts, concerts, parties, advertisements, placards and refreshments—how they all vex the soul."[112] Burne-Jones's comments suggest that the gallery had become too much like some of the local entertainment halls and too little like his idea of an art gallery. All of the activities of which Burne-Jones complains, however, are integral features of the modern-day museum or gallery, and though they may have appeared crass to such a purist as Burne-Jones, they are necessary parts of any cultural arena that wants to enliven the atmosphere and increase the audience for its exhibits. Many modern museums have elaborate celebrations in their galleries to open their shows as well as a concert series, special dinners, and benefit balls. Lindsay did not begin to take out larger commissions on artists' works to recoup his financial straits, but rather created these other activities to bring in money. There is no evidence that he abused his artists during his financial troubles. Nevertheless Burne-Jones left the Grosvenor with Hallé and Carr, who formed the New Gallery in 1888 in Regent Street, which drew off the Pre-Raphaelite circle and the classicists from the Grosvenor. Lindsay continued to bring in other important young artists to replace these two groups, such as the Glasgow Boys.[113]

Despite its monetary failure, the Grosvenor Gallery provided an important exhibition model for other Victorian institutions and served as an example for later avant-garde exhibition halls. Lindsay could be said to have brought the history of galleries full circle. In his attention to domestic interior design, he recreated the kind of aristocratic space in which picture galleries were first found. Thus, Lindsay transformed the role and the appearance of the exhibition hall, as well as the viewers' attitude taken toward it. His "Palace of Art" represented a turning point in the history of art exhibitions.

23. Joseph Middleton Jopling, *Sir Coutts Lindsay Outside the Grosvenor Gallery*, 1883. Watercolor. Courtesy of the National Portrait Gallery, London (cat. 26)

2
Art Audiences at the Grosvenor Gallery

Paula Gillett

THE GROSVENOR GALLERY, especially during the years of Lady Blanche Lindsay's participation (from 1877 to 1882), was a phenomenon of major social as well as artistic significance. The heady excitement of its opening (saluted even by critics who sensed the presence of alien and subversive aesthetic values) was intensified during the following year by the acrimonious Whistler-Ruskin lawsuit, an event reported in close detail and widely publicized by newspapers and journals of art and general culture.[1] By the end of the Grosvenor's fifth season, three theatrical satires—as well as a series of brilliant comic drawings of the contemporary aesthete in *Punch*—had crystallized the gallery's public image as a place where imaginative art and high fashion coexisted in an atmosphere that many found exhilarating—even inspiring—while others responded with a measure of uneasiness and, sometimes, strong disapproval.[2] It was possible to admire or dislike the Grosvenor—or to respond, as many did, with an ambivalence that mixed aesthetic values with moral judgments. But no one with even a casual interest in art could have remained unaware of the Grosvenor or of its remarkable combination of aristocratic glamor and challenge to prevailing conceptions of beauty in art, fashion, and home decoration, as well as—more fundamentally—to the purposes of art and the nature of the aesthetic experience.

As an upstart challenging the hitherto unrivaled Royal Academy, whose annual exhibition had long provided structure and focus for the three months of London's social season, the Grosvenor and the women and men attracted to this New Bond Street "Palace of Art" were the objects of considerable commentary. Indeed, the Grosvenor's art public played a role as important as that of the gallery's founders and managers in creating the institution's unique social presence, for, like all other social and cultural organizations, museums and art galleries reflect the interests, concerns, fears, and aspirations of those persons who identify most strongly with their programs and institutional style. Who were the people most closely associated with the Grosvenor? What gave its private views, at-homes, and soirées a character and meaning so special that many prominent people who participated in them took pleasure in reminiscing about these events decades later? Looking to the outer circles of Grosvenor viewers, what led tens of thousands of men and women each year to spend their admission shillings and leisure hours—people whose visits were often linked to far greater expenditures on home decoration and clothing closely identified with the Grosvenor's style and ethos? Finally, why did the throngs who delighted in annual visits to the Royal Academy not patronize the Grosvenor in equal numbers?

The *Art Journal*'s review of the Grosvenor opening provides a starting point for this inquiry into the composition and character of the gallery's art public. The Grosvenor, wrote the reviewer, "is full of interest to people making any pretensions to Art culture."[3] The comment suggests a sizable public of potential Grosvenor visitors—at the same time, implicitly flattering the *Art Journal*'s own, well-informed readership—but one that was far smaller and more select than the enormous crowds that struggled to view the Royal Academy exhibitions. Grosvenor habitué Oscar Wilde alluded to this difference in the opening pages of *The Picture of Dorian Gray,* in Sir Henry Wotton's advice to the painter Basil Hallward concerning the choice of an exhibition place for his latest work: "The Academy is too large and too vulgar. Whenever I have gone there, there have been either so many people that I have not been able to see the pictures, which was dreadful, or so many pictures that I have not been able to see the people, which was worse. The Grosvenor is really the only place."[4] Although attendance at the Grosvenor's much-heralded opening day was reported as 7,000, a figure surprisingly close to the Royal Academy's record attendance of 7,643 (in 1879),[5] numerous comments by contemporaries confirm Wilde's description of the Grosvenor as characteristically far less crowded than the Academy, except for the hectic days of openings and "private" views. The average annual attendance at the Academy during the 1880s was 355,000.[6] Even at the height of the Grosvenor's popularity, its more limited space and typically uncrowded conditions suggest a public considerably smaller than, and perhaps one-third of the Academy's. Figures may well

have been much higher during the peak excitement of the gallery's early years and probably declined with the withdrawal of Sir Edward Burne-Jones to the rival New Gallery in 1888.[7]

THE GRAND OPENING BANQUET

The most socially exclusive segment of the Grosvenor public is easily identified by its well-publicized presence at the gallery's opening banquet, held in its restaurant on the evening of May 9, 1877. The guest list and proceedings were reported in great detail in the next day's *Times,* and the majority of banquet guests were titled friends of the Lindsays, including, most important, the Prince of Wales. It had no doubt occurred to the entrepreneurially minded Sir Coutts that a banquet list headed by royalty was sure to enhance the restaurant's cachet. The prince's support of this event, however, came with strings attached, as he felt free to use his influence on behalf of artists he wished to see included in future shows.[8] No doubt other guests of high degree acted similarly, whether on behalf of artist friends or for themselves; a substantial number of exhibits at the Grosvenor shows were the work of titled amateurs, a circumstance not overlooked by reviewers. For example, the 1877 and 1878 lists of exhibitors included the Honourable Captain and Lady Louisa Charteris, Count Gleichen, the Honourable George Howard, Sir John Leslie, the Honourable Mrs. Loyd-Lindsay (Sir Coutts's sister-in-law), Princess Louise, Baron H. de Lyoncourt, Frances, Countess of Warwick, and Louisa, Marchioness of Waterford—in addition to the Lindsays themselves, who exhibited regularly in the Grosvenor shows. The satirical journal *Fun* commented on this Grosvenor characteristic in a cartoon in its May 9, 1877, issue in which "Brown, a hard working artist," asks a top-hatted "Swell Amateur" if he is showing anything at the Academy this year (fig. 24). "No sir," replies the Swell, in aristocratic diction, "I exhibit by invitation at the Gwovenor."[9] The presence of these aristocratic amateurs and of others who exhibited later, as well as the numerous portraits of titled sitters featured in the annual shows, strengthened the powerful aristocratic ethos conveyed by the Grosvenor's palatial architecture and opulent

VERY SELECT.

Brown (a hard working artist, to Swell Amateur) :— "Got anything at the Academy this year?"

Swell Amateur :— "No sir, I exhibit by invitation at the Gwovenor."

24. "Very Select," *Fun*, May 9, 1877.
Wood engraving

décor, no doubt motivating numerous gallery visits by upper-class friends and relatives, whether art lovers or not.

But important as this aristocratic component of the Grosvenor's public was, it was only part of a more complex picture, for the special identity of this "insider" gallery public reflected the Lindsays' ability to link the aristocracy of birth with an aristocracy of merit that recognized achievement in the professions as well as in literature and the arts. The avant-garde social savor of Grosvenor gatherings—a fitting counterpart to the more daring of the exhibited works—resulted from the commingling of men and women of high birth or professional achievement with members of the world of artistic creativity. Influenced by John Ruskin and Walter Pater to revere those whose lives were dedicated to the creation of beauty, the social elite could also enjoy their engagement with the intriguingly suspect aura of bohemia. Merit in the world of business and industry (as opposed to banking) was underrepresented in

this inner circle, although the absence of James McNeill Whistler's and Edward Burne-Jones's industrialist–art patrons, William Graham and Frederick Leyland, was probably due to external causes—Graham's withdrawal from social life after the death of a beloved son and Leyland's recent bitter dispute with Whistler.[10]

Sir Coutts and Blanche, Lady Lindsay, titled artists and gallery proprietors, personally exemplified the intersection of social worlds they promoted; this crossover identity is epitomized in Watts's much-admired portrait of Lady Lindsay playing the violin that hung in the opening exhibition (pl. 24). Another notable example of this reconstituted aristocrat-cum-artist identity within the gallery's inner circles was George Howard (later, Earl of Carlisle), whose interest in art eclipsed his interest in politics, even during his years as Member of Parliament. Admirers and patrons of Burne-Jones's work long before the Grosvenor's opening, Howard and his wife, Rosalind, who later became a temperance leader, entertained artist friends in their Kensington house, which had been designed and decorated by William Morris's firm.[11]

Two other banquet guests are equally interesting in their combined affiliations with the world of art and the heights of the social pyramid. These were Princess Louise, Queen Victoria's fourth daughter, a sculptor (and, like her friend Blanche Lindsay, an author), and the eminent surgeon and art collector Sir Henry Thompson. As a young woman the talented Louise had found the atmosphere of the studio far more congenial than the restrictive life at court. She overcame maternal opposition to her artistic ambitions and in 1869 was granted permission to sculpt a bust of the queen, who proudly presented her daughter's completed work to the Royal Academy. The princess's art education included modeling classes at the National Art Training School at South Kensington and private study with the sculptor Joseph Boehm, a fashionable artist patronized by the royal family and a frequent Grosvenor exhibitor. She also studied watercolor with the landscape painter Alfred Parsons, another Grosvenor exhibitor and a future Royal Academician.[12] In 1878 and 1879 Louise's work was displayed at the Grosvenor; a portrait of her by Lady Lindsay hung in the 1878 exhibition. During these years Louise socialized a great deal with artists, frequenting the studio of Frank Miles, a friend and neighbor of Oscar Wilde and the first artist to publicize the beautiful Lillie Langtry, another personality closely associated with the Grosvenor.[13]

Sir Henry Thompson, knighted in 1867, was well known by the time of the Grosvenor's opening as the surgeon who had treated King Leopold of Belgium and Napoleon III of France. The painter and Royal Academician Lawrence Alma-Tadema, a fellow banquet guest, had also been a patient and continued to be a friend. An amateur artist who exhibited regularly at the Royal Academy during the 1870s and 1880s, Thompson had anticipated the Aesthetic passion for blue and white china; a catalogue of his collection, featuring Thompson's drawings along with those of Whistler, was published in 1879. In addition to his professional eminence and varied art interests—he later published a guidebook to the picture galleries of Europe—Thompson was known for his exclusive dinners, known as "octaves" for the combination of eight eminent guests (the list included the Prince of Wales) and eight elegant courses. During the early years of the Grosvenor, Thompson played a valuable role as president of the society for the Sunday opening of national museums and galleries, in attempts to widen the gallery's social reach.[14]

The Grosvenor's inner circles also included persons eminent in government, banking, journalism, and music; all these spheres were present at the banquet and regularly thereafter at elite Grosvenor events. Benjamin Disraeli, prime minister at the time of the gallery's opening, was represented at the banquet by his personal secretary, Montagu Corry, who would soon be raised to the peerage as Baron Rowton.[15] Mr. and Mrs. Gladstone also attended, Gladstone later commenting in his diary that the banquet was very well organized and that "I was much pleased with the pictures."[16] The Lord Mayor of London was present, as were several ambassadors.

Among the members of London's powerful banking families who attended the banquet were several of Lady Lindsay's Rothschild relations: Alfred de Rothschild, who in 1868 had become the first Jewish director of the Bank of England;[17] Sir Nathaniel de Rothschild, an MP who, in 1885, became the first Jewish peer; and Baron Ferdinand de Rothschild, a noted art collector known also for the lavish entertainments he put on at his palatial French Renaissance mansion, Waddesdon.[18] Ferdy, as his friends called him, accompanied "Miss de Rothschild"—probably Hannah, who was soon to marry the Baron's close friend, the Liberal politician Lord Rosebery. Hannah de Rothschild's portrait by George Frederic Watts would be shown at the Grosvenor in 1882.

The venerable banking house of Baring was represented by Mr. and Mrs. Edward Baring; he later became Lord Revelstoke. Lindsay himself had strong banking antecedents, having inherited his title from his maternal grandfather, Sir Coutts Trotter, a partner in the banking firm of Coutts and Company. The Lindsays, *Vanity Fair* had observed in 1876, were one of the oldest families in Scotland, "having in more than one matrimonial adventure fallen among bankers."[19] The comment referred directly to Sir Coutts's younger brother, Colonel James Loyd-Lindsay, who attended the Grosvenor banquet with his wife, the daughter of the banker Samuel Loyd, Baron Overstone. The baron, whose rise to wealth was noted in Samuel Smiles's widely read book *Self-Help* (a paean to the virtues and rewards of ambition and self-discipline), was one of the richest men in England. Loyd-Lindsay and his wife inherited her father's fortune upon the latter's death in 1883; two years later, Loyd-Lindsay, who had served with distinction in the military service, became a peer, with the title of Lord Wantage. Lord Overstone's portrait by Frank Holl was exhibited at the Grosvenor show of 1885.

The strong representation of banking families at the Grosvenor banquet—including several soon to be ennobled—was a reflection of the high social status this group had attained by the late nineteenth century. By virtue of their combination of wealth and gentlemanly leisure, bankers had successfully assimilated into the aristocracy.[20] The writer James Payn (whose portrait was exhibited at the Grosvenor) gave a more cynical account of the coexistence of respect for bankers with aristocratic disdain for commerce. The reason, Payn said, was the reliance of the nobility on their bankers, "whom they dared not despise."[21] The presence of Jews at the highest social levels, mirrored at the Grosvenor in Lady Lindsay's Rothschild antecedents and banker relatives, was a much-noted (and sometimes deplored) feature of late Victorian England. Their social acceptance was encouraged by the Prince of Wales's friendships with the Rothschilds and other Jewish financiers.[22]

Those who reached the top of the social pyramid by acquiring wealth did not always find a warm welcome there, even with the sponsorship of the future king; disapproving comments were regularly heard in aristocratic circles about the Prince's choice of friends. A *Vanity Fair* feature article held that wealth had a claim to the highest respect only when strongly associated with contributions to national honor: because the thousands of pounds that make up a great fortune contain the entire history of their acquisition, "the riches of a Marlborough or a Wellington . . . yet scintillate with the splendour of great deeds. There is here something of the fame and glory of the State. . . . We have no such feeling about the piled-up moneys of a Rothschild or a Baring. Their possessors may be respected, but there is no sentiment about the matter." If society is correctly moved to worship wealth, *Vanity Fair* advised, "its well-understood interests inculcate a certain reserve in this religion."[23] If there was some overlap between the Prince of Wales's Marlborough House set and the Grosvenor's more meritocratic selection of upper-class insiders, the higher tone that prevailed at the gallery (and the altruistic implications of support of the arts) may have contributed some veneer of "national honor" to members of the latter group, including the recently and soon-to-be ennobled who lacked ancient lineage and ancestral deeds of valor.[24]

Although the honor associated with art sponsorship lay outside *Vanity Fair*'s limited definition, art collecting had long been a traditional function of nobility. Art patronage in Victorian times had passed into the hands of

newly rich industrialists, but this innovation was less than two generations old. In this context the Grosvenor Gallery can be seen as a reaffirmation of the value and power of aristocratic taste. Reviews of the Grosvenor's opening implicitly recognized this meaning by ascribing Sir Coutts's founding of the gallery to his spirit of noble generosity—the aristocrat sharing his cultivated taste and inviting his countrymen to delight in art works in a setting of palatial opulence. Even John Ruskin, critical as he was of the Grosvenor's overly rich decoration, praised Lindsay as "a gentleman in the true desire to help the artists and better the art of his country."[25]

Although such reassertion of traditional claims to cultural leadership served class interests, the Lindsays' friends were hardly typical members of the upper classes, for art and art patronage were not subjects to which most late Victorian aristocrats gave much thought. In the judgment of the Countess of Warwick, a well-known member of the Marlborough House set, the aristocratic segment of society was strongly prejudiced against artists, writers, and musicians as well as lawyers: "We acknowledged that it was necessary that pictures should be painted, books written, the law administered; we even acknowledged that there was a certain class whose job it might be to do these things. But we did not see why their achievements entitled them to our recognition; they might disturb, over-stimulate, or even bore. On rare occasions, if a book made a sufficient stir, we might read it, or better still, get somebody to tell us about it, and so save us the trouble."[26]

Insofar as aristocratic Grosvenor participants could create a counterimage to the view of aristocracy as exclusively pleasure-driven and self-serving, insofar as they could play (or be perceived as playing) the role of serious art patrons (even if their commissions were limited to family portraits), the gallery was almost as useful to them as they were to it. A far greater—and remarkably well-timed—service was rendered by the Grosvenor to artists. The gallery's opening coincided with the early stages of severe contraction in the demand for works of contemporary art; canvas prices and incomes of all but the most famous artists of the day were beginning to decline, and many artists of the late 1870s and 1880s abandoned their preferred genres and subjects to take up the more secure practice of portraiture. Introductions to the social elite were therefore especially valuable to artists at this time, particularly as the financial benefits of such contacts were combined with the Lindsays' gracious recognition of their high calling. Grosvenor artists were welcomed to the gallery's most prestigious events in a manner that sharply contrasted with the inconsiderate and demeaning treatment of "outsider" (non-member) exhibitor artists at the Royal Academy, who could attend its Private View only by culti-vating the friendship of Academicians.[27]

The Grosvenor's mixing of aristocrats and artists was not unprecedented—a number of fashionable hostesses enjoyed "raiding bohemia" to add zest to a luncheon or dinner party. But the Lindsays' mingling of the aristoc-racies of birth and artistic talent was not occasional but programmatic. Artists, it was said over and over again, are treated like guests at the Grosvenor. The alliance between the Lindsay-constituted art aristocracy and gallery-insider aristocrats of birth was seen on the walls of successive Grosvenor Gallery exhibitions where, alongside the commissioned portraits of those born to high status, hung a remarkable number of images of men and women eminent in the arts—painters and sculptors, writers, musicians, and actors. Among the artists por-trayed in canvases and sculptures were Burne-Jones (by Watts), Alphonse Legros (by Burne-Jones and Rodin), Whistler (by Boehm), Louise Jopling and Kate Dickens Perugini (by Millais), Barbara Bodichon (the landscape painter and feminist leader, by Emily Mary Osborn), and Holman Hunt (by W. B. Richmond and Alma-Tadema). Alma-Tadema also showed a portrait of the etcher L. Lowentam and a life-size portrait of the sculptor Giambattista Amendola working on a silver statuette. Among the writers portrayed were Andrew Lang (by Richmond), Robert Browning (by Legros and by gallery co-manager C. E. Hallé), Thomas Car-lyle (by Legros and Whistler), and the novelists Wilkie Collins and James Payn (by Rudolph Lehmann). Musicians' portraits included Hans Richter (by Alma-Tadema), Franz Liszt (by

Boehm), the composer Charles Villiers Stanford and the violinist Joseph Joachim (both by Herkomer), and a portrait of the eminent pianist and conductor Charles Hallé by C. E. Hallé, his son. Portraits from the world of theater included three of the great actor Henry Irving (by Millais, John Collier, and—in the role of Philip the Second—by Whistler). Sarah Bernhardt was painted by Jules Bastien-Lepage; the actor-manager Squire Bancroft, by Carlo Pellegrini; and the celebrated American actress Mary An-derson, sculpted by Count Gleichen. Whistler also contributed a painting of the eleven-year-old dancer at the Gaiety Theatre, shown with the title *Harmony in Yellow and Gold: The Gold Girl—Connie Gilchrist* (pl. 33).[28]

Several of these artists and sitters had been guests at the opening banquet, where artists represented the largest single occupational group. Whistler, Albert Moore, James Tissot, and Alphonse Legros attended the banquet unaccompanied, while Alma-Tadema, Edward Poynter, John Everett Millais, and Louise Jopling came with spouses. Several painters represented the new Victorian profession of art administrator: Poynter and Legros served as director of art at South Kensington and Slade Professor at University College, London, respec-tively. Sidney Colvin, Slade Professor at Cambridge, had been since 1876 director of the Fitzwilliam Museum, and Frederick W. Burton, director of the National Gallery, was also a Grosvenor exhibitor. Although women artists were to form a significant presence in the Grosvenor exhibitions, Louise Jopling, a friend of the Lindsays, appears to have been the only professional female painter at the banquet. Robert Browning, a ubiquitous figure in late Victorian high society, was the only major writer present.

In keeping with Lady Lindsay's activities as a gifted musical amateur (and with her plan to feature concerts at the gallery), the guest list included a number of prominent musicians: Charles Hallé; Wilma Norman-Neruda, eminent violinist and Hallé's future wife; Alberto Ran-degger, an Italian composer and voice teacher who had settled in England; Auguste Rouzeaud, husband of the international opera star Chris-tine Nilsson, a friend of the Lindsays; and the indefatigable George Grove, editor of *Macmillan's Magazine,* who was soon to publish the musical dictionary that still bears his name. In 1883 Grove was knighted and became the first director of the Royal College of Music.[29]

Like Grove, several banquet guests held important positions as editors, proprietors of, or writers for leading journals and newspapers. Coverage in the press was essential to the Grosvenor's success, and the rapidly growing readership of these publications gave a great deal of influence to these men who were much sought after by political leaders and ambitious hostesses.[30] The most important journalists at the banquet were Edward Dicey of the *Observer;* Algernon Borthwick of the *Morning Post,* who later became one of the first editors to receive a peerage; Edward Levy-Lawson of the *Daily Telegraph,* a major figure in Victorian journalism who later became Lord Burnham; and Tom Taylor, art critic for the *Times* and (since 1874) editor of *Punch.* The *Observer* was the oldest Sunday paper in England, and the *Post* the favored paper of the social elite. Lawson's *Telegraph* was known for its lively style, cheap price, and enormous circulation. Although not present at the banquet, its noted foreign correspondent George Augustus Sala became an important member of the Grosvenor's inner circle; in 1881 Sala was listed as a director of the company that Sir Coutts established to finance the Grosvenor Gallery Library.[31] The welcome Sir Coutts gave to representatives of the press no doubt contributed to the fact that Grosvenor exhibitions regularly received coverage comparable to that given the Royal Academy, and reviews of the two shows were frequently juxtaposed for ease of comparison. But articles in the press were frequently critical of the Grosvenor's choice of works, although they usually combined negative comments with statements of respect for the gallery's high goals. An unusually relentless campaign of criticism was carried on by Tom Taylor's *Punch*—especially through the work of its cartoonists, George Du Maurier and Edward Linley Sambourne, who scathingly satirized the Aesthetic Movement and its famous venue; Taylor himself testified against his fellow ban-

quet guest, Whistler, in the artist's 1878 lawsuit against Ruskin.[32]

One additional banquet guest merits special mention: Arthur Sullivan, whose partnership with W. S. Gilbert had begun two years earlier with the operetta *Trial by Jury,* was a close friend of the Lindsays. He visited them at their home at Balcarres and traveled with them on the Continent; he also served as music mentor to Blanche Lindsay, instructing her in harmony and counterpoint and advising her on the publication of one of her songs.[33] Relying on Sullivan's finely tuned knowledge of the unwritten rules of high society, she called on his advice again, when last-minute changes became necessary in the delicate matter of banquet seating arrangements.[34]

THE PRIVATE VIEWS

Blanche Lindsay's success in attracting this dazzling and varied group of celebrities to the Grosvenor's private events over the course of her six-year involvement in the gallery brought her recognition as one of London's most successful hostesses. It was a kind of success fervently sought and highly valued during this period of intense social competition, when people on the fringes of society vied to enter, and people on the inside competed for status among all the others who counted. Accounts of Grosvenor Gallery private functions, which, like the private views, were often described in the press, encouraged attendance at the gallery by the socially ambitious who, by paying their admission shillings, could at least walk in the footsteps (and sometimes get a glimpse) of those fortunate enough to take part in the more exclusive gallery events. One example of such social emulation that often followed this experience was Du Maurier's brilliant creation, the social climber Mrs. Ponsonby de Tomkyns, whom Henry James (a close friend of Du Maurier and frequenter of the Grosvenor) described as "the modern social spirit . . . the little London lady who is determined to be a greater one."[35] Du Maurier's cleverness in satirizing the relentless pursuit of social status as manifested in the art world takes on poignant overtones when one learns from his biographer of how greatly the cartoonist cherished the legend of his own noble origins, ignorant that they were a fabrication.[36]

The emphasis of many Du Maurier cartoons on dinner parties, balls, and guest lists reflected an important component of upper-class social reality; a woman's ability to entertain in elegant style and to attract high-status guests was one key to success—for both herself and her husband. Because in the political world friendships with influential people could enhance a man's chances of getting into Parliament or gaining a title, even the most amusing parties were a serious business. *Vanity Fair* helped its readers to plan entertainments strategically, advising them to give special care to the numbers on their guest lists: one must invite more guests to a party than are really wanted, since too few produce a dismal event, but if too many come, the hostess is considered guilty of "packing." The journal suggested that a good party "in a popular house" would probably attract two-thirds of those invited, especially if a well-known entertainer was invited or a member of the royal family was there (then, of course, there would be the problem of those who came without invitations).[37]

Financial resources were a precondition for this level of party-giving. Private establishments of substantial size and opulent decoration were essential, for although the number of those eligible for invitations to parties and balls had greatly increased by the last quarter of the nineteenth century, the rental of public spaces for such functions was considered out of the question. As *Vanity Fair* reported in 1878:

London Society, already overgrown, is daily becoming larger, and the small rooms of private houses are entirely insufficient to contain those who are bidden to them. There is, nevertheless, the greatest prejudice against meeting elsewhere than at private houses, and any assembly in a public room is regarded with aversion and contempt. What is certain is that quarts cannot continue for ever to be put into pint pots, and that either London Society must provide itself with some common meeting places of sufficient dimensions, or else that the select must be made more select by the weeding out of a large proportion of their numbers.[38]

There were numerous complaints about the London "crush," which one contemporary described as a process of "painfully struggling up a staircase," forcing one's way into a drawing room so packed that it was an ordeal to reach the other side of the room, and then failing to be able to engage in an audible conversation with another guest.[39] Despite these inconveniences people would push themselves into the most crowded venues if the attractions were sufficient (and especially if they were strikingly different and original): excellent food, memorable decorations, entertainment or a royal guest, and—perhaps even more of a draw—the presence of one or more "professional beauties." That term referred to attractive society women who allowed their photographs to be sold and widely displayed—even in shop windows—a craze that led some enterprising hostesses to add a note to their invitations promising the presence of one or more "PB's."[40]

In this intensely competitive world of hostessing, Lady Lindsay's ability to use the Grosvenor Gallery as party site was a tremendous advantage and one which she knowingly exploited. Notices in the press regularly reported these "private" events, from the five hundred guests entertained after the 1877 opening night banquet to the Sunday afternoon parties, Monday parties at ten in the evening, and, of course, the annual private view.

The Grosvenor's private view was, like that of the Royal Academy, a stellar event of the social season: detailed reviews of the art works—accompanied by descriptions of the viewers—enhanced the gallery's charisma, motivating new visitors to attend and former patrons to return. Especially during Blanche Lindsay's years as hostess the private view was a "crush," although the crowding was moderate when compared with the feverish press of crowds at the Academy's event, brilliantly depicted in a drawing of the Academy's "Strictly Private View" (fig. 25). While the *Punch* cartoon of the 1882 Grosvenor private view shows a crowded scene, Du Maurier's drawing of the event for Lucie Lillie's novel *Prudence,* published in the same year (see fig. 21), shows conversational space at seating areas located at a comfortable distance from the exhibition walls. Such space was required by Lillie's narrative,[41] and it seems likely that Grosvenor private

STRICTLY PRIVATE VIEW, ROYAL ACADEMY.

25. Harry Furniss, "Strictly Private View, Royal Academy," *Punch*, May 3, 1890. Wood engraving. Yale Center for British Art, Gift of Henry S. Morgan

view day, however crowded, allowed for some degree of conversational interchange and was generally a more decorous affair than the Academy's dressy mob-scene. This interpretation is supported by the accounts of society journalists who described the Grosvenor's private views as more "intellectual" and "select" than those at the Academy.[42] For the unsophisticated viewer invited by a well-connected friend or relative, such attributes were not necessarily seen as advantageous. The critic for *Vanity Fair*, in his account of the 1878 Grosvenor private view, related the comments of one young woman who attributed her preference for the Academy's over the Grosvenor's private view to the fact that the Burlington House event provided so many more people to look at.[43]

Admission to the Grosvenor private view was, as at the Academy, by ticket;[44] the limited supply of tickets to both events greatly enhanced their value, as did the promise of rubbing shoulders with celebrities. The Lindsays carefully shaped the composition of the influential private-view audience. One gets a glimpse of this informally directed process in a letter George Eliot wrote in 1877, thanking her friend Georgiana Burne-Jones (wife of Edward Burne-Jones) for the offer of tickets to the gallery's first private view. Eliot was very much

interested in plans for the Grosvenor; she had expressed great pleasure at news of the completion of the building early in 1877 in a letter to her goddaughter, Emilia Pattison. But she had no need of the Burne-Jones's tickets, as Lord and Lady Lindsay had already provided them for herself and George Henry Lewes.[45] Numerous ticket exchanges similar to this one among Grosvenor artists, patrons, and friends of the Lindsays combined to constitute the unique public that was the source of so much excited commentary in newspapers and, many years later, of nostalgic recollections in memoirs.

As it happened, Eliot's presence at the Grosvenor's first private view provided a kind of unanticipated centerpiece for the event, even in the midst of many other celebrities and attractions. The papers of Jeanie Adams-Acton, wife of a sculptor who showed two works in the exhibition, include a vivid description of the occasion. Her account emphasized the high pitch of excitement generated by the gallery and its featured art works, Lady Lindsay's extraordinary skill as hostess, and the lionizing of Eliot:

All the world was—bewilderingly—there! . . . Lady Lindsay was extremely kind, gushing and amiable, and all over everywhere at once. Every now and then there was another rush through the crowd, and it was

Lady Lindsay again, seeing some interesting person enter, and flying to greet them. . . .

We soon picked out our friend Robert Browning, with his white beard and pale face. . . . Whilst standing listening to him I caught sight of the cause of his sudden animation, two familiar figures among those entering—George Lewes and George Eliot. . . . [They] had come to see the pictures in the New Exhibition, and to judge these solemnly according to their lights.

Lady Lindsay had greeted the couple rapturously, and they were slowly making their way towards us, when the surging crowd almost thrust us into their arms; and the next moment we were all talking together—Robert Browning and that quaint couple, the cynosure of all eyes. That plain-faced woman, then at the height of her fame—one could not but listen to every word she said and be astonished at its simple commonplaceness! Soon she was again claimed—claimed on every side simultaneously. Her position at that time was anomalous; yet here in the most fashionable place in all London that day there was not one who would not have given much to be seen speaking to her. . . .

The next instant we were pushed aside by other claimants on her attention. She made conscientious efforts to fulfill the intention with which she had come—to study the works of art—but she had no chance of doing this, so great was the crowd pressing round her; and I realised more fully than I had done before what a grip she now had on London society.[46]

The enthusiastic reception of Eliot, who up to her death in 1880 remained a devoted Grosvenor visitor, suggests an aspect of the gallery's aura that enhanced its appeal to those who welcomed some relaxation of strict Victorian propriety, while it gave notoriety to the gallery among the strictest upholders of conventional mores. Of the two artists most closely associated with the gallery's first years, Whistler was notorious for flouting central Victorian beliefs on art, especially the value of detail and finish (typically interpreted as evidence of the artist's devotion to the gospel of work) and the artist's responsibility to serve "higher" (i.e., morally elevating) goals. While lacking Whistler's combativeness, Edward Burne-Jones had also affronted Victorian mores: his long absence from public view was his response to the scandal created by his 1869 exhibition of *Phyllis and Demophoon*, a picture with a male and female nude couple and an epigraph that some interpreted as a veiled reference to his

own marital infidelity.[47] Even among his admirers at the Grosvenor there were murmurs of uneasiness at the withdrawn and disconsolate character of his female figures and, especially, at the effeminacy of his medieval knights—"underfed," "unhealthy," and "unmanly" are words encountered again and again in press reviews of his paintings. The corsetless, clinging dresses of the "aesthetic" women who set the tone at the private views became closely identified with the Grosvenor Gallery and so well-known that the lower-middle-class readership of the new journal *Ally Sloper's Half-Holiday* could be expected to appreciate

FASHION FANCIES.—By Miss Sloper.

26. "Fashion Fancies.—By Miss Sloper," *Ally Sloper's Half-Holiday*, May 17, 1884. Wood engraving. Lilly Library, University of Indiana, Bloomington, Indiana

the humor of a drawing called "Fashion Fancies," in which a frizzy-haired young woman wears a tight, sunflower-decorated dress labeled "The Grosvenor (not intended to be sat down in)" (fig. 26).[48] Although women's aesthetic dress moved into mainstream fashion during the 1880s, its early and more extreme manifestations, associated with the clinging-nightgown look of Burne-Jones pictures and satirized by the aesthetically draped "twenty love-sick maidens" of Gilbert and Sullivan's *Patience,* challenged corseted convention as provokingly as did Whistler's harmonies and nocturnes.

LADY LINDSAY'S INVITATIONALS
The avant-garde aura of Grosvenor private views also characterized Blanche Lindsay's exclusive invitational gatherings. As the most celebrated of these parties were held on Sunday afternoons, the Grosvenor's challenge to convention took on an anti-sabbatarian flavor. Marian Adams, wife of the American historian Henry Adams and a London visitor during the late 1870s and early 1880s, described a Sunday afternoon reception at the gallery in an 1879 letter to her father as "an anti-Sabbath protest by the 'high art' folks."[49]

Mrs. Adams's pungent expression pointed to the important Grosvenor policy that allowed Sunday viewing to a restricted public. Months before the gallery's 1877 opening, the *Times* (March 12) had noted an innovation that contrasted with practice at the Royal Academy (which was always closed on Sunday): a limited number of season tickets would be issued to admit the bearer and a guest into the Grosvenor any day of the week, including Sunday. Lindsay maintained this pattern through the years; the gallery was open to visitors on Sunday, but only to a specially constituted group. Thus Sunday was the most exclusive visiting day of the week.

Lady Lindsay's weekly afternoon parties are best understood within the wider context of late-Victorian Sunday practice among artists and the social elite. During the 1870s artists and art lovers developed an informal institution known as Show Sunday. Painters opened their studios on a designated Sunday in April so that the most interested members of the public could get an early view of paintings destined for the May exhibitions.[50] The custom served many artists as a genteel marketing strategy, particularly during the 1880s, when what had first appeared to be a temporary downswing in the demand for contemporary art was increasingly recognized as a more ominous structural market decline.

At the same time that artists were becoming accustomed to using one (and sometimes more than one) pre-season Sunday to increase publicity and sales, upper-class practices were testing, and increasingly widening, the range of acceptable Sunday activities. Comments in *Vanity Fair* provide a sense of the rapidity of this change. Just a few days before the Grosvenor opened its doors, the society journal discussed the controversy over a "theatrical party" given the previous Sunday by Lady Sebright, whose keen interest in theater subsequently led her to take up acting as a career. Invitations to the Sunday party had elicited vacillating responses "during the gossiping afternoon which weekly follows the virtuous effort of church-going." The problem lay not only in the choice of Sunday but in the rumor that the event was to include the performance of a play. The "wicked," so named by *Vanity Fair,* announced that they would attend—although many of them did not—while the "more virtuous" said they would not go, although a number of them did. As it happened, there was no play, but actors were present and guests enjoyed comic songs and supper. The evening, the journal commented, was a great success and one likely to be repeated, "thus introducing a new and much-wanted element into a very much neglected evening of the week."[51]

Two years later—again, just before the opening of the season—*Vanity Fair* continued its discussion of changing Sunday practices. Having guests for Sunday dinner, which would have been considered wicked a mere fifteen years before, was now completely acceptable; the real issue was "whether we ought to be allowed to go anywhere after dinner on Sunday evening." The grounds of the controversy had shifted to a concern for a more efficiently organized Sunday schedule: it was suggested that Sunday afternoon parties, such as Lady

Lindsay's at the Grosvenor, be moved to an hour *after* dinner. This change would allow many ladies to welcome afternoon visitors, a convenience for men too busy to make these visits during the week. And everyone would then be able to increase the sum of social pleasures by adding Sunday night to the heavily scheduled season.[52] In keeping with the pragmatic tone of *Vanity Fair*'s discussion of the contentious public issue of Sunday observance was Lady Greville's judgment that a weekly day of rest was "oddly inappropriate" for the leisured classes: for those "who never have any work in particular to do, a day of enforced rest loses all *raison d'être.*"[53]

AMERICANS IN THE GROSVENOR SOCIAL CIRCLE

If Sunday parties at the Grosvenor were, as Marian Adams told her father, "an anti-Sabbath protest," they were hardly unique in this regard. A more knowing observer of the Grosvenor scene was Henry James, a frequent guest at the Sunday receptions and at Lady Lindsay's ten P.M. Monday invitationals. A friend of Blanche Lindsay, James had resided in London since 1876 and was a much-sought-after dinner guest—during the winter of 1878–79, he dined out 140 times.[54] James had more than a passing interest in art: his reviews of the Grosvenor Gallery and other London exhibitions appeared in the American *Nation* and other publications, and much of his fiction dealt with art and artists.[55]

James had been introduced to the London social scene by George W. Smalley, the most important American journalist then working in London, whose home served as "an Anglo-American meeting ground."[56] Smalley, whose articles on English society, politics, and culture appeared in the *New York Tribune*, gave detailed coverage to the London art scene in reviews that encouraged Americans planning trips to London to place the Academy and Grosvenor exhibitions high on their sightseeing lists. Transatlantic travelers could see headlines like the following, from the *Tribune* on May 22, 1879: "ART DISPLAYS IN LONDON. Nearly two thousand pictures on view; the exhibitions of the Royal Academy and Grosvenor Galleries

opened." Like the *Tribune,* the *New York Times* regularly covered the London art season, and its May 18, 1880, review took special note of "Women's work in the Grosvenor Gallery." This reflected contemporary interest in new fields of female endeavor, as well as an awareness of the substantial number of mothers and daughters who would be crossing the ocean without male companions and might be especially interested in a show that featured women artists.

American tourists who had not read about the Grosvenor before their departure were likely to find it recommended by a thorough guidebook such as John Murray's 1879 *Handbook to London As It Is.* Murray's guidebook also mentioned the advantage of the Grosvenor's innovative restaurant, a boon to the weary art-tourist. Whether they first heard of the gallery from accounts of the 1878 lawsuit by the assertively American Whistler or from friends, the press, or tourist guides, many Americans visited the Grosvenor. The 1882 publication in New York of the "aesthetic" novel *Prudence*, with a high moment of its drama set at the Lindsays' private view, assumed this kind of knowledge on the part of its American audience.

Although the great majority of American tourists could not have aspired to attend Grosvenor invitational events, some would have heard news of them, given their regular press coverage and the prominence of the American socialites who entered the charmed circle. Tourists from Boston would certainly have known the name of Mrs. Jack Gardner, the flamboyant art collector. Marian Adams met Isabella Stewart Gardner at a Grosvenor party, where the two women "smile[d] pityingly on the Britons" for their obsequious behavior toward the two princesses present.[57]

The other American woman whose presence Adams rather disparagingly noticed was Mary Frances Ronalds, a singer of considerable talent and a former belle in New York's high society who had been separated from her husband for more than a decade.[58] Mrs. Ronalds was a member of the Marlborough House set, and the Prince of Wales once said that he would travel across England just to hear her sing Arthur Sullivan's "The Lost Chord." Guests at Ronalds's musical parties knew that they would always meet Sullivan there. In fact, the two had an intimate relationship over the course of many years, which had to be kept secret because, as another Marlborough set member said, "What a man or woman might feel or do in private was their own affair, but our rule was No Scandal!"[59] Adams's comments on Ronalds, included in letters written in 1879, reflect the ambiguity of the latter's status as a woman highly placed in English society but one whose past could not be wholly overlooked. Of her first excited visit to a Grosvenor Sunday "at home" on July 13, Adams wrote to her father that Henry James was present "[and] even Mrs. Ronalds was there, whose usual sphere is far above ours, in a red straw bonnet trimmed with pink roses; pretty still, but faded, and not, to my jaundiced eye, highbred-looking, but gracious and subdued." Two weeks later she wrote to "Dear Pater" of seeing Ronalds again, accompanied at this event by her "poor little lame daughter." This time there is a trace of smugness in the description of Ronalds, who in pale blue appeared to her compatriot "common-looking and little beauty left."[60]

MUSICIANS AND ACTORS

As at the opening banquet, musicians had an honored place at all Grosvenor receptions. Blanche Lindsay, an accomplished violinist and pianist, was capable of accompanying the great violinists, Joseph Joachim and Wilma Norman-Neruda, who, like Charles Hallé, were frequent Grosvenor guests. The Czech-born Neruda had been a London celebrity since 1869. Although she did not identify with feminist issues, her life was unorthodox by Victorian standards. For a number of years she lived apart from her husband, and in 1885, three years after his death, she married Hallé, her concert manager in England. Neruda continued to give concerts after her remarriage and, after Hallé was knighted, continued to perform as Lady Hallé. Hallé and Neruda gave many concerts together at the London Popular Concerts and the Grosvenor Gallery.

George Eliot and G. H. Lewes were ardent music lovers whose frequent concertgoing included musical evenings at the gallery. Both were friends of Rudolph Lehmann, whose por-traits were hung at the gallery in each season from 1877 to 1889. Lewes and Lehmann, through close mutual connections with the Scottish writer and publisher Robert Chambers, were at the center of an interesting social network. Chambers played an important role in Victorian intellectual history; the ideas on evolution presented in his book, *Vestiges of the Natural History of Creation*, published anonymously in 1844, stirred up a great deal of controversy and set the stage for Darwin's *Origin of Species*. As a young journalist, G. H. Lewes had worked for Chambers and was a frequent guest at his home. Evenings there were filled with music—Robert Chambers played the flute and his wife played piano and harp.[61] Amelia Chambers, a gifted singer and composer, became the wife of Rudolph Lehmann; sharing Blanche Lindsay's musical interests and professionally involved with the Grosvenor Gallery, the couple became her friends and continued that relationship even after her marital breakup. Their daughter Liza became a noted composer of art song; one of her compositions, "The Exile," was written to words by Blanche Lindsay.[62]

Rudolph Lehmann's brother Frederick, a businessman and a serious amateur violinist, married Nina Chambers, sister of Amelia and a gifted pianist. Frederick Lehmann said that his instrument had been "the key which opened the [Chambers's] house to me."[63] He and Nina were friends of the novelists Wilkie Collins and James Payn—like G. H. Lewes, Payn had been associated with *Chambers's Journal*. Rudolph Lehmann's portraits of Collins and Payn hung in the Grosvenor exhibition of 1882. Joseph Joachim was another friend of the Lehmann families who sat to Rudolph Lehmann for his portrait. The Lehmann circle of musicians and writers included Arthur Sullivan and George Grove, both of whom were close friends of Frederick and Nina.

While writers, painters, and musicians had an honored place at the heart of Grosvenor Gallery's most exclusive society, members of the acting profession received a more ambiguous welcome. This is all the more striking given the fact that London society was "stage struck," in the words of an acute observer of social practices T. H. S. Escott.[64] There were ample connections between the Grosvenor and the theatrical world; as a young man, Coutts Lindsay had scandalized his family by consorting with actors and actresses and had tried his hand at playwriting.[65] A more direct connection to the stage was provided by Joseph Comyns Carr, a playwright as well as Grosvenor manager, and his wife, Alice, a costume designer who numbered among her many theatrical friends Ellen Terry (who had been married to G. F. Watts). Yet, despite these close connections and the growing respectability of the late Victorian theater,[66] actors were noticeably rarer in Grosvenor society than were other art professionals. Although *Vanity Fair,* in its appreciative 1878 profile of Lady Lindsay as one of the "Hostesses of the Season," said that the charm of her parties at the Grosvenor was the result of their inclusion of "every kind of excellence and distinction," the journal qualified its remark by adding that Grosvenor invitations to members of the theater world went only to "the best actors."[67] It is consistent with the prejudices of the time to interpret *Vanity Fair*'s statement as more favorable to the men than to the women of the profession; for example, George Grossmith, the comic actor and star of Gilbert and Sullivan operettas, was a frequent and very welcome guest. But neither the strong contemporary interest in theater nor the celebrity status of Ellen Terry was a sufficient counterweight to upper-class prejudice against actresses; the prejudice hung on for many years, despite well-publicized romances—and some marriages—between the nobility and women of the stage. A symptom of this prejudice can be seen in the lapse of three decades between the first awards of knighthood to male actors (in the mid-1890s) and parallel awards to women.[68]

One striking exception to this picture was the enthusiastic reception that London society gave to the American actress Mary Anderson. Count Gleichen, who sculpted a bust of Anderson at the request of the Princess of Wales, had a replica of it made for the Grosvenor Gallery exhibition of 1884.[69] A month before the season opened *Punch* reflected on Anderson's appeal to men of diverse walks of life:

The Actress and Her Suitors

Dear Mr. Punch,—There is not the least particle of truth in the rumour that Miss MARY ANDERSON is about to be married to Mr. GLADSTONE, the Speaker of the House of Commons, Sir ROBERT PEEL, the Governor of the Bank of England, Lord WOLSELEY, Lord Tennyson, the Master of Balliol, Lord RANDOLPH CHURCHILL, . . . Mr. J. L. TOOLE [comic actor], the LORD CHAMBERLAIN, Marquis of Bute, the President of the College of Surgeons, Mr. LABOUCHERE, Captain Burton, the Archbishop of Canterbury, the LORD MAYOR, Baron ROTHSCHILD, . . . Sir FREDERIC LEIGHTON, or the Maharajah DULEEP SINGH. I must beg you at once to deny all or any of these rumours which have, in some unaccountable fashion, gained currency. I happen to know that many of the above-mentioned are married men,—and so their pretensions are out of the question; and, moreover, I also happen to know that the accomplished American Actress has long been engaged to yours most faithfully,

THE ONLY ONE SHE EVER LOVED.[70]

Mary Anderson wrote in her memoirs, "I shall always owe a debt of gratitude to my profession for opening to me the doors of the artistic and literary world of London."[71] Perhaps the warm reception given her by London society was to some extent the result of what one contemporary described as an aura that made Anderson seem different from the prevailing image of the actress: as one reviewer commented, she seemed less an actress than "a woman of surpassing loveliness with some taste for acting."[72] Perhaps Anderson's acting somehow communicated the ambivalence about theatrical self-display that she cited as a major reason for her retirement from the stage in 1889 at the age of twenty-nine.[73] Without doubt, the innocence of manner that set off her personal beauty and striking Grecian draped mode of dress had great power to fascinate.[74] In striking contrast to Sarah Bernhardt, the actress who had dazzled London and fanned the Prince of Wales's desires just a few years earlier,[75] Mary Anderson responded with pleasure to his kind words but ingenuously remarked, after being met by the unaccompanied Prince, "I was rather surprised that the Princess did not see me as well."[76] The exceptional nature of Mary Anderson's welcome at the Grosvenor is confirmed by the sour tone of Alice Carr's remark that "we of the Bohemian world" never really belonged to Lady Lindsay's closest, aristocratic circle. That unspoken slur, she said, was behind the delight the outrageously attired and mannered Whistler took in making deliberate faux pas at Lady Lindsay's parties.[77]

One woman soon to embark upon an acting career and a much-noticed presence at Grosvenor Gallery receptions was Lillie Langtry, the professional beauty most prominent among those featured in the windows of photographers' shops. Portrait artists, including Watts, Whistler, Edward Poynter, and Burne-Jones, vied to paint her. One of the first to do so was Frank Miles, whose fashionable studio was visited by actors and actresses, an array of other professional beauties, and even by members of the royal family.[78] An almost color-blind artist known for his flattering drawings of women, Miles was a friend and, for a time, housemate of the young Oscar Wilde, who initiated a public campaign of adulation of Langtry, describing her beauty as "a form of genius." Richard Ellmann points out that Wilde and Langtry were well-matched, each eager to make a mark in society, he by his wit and she by her looks.[79]

An Oxford student in his early twenties at the time of the Grosvenor's opening, Wilde managed, through his friendship with Miles and the aristocrat sculptor Ronald Gower—a Grosvenor exhibitor whose portrait by Millais hung at the 1877 show—to procure an invitation to the gallery's private view on April 30; he also attended its opening day.[80] The gallery's debut served Wilde as the occasion of his own: he appeared in a reddish-bronze custom-made coat which, when seen from the back, had the shape of a cello.[81] Wilde's article on the opening exhibition in the *Dublin University Magazine* was his first published art review. By his subsequent frequenting of the gallery, his recognition as a central figure among the aesthetes of the time, and by the parodies of his person in *Punch* and on the stage, Oscar Wilde added to the Grosvenor's fame and notoriety in a manner never sought by its founders.

During her time as the Prince of Wales's mistress—1879–1880—Lillie Langtry, like Wilde, became a recognized figure at Grosvenor parties as elsewhere in society, for the prince made it known that his presence was conditional upon her receipt of an invitation.[82] "The Jersey Lily" (an epithet coined by her Jersey-born compatriot Millais, who painted her with that flower) elicited a frenzied level of excitement, even within the highest social ranks; ladies at a fashionable ball submitted to the indignity of standing on chairs so as not to miss her entrance into a crowded room.[83] Even the caustic Mrs. Adams was awed by Langtry's beauty; reviewing the highlights of a late Monday evening party at the Grosvenor, Adams named her among the "many people one was glad to see . . . in white, no flowers or jewels, and really very handsome."[84]

THE MIDDLE-CLASS PUBLIC

Although the women and men of the Grosvenor's inner circles gave the gallery its unique social character, the great majority of visitors passed through the turnstile anonymously. Fortunately, we can piece together some of their attributes from numerous descriptions and comments written by reviewers and observers of the social scene. In addition, we know that admission was a shilling, a charge Sir Coutts modeled on the Royal Academy's. That body decided to charge an entrance fee at its very first exhibition in 1769 in order "to prevent the room from being filled with improper persons, to the entire exclusion of those for whom the exhibition is apparently intended."[85] During the Victorian period the Academy's shilling fee allowed for the creation of an audience of great social heterogeneity, ranging from the highest social strata to the lower middle class, and probably including artisans, craftsmen, and highly skilled workers of the labor aristocracy. Many wives and daughters in these groups enjoyed newfound leisure hours and discretionary income for entertainment thanks to the availability of servants to work even in modest homes and the belief among many members of these classes that respectability required that wives and daughters not work outside the home. While some exceptionally motivated viewers no doubt came from poorer segments of society, the shilling admission generally constituted a significant barrier to most of the unskilled,[86] particularly as there was a hidden charge of a second shilling for the catalogue, a near-necessity in the absence of identifying labels. The Academy catered to a wide social range but definitely drew a line that ensured middle-class respectability.

Although the Grosvenor's entrance fee was the same as the Academy's, audience self-selection informally created a far higher social threshold. Many comments attest to the fact that, except for private view days, the Grosvenor was seldom crowded, and the reports of gaucheries almost never suggest the country-bumpkin character of remarks reportedly overheard with great frequency at Burlington House. Given the Grosvenor's high profile and status—and the far greater comfort it offered—how does one account for the lack of interest shown by so many people who were clearly enthusiastic about their Royal Academy visits? Henry James suggested one persuasive answer: many of those who visited the Academy could not afford to pay the admission charge for more than a single annual art show—and that was an expense far higher than a shilling when multiplied by several family members. This limited-income segment of the Academy's art public may well have believed itself far better served there than at the Grosvenor. Many thousands of people new to gallery viewing could respond without specialized knowledge to the grand array of narrative and genre art characteristic of Academy exhibitions; they were excited and entertained by the "blockbuster" experience: the floor-to-ceiling canvases, the rails to protect the "Picture of the Year," the milling crowds creating an atmosphere that bordered on that of a festival.

Quite a few people who felt their shillings well spent at the Academy were likely to have found a Grosvenor visit disappointing; as James pointed out, because this far smaller gallery included only a fifth as many art works as the Academy, they may have judged it to offer far less value for their money.[87] Furthermore, the Grosvenor's more intimate atmosphere and the more recondite nature of its art are likely to have been intimidating to the uninitiated; in the Academy's bustling atmosphere it was far easier for both the unsophisticated and the parvenu to try their wings. James provides a fascinating example of the latter in Mrs. Headway, the so-cially ambitious heroine of his short story "The Siege of London." Shrewd enough to know that she must acquire some knowledge about art before frequenting the elite art events of the London season, Mrs. Headway quickly latches onto a mentor and starts her informal course of study. Others lacking her considerable assets—beauty, time, money, and a knowledgeable tutor—might well have limited themselves to the far less exposed atmosphere of the Academy.[88] The snobbish joke of a *Punch* cartoon entitled "Culture!" published in the issue of May 7, 1881, played on its readers' understanding of the different identities of Academy and Grosvenor publics, the dustman in comically ill-fitting, formal dress holding his arm out to his wife, requesting for her choice: "the hahr-hay, or the Gruv'nor" (fig. 27).

CULTURE!

Our (Reg'lar) Dustman (on first Monday in May). "Now, BETSY, VICH IS IT TO BE, MY DEAR —THE HAHR-HAY, OR THE GRUV'NOR ! ! !"

27. Charles Keene, "Culture!" *Punch*, May 7, 1881. Wood engraving. Yale Center for British Art, Gift of Henry S. Morgan

Mrs. Headway's historical counterparts were equally aware that for an upwardly mobile aspirant to make the best of the Grosvenor required some degree of "cultural capital," defined by theorist Pierre Bourdieu as the ability to decode richly symbolic art works or to appreciate those whose value derives in large part from formal qualities.[89] Countless reviews of Grosvenor shows emphasized their esoteric nature, typically with comments that much of the art was understandable only by the "fit though few." Critics hostile to this tendency referred to Grosvenor art lovers as a "cult," while others were self-congratulatory, as in *Art Journal*'s pompous review of the opening exhibition: "It needs that a person should be possessed of some culture and learning thoroughly to appreciate the more noteworthy works at present on view in the Grosvenor Gallery."[90] As Mrs. Headway well knew, an acceptable minimum of such culture and learning could be acquired and the effect greatly enhanced by a flair for fashion, especially since the Aesthetic Movement dealt as much with dress and decor as with fine art. Instruction that was helpful—even inspirational—was widely available; Oscar Wilde lectured and wrote on these matters, and two writers on art and fashion closely associated with the movement, Mary Elizabeth Haweis and Lucy Crane (whose brother was the Grosvenor artist, Walter Crane), gave well-attended lectures on bringing Pre-Raphaelite principles into daily life.[91]

WOMEN AT THE GROSVENOR

Women were an important component of the Royal Academy's art public; they were even more central to the Grosvenor's character and success. Founded during a decade in which women's abilities, opportunities, and rights were matters of pressing concern, the Grosvenor Gallery played a role by the recognition it gave to the talents of female artists. Several women artists who contributed prominently to the Grosvenor shows were participants in the early suffrage movement. Margaret Gillies, a perennial Grosvenor exhibitor, was one of the earliest signers of the female suffrage petition; Louise Jopling, a signer of the 1889

Declaration in Favour of Women's Suffrage, eventually left her painting career to work in the campaign for women's rights. Among other Grosvenor exhibitors who signed petitions for women's suffrage were Emily Mary Osborn, whose large portrait of Barbara Bodichon hung at the 1884 exhibition, the Pre-Raphaelite painter Evelyn Pickering De Morgan, Emily Ford, Constance Phillpot, Louisa Starr, Mary Waller, Elizabeth Forbes, Kate Perugini, Henrietta Rae Normand, Clara Montalba, and Annie Swynnerton, whose portrait of the feminist leader Millicent Fawcett was purchased for the nation by the Chantrey Bequest.[92] The participation of these feminists in Grosvenor exhibitions is likely to have attracted fellow suffragists who knew of some of these artists, as well as many of the rapidly growing numbers of women art students from schools in and outside London.

Women were beginning to enter the profession of journalism during the 1870s and wrote not only about "female" subjects like dress and home decoration but also about female advancement in male-dominated professions. Even journals that kept a distance from feminist ideas had an interest in advancing women's education and in expanding the areas in which respectable women could be self-supporting. It was in this spirit that the upper-class magazine *Queen* reported, with evident pride, on the significant presence of women artists in the Grosvenor's opening exhibition.[93]

The leisure hours enjoyed by middle- and upper-class women who employed servants and governesses meant that weekday Grosvenor audiences must have been preponderantly female. Many were suburbanites who came into town for the day on trains that brought them to and from London in an amount of time comparable to today's transit schedules. Amy Levy, a poet and essayist of the 1880s, included the "high-school mistress" among those who came to town "for a day's shopping or picture-seeing."[94] One much-noted example of a town planned for London commuters was Bedford Park, the first garden suburb. Built in the mid-1870s under the directorship of Jonathan Carr, a brother of the Grosvenor's manager, J. Comyns Carr, it was home to artists and aesthetically inclined professionals. Residents of this Queen

Anne-style village could take the train at Turnham Green and arrive in central London within a half hour. With its own art school, a club with books supplied by the Grosvenor Library, and the directorship of a Carr brother at each place, Bedford Park must have provided frequent visitors to the Grosvenor Gallery.[95]

Even people living in towns at a far greater distance from London, such as Bath and Cambridge, could easily make a day's trip to London for shopping and gallery visits during the 1870s. Sir Coutts and his managers understood the unmet needs of these visitors, especially of the upper-class women. They knew that, although women could travel to the city, their visiting time was often truncated by the lack of amenities once they arrived. Restaurants were few in London even as late as the 1880s and could be appropriately patronized by respectable women only in the company of a male relative. Although the first public toilets were installed during the eighties, women of high status would have found it embarrassing to frequent them.[96]

An article in *Queen* magazine at the start of the 1878 social season entitled "Refreshments for Ladies at the Grosvenor Gallery" attests to the important presence of upper-class women at the gallery and to the proprietor's careful cultivation of this segment of his public. The occasion for this article was the (temporary) refusal of the Grosvenor's request for a license to sell liquor in its restaurant: "There are so few places in London where, free from all objectionable surroundings, ladies can obtain even light refreshment, not to speak of so serious a repast as a dinner, that the closing of any one of them is a matter of some importance to many of our readers. It is therefore with regret we hear of the refusal of a licence to the restaurant connected with the Grosvenor Gallery in New Bond-street."

The article goes on to explain that in the first year of the Gallery's establishment its "large, commodious restaurant" was awarded an interim license for the sale of wines and spirits, the facility having been opened too late for a regular license to be obtained: "We have no hesitation in saying that the existence of the refreshment room during the past year has been highly useful to many thousand visitors, espe-

cially to those ladies who, far distant from their homes, had no alternative but the fatty, dyspepsia-bearing tarts of the pastrycook." Sir Coutts's application for a liquor license had apparently been refused because of the magistrates' pique over his success in gaining an interim license pending their own regular meeting. The article concludes with a strong statement of support for Sir Coutts and confirmation of the importance of this amenity to its readers: "The granting of a licence to the Grosvenor could by no possibility affect the licensed houses in the neighbourhood. Its frequenters belong to the classes in society that cannot patronise ordinary public-houses: and it is really an unjust action to deprive the ladies visiting the gallery of a glass of claret or other needful refreshment, simply because the magistrates choose to pick an undignified quarrel with the Board of Inland Revenue, to the inconvenience of the public, and the pecuniary loss of the projectors of this well-conducted and important institution."[97]

The Grosvenor restaurant's licensing problem was bothersome to men as well as to women—the newspaper *Truth* referred to the refusal as a "monstrous" injustice, pointing out that the restaurant was "a great convenience to thousands."[98] But men had far greater choice of places for food and drink—upper-class men had their clubs, while clubs for women were just beginning to develop in the mid-eighties—Amy Levy's 1888 article on women's clubs mentions just four.[99] The benefits to patrons listed on successive Grosvenor catalogues clearly show a market strategy designed to appeal to cultured women poorly served by commercial establishments and the still-limited development of women's clubs. From 1880 the Grosvenor Gallery Library and Club offered the use of a Ladies' Drawing Room as a privilege of the annual two-guinea membership. The 1883 catalogue added the option of private dinners in the restaurant, as well as afternoon tea, coffee, chocolate, and patisseries. The 1885 catalogue announced, "in response to numerous applications arrangements have been made for the opening of new and commodious LADIES' READING ROOMS." In 1888 and 1889, as Sir Coutts worked to shore up gallery finances, he again appealed to the female market with a "ladies' restaurant par excellence."[100]

SUNDAY OPENINGS

A very different area of Grosvenor innovation in the accommodation of art publics took place as part of the national campaign for Sunday openings of museums and galleries, a movement led by the National Sunday League. Founded in 1855 by a group of London artisans, the League had soon gained the support of John Stuart Mill and other liberal intellectuals.[101] Pressure for Sunday admission had already met with some success outside London before the Grosvenor was built; in 1876 a procession of 20,000 men had lined up to present a petition for the Sunday opening of the British Museum.[102] As onetime president of a section of the reformist National Association for the Promotion of Social Science (and having already opened his gallery on Sunday, albeit to a limited number of season-ticket holders), Coutts Lindsay was a natural ally of the Sunday Society. He was joined by several other prominent men associated with the Grosvenor, among them Lord Rosebery, the Duke of Westminster, Sir Henry Thompson, and George Howard; a Member of Parliament in 1882, Howard would introduce a motion for the Sunday opening of all museums and galleries, to be supported by national funds.[103]

The columns of the *Times* during July 1878 provide an overview of the Grosvenor's role in the movement for Sunday museum opening. Having readily acceded to the League's request for Sunday hours, Sir Coutts found that he needed to work around the laws that regulated licensed houses. Because such establishments were required to close on Sunday between three and six P.M., the Grosvenor premises, which included a licensed restaurant, would have to close as well during those hours, even though the restaurant was itself closed, since the liquor license extended to both the gallery and the restaurant.[104]

At a meeting of highly placed friends of the Sunday Society, Mark Judge, the society's founder, recommended a schedule of Sunday hours chosen to work around the licensing law. Sir Coutts assured the public that if the strictest Sabbatarians were to visit his gallery on Sunday,

they would clearly see that there was no desecration of the Sabbath or infringement of hours of worship. Even with the brief and belated notice given in the papers of the new opening hours, 563 people turned up for this new Sunday opportunity to visit the Grosvenor.[105]

A week later, "at the usual time in London for opening the publichouses on the Sunday," the Grosvenor opened under the auspices of the Sunday Society, whose president was then Lord Rosebery. The society had issued 3,200 tickets, but a misunderstanding with another organization that had permission to issue limited numbers of tickets meant that an even greater number attended the Grosvenor on a day when, the *Times* pointedly noted, "by the traditions of the country, pictures in public galleries are not to be viewed." The visitors on this July Sunday "were not of one class," for many middle-class titled people and Members of Parliament came "to see the result of this experiment for themselves. The visitors were as orderly as a congregation in a place of worship. There was no money changing in the gallery. Some of the visitors had not provided themselves with catalogues, and they were lent the books on the promise that they would return them on leaving. The famous restaurant, the existence of which was opposed by the licensing magistrates, was not on this occasion opened."[106] A year later (July 1879) Henry Thompson, the new Sunday Society president, announced the continuation of these Sunday hours, thanking Sir Coutts Lindsay for his "generous endeavour to add to the few opportunities now possessed by the people for the study of art on their one leisure day."[107]

How did the Grosvenor balance its two distinct Sunday publics? An answer is suggested in the 1881 profile of Lady Lindsay that appeared in the *Illustrated Queen Almanac and Lady's Calendar*: "At Lady Lindsay's Sunday receptions, held during the season at the Grosvenor Gallery, all London literary and artistic may be seen. Besides these brilliant receptions there are humbler Sunday gatherings later on in the season, when poor people, especially of the artisan class, under the guidance of some cicerones, are admitted by ticket gratis to view the works of art."

The Sunday policy appears to have been renewed annually; it may be that Blanche Lindsay's withdrawal from the scene after the 1882 season and the end of large-scale, fashionable Sunday entertainments at the gallery opened additional hours earlier in the season for Sunday Society viewers. The policy of special Sunday opening was well received, as was evident in an appreciative 1884 notice in Annie Besant's socialist journal, *Our Corner*. The columnist noted the enjoyable opportunity afforded to members of the Sunday Society and their friends by the Grosvenor Gallery, whose rooms were "well filled with busy folk, glad of the opportunity of passing pleasantly some of the hours of their most leisure day."[108]

The Grosvenor Gallery's impress upon the times was far greater than its limited life span would indicate. The level of excitement it generated suggests that its effects were as multilayered as were the social currents with which it interacted. If the satirists were partially right in seeing sham and social climbing in this segment of the art world, their partial view should not be accepted as the whole story. Contemporaries saw the Grosvenor as somehow embodying a new spirit. While there was, indeed, an effort to reassert traditional aristocratic cultural leadership, that effort could not stand alone and was ultimately unsuccessful. It was the work of artists and the acceptance of new understandings of aesthetic experience—the culmination of Romanticism and, especially, of the work of Ruskin and Pater—that gave the Grosvenor its unique charisma. And if Grosvenor proprietors and the members of its publics sometimes muddled the world of art with those of fashion, commerce, and social striving, that confusion seems as modern as any of Whistler's nocturnes and harmonies.

3
"Art Is upon the Town!"
The Grosvenor Gallery Winter Exhibitions

Allen Staley

IN ADDITION TO THE SUMMER EXHIBITIONS of contemporary art, which constituted the prime reason for the gallery's creation, the Grosvenor Gallery annually presented winter exhibitions of a very different kind, often but not exclusively devoted to earlier art. These exhibitions opened on or around the first of the year and continued until the end of March.[1] There were thirteen winter exhibitions, the first in 1878 and the last in 1890; in addition, during the last four years of its existence, the Grosvenor Gallery's premises were used for a third exhibition in the autumn months. The first of these, in 1887, was of works by the peripatetic Russian artist Vassili Verestchagin, which seems not to have been organized by the gallery itself but by the artist, who took over the space to show his work. That entrepreneurial venture was followed by three exhibitions devoted to pastels, the last in 1890 under the auspices of a newly formed Society of British Pastellists.

The winter exhibitions started auspiciously with *Drawings by the Old Masters and Watercolour Drawings by Deceased Artists of the British School*. Joseph Comyns Carr claimed that in presenting old-master drawings to a large public beyond "a limited and learned circle of amateurs," the exhibition marked an "epoch in Art exhibitions,"[2] and most of the critics seem to have agreed. The exhibition was accompanied by a modest unillustrated catalogue (really a checklist), which a visitor could carry around the galleries, and by a folio volume containing fourteen illustrations and a twenty-seven-page introduction by Carr devoted to the old-master drawings on view. The drawings shown included large groups by or ascribed to Leonardo, Raphael, Michelangelo, Titian, Dürer, and Holbein coming from such distinguished sources as the Royal Collection, Chatsworth House, and Warwick Castle. The English watercolors were, in their own way, equally impressive. But to a twentieth-century observer the most remarkable thing about this presentation was not the quality of the works shown but the quantity: a total of 1,238, with 520 watercolors in the West Gallery alone. Apart from the question of how all of them could have been squeezed in, how anyone could have found time to look at them all staggers the mind. Allowing an average of one minute per drawing, even a cursory inspection of the entire exhibition would have required at least ten two-hour visits. No wonder the gallery offered season tickets. In contrast to those 1,258 works, some 200 paintings and drawings had been shown in the same spaces in the gallery's opening exhibition in the preceding summer, a number somewhat more in line with Sir Coutts Lindsay's goal of elegantly uncrowded exhibitions.

The second exhibition in 1879 consisted, like the first, of old-master drawings and English watercolors, but with the important difference that the watercolors were by living rather than deceased artists. The largest group of old-master drawings came from the great collection owned by Christ Church, Oxford, but perhaps the most interesting aspect of the undertaking was a gallery of early nineteenth-century French drawings, almost all borrowed from French collections and including no less than seventy-three by Ingres alone. Once again, the exhibition was huge: 1,151 works, which, as the *Art Journal* pointed out, surpassed the 1,055 on view in the concurrent winter exhibition in the considerably larger galleries of the Royal Academy.[3] The *Art Journal* went on to express fear that such magnificence could not be kept up, a concern which proved prophetic.

After 1879 old-master drawings disappeared from the walls of the Grosvenor Gallery, but exhibitions of contemporary watercolors continued for the next three winters. In 1880 a group of Dutch watercolors, sent by the Society of Painters in Water Colours of the Hague, provided a special feature, and in 1881 there were French watercolors and a contribution from the Liverpool Society of Painters in Water-Colours. But despite these efforts to enrich or enliven the offerings, the watercolors shown in the winter exhibitions seem to have been of decreasing quality and interest; in 1881 the critic Wilfrid Meynell described the selection as profoundly commonplace.[4] Those exhibited the following year were completely overshadowed by the paintings with which they shared the gallery, and after 1882 the watercolor exhibitions ceased.

The old-master drawings, which had co-existed with the watercolors in the gallery's first

two years, were succeeded in 1880 and 1881 by sketches and drawings by contemporary artists, with the main interest provided by the same artists who were the star attractions of the summer exhibitions, in particular Edward Burne-Jones, who was the most substantial contributor in both years. Although the *Magazine of Art* dismissed many of the drawings as "portfolio scraps,"[5] many others were designs and cartoons for stained glass, mosaics, and other decorative schemes of considerable size, ambition, and interest. In displaying them, the gallery gave public visibility to a central impulse of the Aesthetic Movement directed away from the single, self-contained, conventionally framed paintings that constituted the more usual staple of most exhibitions.

A more radical departure came in the winter of 1882 with a retrospective exhibition of 205 works by George Frederic Watts. Strictly speaking, this was not a one-man exhibition, as Watts shared the gallery with the last of the watercolor shows; nonetheless, attention on such a scale was usually reserved for the memorial exhibition following an artist's death and was virtually without precedent for a living artist. A portrait of Lady Lindsay by Watts (see fig. 62) had been exhibited in the first summer exhibition of the Grosvenor Gallery, and it reappeared there in 1882. Sir Coutts had probably known Watts since around 1850; he inherited his studio assistant, Charles Couzens, from Watts, and both men had been in love with the same woman, Virginia, Countess Somers (formerly Virginia Pattle, the sister of Sarah Prinsep, in whose home Watts lived from 1850 to 1875).[6] Watts had been the subject of a smaller exhibition of fifty-six works all lent by one collector at the Royal Institution in Manchester in 1880. In 1882 he was sixty-five years old, looked upon by all as a living old master, and, although a member of the Royal Academy, an uncomfortable one who had been a mainstay of the Grosvenor Gallery's summer exhibitions since their inception.

The next year, having taken the first step, the gallery followed Watts with paintings by Lawrence Alma-Tadema, the recently deceased landscape painter Cecil Lawson, and nine sculptures by Giovanni Battista Amendola, an Italian living in London, and after a two-year interval, a large exhibition in 1886 devoted to John Everett Millais. Of these artists, Amendola's inclusion is possibly explained by his friendship with Alma-Tadema, whose wife's portrait was one of the works Amendola showed. A portrait of Amendola by Alma-Tadema appeared in the summer exhibition of 1884; nevertheless, the sculptor was sufficiently little known to the gallery's directors for them to list him in the catalogue as A. Amendola rather than by his proper initials. Cecil Lawson, on the other hand, was a respected young artist who had made his reputation in the summer exhibitions of the Grosvenor Gallery. Following his death at the age of thirty-one in 1882, a retrospective display of his paintings there was not only appropriate but almost called for. Both Alma-Tadema and Millais were Royal Academicians, whose careers and reputations were closely tied to the Academy, although both regularly sent works to the Grosvenor Gallery as well. In 1883 Alma-Tadema was still only in his forties but already immensely successful. He was also a close personal friend of Joseph Comyns Carr.[7] Millais, one of the original members of the Pre-Raphaelite Brotherhood in 1848, was by 1886 probably the most widely popular artist in England, who was sure to guarantee large attendance and, thereby, income for the by-then financially struggling gallery.

In the 1880s the gallery also presented three monographic exhibitions devoted to English or quasi-English old masters: Sir Joshua Reynolds in 1884; Thomas Gainsborough in 1885 (along with drawings by the illustrator Richard Doyle, who had died in 1883 and, like Cecil Lawson, had close associations with the gallery); and Sir Anthony Van Dyck in 1887. All three were ambitious undertakings in scale and in the scholarly catalogues that accompanied them, a new departure for the gallery and indeed a departure from the skimpy catalogues of most nineteenth-century exhibitions. The illustrated folio with introductory essay by Comyns Carr published in conjunction with the first winter exhibition in 1878 had no immediate successors. Even the handlist catalogues, previously sold for a shilling, became smaller and slimmer affairs and sold for a sixpence from

1880 to 1885. But the Reynolds catalogue contained "Historical Notes" by Frederic George Stephens, who was identified on the title page of the catalogue as author of *English Children as Painted by Sir Joshua Reynolds* but was better known as the art critic of the *Athenaeum*. For the catalogues of the subsequent four winter exhibitions, Stephens wrote similar notes: entries, often quite long, for individual pictures, identifying subjects, discussing dates and the works' histories, and providing other basic information in the manner of a detailed modern catalogue.

The entries for the Millais catalogue have a special interest, as Stephens had been one of the original members of the Pre-Raphaelite Brotherhood along with Millais and, hence, could write about the works on the basis of firsthand knowledge of events.[8] There were no introductions, but, in the four monographic catalogues he wrote, Stephens made his entry for a self-portrait by the artist the occasion of a brief biographical and critical essay. The Reynolds catalogue was reissued by the Chiswick Press in an edition illustrated by artistically fuzzy "Photo-Intaglio Plates" by Alfred Dawson, who was also responsible for the plates in the earlier illustrated volume of 1878, but like the earlier volume it had no immediate successors. The Millais exhibition, however, did inspire an independently published rival, *Notes on Some of the Principal Pictures of Sir John Everett Millais Exhibited at the Grosvenor Gallery, 1886. With a Preface and Original and Selected Criticisms, by John Ruskin, D.C.L., LL.D.*, consisting mainly of comment about Millais's pictures excerpted from Ruskin's earlier writings.

The resignations of Charles Hallé and Joseph Comyns Carr in the autumn of 1887 signaled a change in the winter exhibitions before the impact of the resignations was felt in the following summer's contemporary exhibition. In the catalogue of the exhibition that opened in January 1888, Sir Coutts Lindsay acknowledged the "valuable aid in forming the collection" of Mr. C. W. Deschamps, and in the following year Deschamps's name was listed on the title page along with that of Lindsay. Deschamps was a nephew of the great Victorian art dealer Ernest Gambart and, unlike Hallé and Carr, was himself a dealer; as manager of Paul

Durand-Ruel's Society of French Artists between 1872 and 1875 Deschamps had helped introduce French Impressionism to the English public. In the winters of 1888 and 1889 Lindsay and Deschamps put on exhibitions entitled *A Century of British Art from 1737 to 1837*. The two were full of wonderful pictures running from Hogarth to Constable and Turner, but by their nature they lacked the focused interest of those of the preceding six years. Also, although the Grosvenor Gallery was never a commercial gallery with its own stock to sell, and although many of the loans still came from aristocratic owners and from Queen Victoria, who lent to both exhibitions but was not about to sell off her inherited treasures, many came from more enterprising collectors, including the artists Thomas Woolner and James Orrock, who actively bought and sold pictures and certainly benefited from the opportunity of putting their goods on prominent display. It is also fascinating to note how many pictures included in the two exhibitions not only changed hands in the following few years but crossed the Atlantic to find their way onto the walls of American museums. Gainsborough's *Mall in St. James's Park*, for example (now in the Frick Collection), was in the exhibition of 1889. F. G. Stephens wrote the notes for the catalogue of 1888 but was replaced in 1889 by Walter Armstrong, a prolific younger critic and art historian, who worked extensively with and for the art trade and in 1892 became director of the National Gallery of Ireland.

The gallery's final winter exhibition in 1890 was *Works of Art Illustrative of and Connected with Sport*. It was a socially grand affair, under the patronage of four royal princes, and organized by an executive committee whose chairman was His Royal Highness the Duke of Edinburgh. Sir Coutts Lindsay was listed only as one of the committee's dozen members rather than coming first on the title page as "Proprietor and Director," as he had in the twelve preceding catalogues. Deschamps seems to have departed, and no author received credit for the catalogue notes. Like the previous two exhibitions, this one had its quota of major masterpieces, including the great Rubens *Wolf and Fox Hunt* now in the Metropolitan Museum of Art, fifteen paintings by George Stubbs, and fifty-four by

Edwin Landseer. But it was also an amazing grab bag, including not only sporting paintings but also sculptures (including the model for *The Falconer* by George Simonds which overlooks the Seventy-Second Street Transverse in Central Park in New York), plate, arms, "Gloves, Hoods, Lures, Jesses, Swivels, Bells, etc." used for falconry, stuffed hawks, and 148 "Trophies," meaning the stuffed heads (and occasionally more) of big game, ranging from African boars and warthogs to three North American moose heads "brought back by Lord Lonsdale from his recent Arctic Expedition." Fascinating things in their own right no doubt, but a far cry from what the Grosvenor Gallery had initially been intended to display.

The "Proprietor and Director" and his wife were both artists, members of the New Watercolor Society, and both showed their works in their gallery's winter watercolor presentations from 1879 to 1882, as they did also in its summer exhibitions. In 1880 and 1881 Lindsay additionally exhibited several of his designs for his most ambitious undertaking as an artist: the decoration of Dorchester House, the palatial residence built in Park Lane in London by his sister's husband, Robert Holford. Otherwise, Sir Coutts and Lady Lindsay lent only a few watercolors by such relatively minor artists as Samuel Prout and William Leighton Leitch to the winter exhibitions. They were not serious collectors, although each had wealthy relatives or in-laws who were. Holford formed one of the greatest collections of pictures in Victorian England, and the Baron Ferdinand de Rothschild (a cousin of Lady Lindsay, whose mother was a Rothschild), built the country house Waddesdon Manor between 1874 and 1889 and filled it with the awe-inspiring collections that are still there. The most publicized and discussed loan to the first winter exhibition, a celebrated volume of drawings ascribed to Mantegna, was lent by another cousin, Hannah de Rothschild, but, by and large, the gallery's program does not appear to have been directed or influenced by any particular interests of family members. The relative who would have probably had the greatest potential influence on Lindsay was Alexander Lindsay, his first cousin and brother-in-law, who became twenty-fifth Earl of

Crawford. In 1847, under his then title of Lord Lindsay, Alexander published *Sketches of the History of Christian Art,* a book written in the form of letters to a promising young artist with whom the author had "spent many a happy day in exploring the pictorial treasures of Umbria and the Appenine, and for whose use they were originally designed, Sir Coutts Lindsay, Bart."[9] This book made a seminal contribution to the rediscovery of Italian fourteenth- and fifteenth-century painting that would underlie significant developments in English painting in the following years, such as the formation of the Pre-Raphaelite Brotherhood in 1848, as well as in taste more generally. Sir Coutts, to whom the *Sketches* were dedicated, was expected to play a role in these developments: "I see no reason why he should not be a second Benozzo Gozzoli."[10] But by the time of the establishment of the Grosvenor Gallery, thirty years had passed since publication of *Sketches of the History of Christian Art*; the revolution in taste which it had helped to encourage was no longer at the cutting edge of fashion and was not significantly reflected in the gallery's winter exhibitions.

The available evidence suggests that the gallery's loan exhibitions prior to 1888 were less directly shaped by Sir Coutts Lindsay than by his two younger assistant directors, Charles Hallé and Joseph Comyns Carr, who did the real work of organizing them. Hallé, the son of Sir Charles Hallé, the musician after whom the Hallé Orchestra in Manchester is named, was a painter who never had much professional success. He had studied in Paris under a former pupil of Ingres, and the Grosvenor's major display of Ingres's drawings in the winter of 1879 was due to his connections.[11] In his memoirs Hallé recorded the profound impression that the huge *Art Treasures* exhibition of 1857 in Manchester (where his family lived) had made upon him, and memories of the grandest art exhibition ever to take place in the British Isles surely lurked in the background of the exhibitions he subsequently helped to stage.[12] As an eleven-year-old Hallé learned to love Italian art under the guidance of Richard Doyle, who came to Manchester to see the exhibition and stayed for three months as the Hallés' guest. Twenty years later that friendship was still alive: Doyle was at

the meetings in which the Grosvenor Gallery was conceived; he helped select old-master drawings for its first winter exhibition;[13] his drawings became an expected feature of its shows; and following his death almost two hundred of them were included in the winter exhibition of 1885.

Unlike Lindsay and Hallé, Joseph Comyns Carr was not a painter and, hence, did not share their practical goal of establishing a new venue for themselves and like-minded friends to show their own work. Perhaps because of that, he only officially joined the team after the first two exhibitions, although he had participated in the discussions in the autumn of 1876 that preceded the gallery's formation. He was a writer, a man of the theater, and playwright and in the 1870s was the art critic for several periodicals. As a critic he championed the living artists who would be associated with the Grosvenor Gallery, but he also wrote about earlier art, including a five-part series in the *Pall Mall Gazette* about the old-master drawings in the British Museum.[14] That endeavor may well have prompted the decision to show old-master drawings in the first winter exhibition at the Grosvenor Gallery and undoubtedly prepared Carr to participate in organizing the exhibition and to write the catalogue essay for it, although none of its contents came from the British Museum. His essay was a surprisingly scholarly and focused discussion of specific drawings shown, with attention to details of dating, provenance, and attribution in which Carr frequently asked if the works (which were listed under the names provided by their owners) were correctly labeled, doubting, for example, whether the drawings in the volume lent by Hannah de Rothschild were indeed by Mantegna.[15] During the 1880s F. G. Stephens, rather than Carr, wrote catalogue notes for the gallery, but Carr did write an appreciative essay about Reynolds after the exhibition of 1884 and a slightly less appreciative one about Gainsborough, the subject of the following year's exhibition.[16]

In undertaking a program of winter exhibitions, Lindsay and his colleagues were following the lead of virtually every other gallery in London. "Art is upon the town!" declared James McNeill Whistler in 1885 in his "Ten O'Clock

Lecture." In February 1878 the *Art Journal's* review of the Grosvenor Gallery's initial winter exhibition appeared in the second installment of a three-part series of reviews under the heading "The Winter Exhibitions." Other exhibitions discussed included those of the French Gallery in Pall Mall, the Everard Galleries, the Fine Art Society, the McClean Gallery, Mr. Tooth's Gallery, the Society of British Artists, the Dudley Gallery, the Old Water-Color Society, the New Water-Color Society, the Guardi Gallery (antecedent of the modern Colnaghi's), the Burlington Fine Arts Club, and the Royal Academy.[17]

Loan exhibitions of old-master paintings were introduced to London early in the nineteenth century by the British Institution, an organization founded in 1805 by a group of collectors and patrons, in covert rivalry with the Royal Academy, as a place of instruction and of exhibition of contemporary work. In 1806 its directors started to borrow old-master paintings, not for the sake of exhibitions per se, but for instruction, for students to copy. In the summer of 1813, the Institution staged a public exhibition of Sir Joshua Reynolds, following it in 1814 with one of Gainsborough and three other eighteenth-century British painters and in 1815 with one of Dutch and Flemish pictures. Thus began the annual exhibitions of works by old masters and recently deceased British artists which the British Institution put on every summer until 1867, when it lost the lease on its building in Pall Mall and went out of business.[18] The Royal Academy, which was in the process of moving into its present home in Burlington House, thereupon assumed the burden, reversing the British Institution's pattern of winter exhibitions of contemporary art and summer loan exhibitions. Its first winter exhibition of old masters and paintings by Charles Robert Leslie and Clarkson Stanfield, Academicians who had died in 1859 and 1867, respectively, opened in January 1870, and its tradition of major loan exhibitions continues to this day (now no longer confined to one annual winter offering). In the 1870s and 1880s the Academy's winter exhibitions were usually devoted to somewhat heterogeneous displays of "Old and British Masters," but often with a

gallery or galleries set aside for individual artists or specific themes.[19] The exhibition of 1878, with which the first winter show at the Grosvenor Gallery competed, included a gallery of mezzotint engravings (which were to have an immense vogue in subsequent years) after Reynolds, George Romney, and Gainsborough and a gallery of landscape paintings by the early nineteenth-century Norwich School. The next year, following the Grosvenor Gallery's inaugural showing of drawings (and probably inspired by it), the Academy devoted four of its galleries to old-master drawings, with additional displays of miniatures and Venetian, Spanish, and Dutch paintings. Succeeding those of the moribund British Institution, these were ambitious exhibitions on a large scale in the vast and splendid new galleries in Burlington House, and to them has been ascribed a major influence upon the collecting of old masters in the last quarter of the nineteenth century. They provided the chief model, as well as competition, for the rival offerings at the Grosvenor Gallery.

Of the other winter exhibitions cited by the *Art Journal*, after 1862 those of the watercolor societies were of sketches and studies, as opposed to the finished works that appeared in the societies' summer exhibitions, and they may have prompted the decision to show sketches and studies at the Grosvenor Gallery in the winters of 1880 and 1881. Art historically, the exhibitions of the Burlington Fine Arts Club, founded in 1866, were the most adventurous and interesting taking place in late Victorian England. The members of this club of "Amateurs, Collectors, and others interested in Art" annually organized two or three exhibitions, often built around their own collections but also intended to elucidate, with the help of serious scholarly catalogues, "some school, master, or specific art."[20] It was probably to this club's offerings, which were not open to the general public and which included a show of drawings by Raphael and Michelangelo in 1870, that Comyns Carr, without naming them, intended to allude in commending the Grosvenor Gallery for exhibiting drawings to the larger public "beyond a limited and learned circle of amateurs." The Grosvenor's display of watercolors by deceased artists alongside the old-master drawings in 1878 also gave a public dimension to what had previously been on private view at the Burlington Fine Arts Club, in exhibitions of watercolors by artists born before 1800 in 1871, by David Cox and Peter De Wint in 1873, and by Thomas Girtin in 1875.

The attention given in these exhibitions of landscape watercolors to artists such as Girtin, Cox, and De Wint—whose broad, atmospheric styles were the antithesis of the bright color and minutely stippled detail of Victorian watercolors inspired by the precepts of Ruskin and the example of the Pre-Raphaelites, was echoed in the showings of Dutch and French watercolors at the Grosvenor Gallery in 1880 and 1881.[21] It could be seen on a different scale in 1883, in more than one hundred pictures and watercolors by Cecil Lawson, who was described in the same year by Edmund Gosse as having taken up the tradition of landscape in the grand style where Constable had dropped it at the beginning of Victoria's reign.[22] Lawson's paintings, such as the large and murky *August Moon* (fig. 28), which had appeared initially in the summer exhibition of 1880 and was re-exhibited in 1883, were criticized for looking "as if they

had come out of the National Gallery,"[23] but he was admired by Whistler (who even made an etching after one of Lawson's paintings) and championed by Comyns Carr.[24] He was immortalized by George Bernard Shaw in the description in *Pygmalion* of Henry Higgins's mother's Chelsea drawing room, which was decorated "with a few good oil paintings from the exhibitions in the Grosvenor Gallery thirty years ago," including one landscape, "a Cecil Lawson on the scale of a Rubens."[25]

Because of his untimely death, Lawson was honored by a memorial exhibition in the tradition of exhibitions of recently deceased artists at the British Institution, the Royal Academy, the Burlington Fine Arts Club, and elsewhere. He died in the same year as Dante Gabriel Rossetti, and, at the same time that the Grosvenor Gallery was showing his paintings, the Royal Academy and the Burlington Fine Arts Club both mounted memorial exhibitions devoted to Rossetti. As Rossetti was a virulent anti-establishment artist who loathed the Royal Academy and never exhibited there, its posthumous exhibition was dubiously appropriate and was even characterized at the time as "a deliberate plot to stab poor Rossetti in the back."[26] Although

28. Cecil Gordon Lawson, *The August Moon*, 1880, exh. 1880. Oil on canvas. Tate Gallery, London

Rossetti never exhibited at the Grosvenor Gallery, either (he never exhibited anywhere), the exhibition should have been there; that it was not can probably largely be ascribed to the energy, enterprise, and influence of Frederic Leighton, the president of the Royal Academy, but a show of Lawson rather than Rossetti in 1883 was consistent with the prevailing pattern of the Grosvenor Gallery's winter exhibitions. A retrospective exhibition of the art of Burne-Jones, the artist most closely identified with the gallery, never took place there and had to wait until 1893 at the New Gallery. That delay can not be explained by the argument that in the 1880s Burne-Jones was still too young for such recognition, as he was six years older than Alma-Tadema, who was given a showing in the winter of 1883 along with Lawson.

The old masters that admirers of Burne-Jones (and hence habitués of the Grosvenor Gallery) might have been expected to want to see, namely Botticelli and other fifteenth-cen-tury Italians, were represented in the exhibi-tions of drawings in 1878 and 1879 but not in large numbers and not nearly as well as at the Royal Academy, which for several years had devoted a special gallery to quattrocento art. After 1879 early Italian art disappeared entirely from the Grosvenor Gallery. By then the Botti-celli craze, which had peaked at the beginning of the decade with Walter Pater's essay "A Frag-ment on Sandro Botticelli" and Ruskin's Oxford lectures, was old news.[27] In contrast, Sir Joshua Reynolds, to whom the Grosvenor Gallery de-voted its first one-man old-master exhibition in 1884, was fresh and exciting. Reynolds, the Royal Academy's first president, belonged at the Academy as emphatically as Dante Gabriel Rossetti did not (fig. 29), and a Reynolds exhibi-tion at the Grosvenor Gallery may have been in part Lindsay's, Hallé's, and Carr's form of retali-ation against Leighton's stealing Rossetti from under their noses the year before. Nevertheless, the Reynolds exhibition was not a one-shot

JANUARY 12, 1884.] PUNCH, OR THE LONDON CHARIVARI. 15

NOT PARTICULAR TO A SHADE; OR, A COLLECTION IN THE GROSVENOR GALLERY.

Sir Frederick Leighton, P.R.A. (1884). "I THINK YOU OUGHT TO HAVE COME TO US!"
Sir Joshua Reynolds, P.R.A. (1769) (*with his ear-trumpet up*). "EH! WHAT!" (*Sir Frederick repeats.*) "AH—UM—WELL—WHY DIDN'T YOU THINK TO ASK ME!" (*Takes snuff.*)

29. Linley Sambourne, "Not particular to a shade; or, a collection in the Grosvenor Gallery," *Punch*, January 12, 1884. Engraving. Yale Center for British Art, Gift of Henry S. Morgan

affair dictated by spite but would be succeeded by Gainsborough in 1885 and Van Dyck in 1887. What was happening was the rediscovery of a type of painting that Ruskin, the Pre-Raphaelites, and the mid-Victorians in general had scorned, a rediscovery paralleling the effort in artistic practice of a painter such as Lawson to rediscover and reaffirm the qualities of a pre-Victorian, pre-Ruskinian, and pre-Pre-Raphaelite tradition of landscape. It is no coincidence that in 1882 John Singer Sargent started to exhibit in London at the Royal Academy and at the Grosvenor Gallery, two years before the gallery began to celebrate and consecrate grand-manner portraiture from the seventeenth and eighteenth centuries.

Long after the fact, Comyns Carr wrote, "In the seventies, when I first became actively engaged in the study of painting, the stirring spirit of English Art still throbbed in response to the message that had been delivered by the Pre-Raphaelite Brotherhood more than twenty years before. . . . We did not, perhaps, then quite realize that the revolution, so far as they were concerned, was already complete."[28] In the thirteen years of the Grosvenor Gallery's existence, the most conspicuous new developments in English art were in the work of such artists as Lawson, Sargent, and the painters associated with the New English Art Club, and these developments carried with them new attitudes toward the art of the past. For the young Pre-Raphaelites in 1848, the name which they gave to themselves announced to the world what they admired, whereas for them Sir Joshua Reynolds was "Sir Sloshua," *fons et origo* of debased practices from which they were trying to break free. As for Reynolds's great contemporary, as late as 1896 Burne-Jones could declare Gainsborough an impostor: "He just scratches on the canvas over loose flimsy stains and puts markings in black around them." Burne-Jones's attitudes toward old and new were of a piece: "I can't imagine a more detestable kind of painting than Sargent's. Unless it were Gainsborough's."[29] How he must have gritted his teeth not only before the Gainsboroughs at the Grosvenor Gallery in the winter of 1885, but before Sargent's portraits that hung there alongside his own works in the preceding and following sum-

mers. Despite his distaste, the cult of Reynolds and Gainsborough was as vigorous and vital, and as closely linked to contemporary art, as the fervor for Botticelli had been only a few years before, and there were many more English portraits than Italian quattrocento pictures in English collections waiting to be rediscovered, reassessed, and exhibited. Van Dyck, whose works followed in 1887, was exhibited as a foreign-born English portraitist, the starting point of what was once again, after a period of eclipse, perceived as a great tradition which flowered in the late eighteenth century in the work of Reynolds and Gainsborough, and which was seen to be flowering again at the end of the nineteenth. In the words of Auguste Rodin, Sargent was "the Van Dyck of our times."[30]

If Sargent was compared to Van Dyck, his slightly younger contemporary, Philip Wilson Steer, would be claimed as "the modern successor of Constable."[31] Steer started to exhibit at the Grosvenor Gallery in 1885, and Constable himself, although not honored on the scale of Van Dyck, was well represented in the two exhibitions of British art from 1737 to 1837 that took place there in 1888 and 1889. The second included eighty-nine of his works with one room devoted entirely to oil sketches, mainly from the estate of his daughter Isabel Constable (fig. 30). Such a display would have been unthinkable a dozen years earlier when the gallery opened. In 1871 Ruskin dismissed the work of Constable and David Cox as "wholly disorderly, slovenly and licentious . . . the mere blundering of clever peasants."[32] By 1888, however, growing awareness of recent French painting made it possible to appreciate Constable anew: "The intelligent young painter, fresh from Parisian studios, is apt, while falling foul of everything else that is English, to be absolutely hysterical in his admiration of Constable."[33] By 1890 Constable was proclaimed the fountainhead of what was best in modern painting: "He is the father of genuine nature-study amongst French landscape painters, and they have been led into his ways of study, which have become almost universal amongst them."[34] As French influence swept over progressive English painting—or what claimed to be progressive—English antecedents for what had been

30. John Constable,
Cloud Study, 1821. Oil
on paper laid on board.
Yale Center for British
Art, Paul Mellon
Collection

happening in France were being sought out not only in obvious places, such as Constable's *plein-air* sketches, but also in less expected ones. In 1891, in an evening of papers about Impressionism, Wilson Steer called even Reynolds and Gainsborough "Impressionists."[35] The past is always seen through the eyes of the present.

The three living painters shown in the winters of 1882, 1883, and 1886—Watts, Alma-Tadema, and Millais—seem less of a piece than the deceased masters just discussed. Nevertheless, in their varying ways all three stood for something quite unlike the second-generation Pre-Raphaelitism of Burne-Jones and his disciples John Melhuish Strudwick, Roddam Spencer Stanhope, and Evelyn De Morgan. The choice of these artists for major shows would seem in part to reflect the desire of the gallery's directors to avoid being identified too exclusively with a single type of painting. Watts throughout his career aspired to a rich, old-masterly breadth of handling, as did Millais after about 1860 when he abandoned his youthful Pre-Raphaelite style. In this respect they had some of the same appeal as Reynolds, Gainsborough, and Van Dyck vis-à-vis the newer developments becoming visible in English painting during the 1880s. Millais, in fact, modeled much of his painting of the 1870s

and 1880s on eighteenth-century English portraiture. His *Hearts Are Trumps* of 1872 (fig. 31), for example, was painted in obvious emulation of and competition with Reynolds's *The Ladies Waldegrave* (fig. 32), as critics recognized.[36] Both pictures were included in their artists' displays in the winter exhibitions, where one following the other gave visual demonstration of the ambitions of Millais, along with many younger artists, to make their painting part of an increasingly admired tradition.

Ironically, however, by providing the public and, indeed, the artist himself an opportunity to see Millais's early pictures, which hitherto had been effectively forgotten, the main achievement of the Millais exhibition was not widespread recognition that he had earned a position in the pantheon next to Reynolds, Gainsborough, and Van Dyck, but rather the discovery that he had been a much better painter at the beginning of his career, when as a young member of the Pre-Raphaelite Brotherhood his goals had been radically different. One of the highlights of the exhibition was *A Huguenot, on St. Bartholomew's Day, Refusing to Shield Himself from Danger by Wearing the Roman Catholic Badge* (fig. 33), which the artist supposedly had not seen since shortly after it was first exhibited in 1852, when it had been

31. Sir John Everett Millais, *Hearts Are Trumps*, 1872. Oil on canvas. Tate Gallery, London

32. Sir Joshua Reynolds, *The Ladies Waldegrave*, 1781. Oil on canvas. National Gallery of Scotland

33. Sir John Everett
Millais, *A Huguenot, on
St. Bartholomew's Day,
Refusing to Shield Him-
self from Danger by
Wearing the Roman
Catholic Badge*, 1852.
Oil on canvas.
Makins Collection

bought by a collector in Preston in northern
Lancashire. Millais saw it unpacked when it
arrived for the exhibition and pronounced it
"not so bad for a youngster."[37] Inspired by the
sight of it, he painted the thematically related
but not very similar *Mercy: St. Bartholomew's
Day, 1572* (fig. 34), which appeared at the Royal
Academy the following year, and whose heavy-
handed treatment, both in conception and in
execution, compared to the tender delicacy of
the *Huguenot*, demonstrates the gulf between
Millais's early and late painting. According to
Comyns Carr the sight of his earlier works was
not a source of unalloyed pleasure for the artist
but undermined his belief in the steady progress

of his art.[38] In a story that may be apocryphal
but must also contain a kernel of truth, William
Holman Hunt recounted that a mutual acquaintance found Millais leaving the Grosvenor
Gallery in tears. When accosted, the artist explained: "You see me unmanned. Well I'm not
ashamed of avowing that in looking at my earliest pictures I have been overcome with
chagrin that I have so far failed in my maturity
to fulfill the full forecast of my youth."[39]

This view was also that of many critics, who
in 1886 were able to see for the first time how
different the dazzling colors and scrupulous
naturalism of early Pre-Raphaelite pictures
were not only from Millais's mature style, but

34. Sir John Everett
Millais, *Mercy: St.
Bartholomew's Day,
1572*, 1886. Oil
on canvas. Tate
Gallery, London

also from the later Pre-Raphaelitism which in the hands of Burne-Jones had evolved into the Aestheticism that dominated the summer exhibitions of the Grosvenor Gallery. The discovery was made by artists as well, and in the same year that the New English Art Club was supposedly burying what was left of the Pre-Raphaelite impulse under a load of fresh ideas imported from France, the seeds were being planted for a neo-Pre-Raphaelitism that appeared first in the works of John William Waterhouse and blossomed in the following decades in those of John Byam Liston Shaw and Eleanor Fortescue-Brickdale. According to an appreciation of Waterhouse published in 1909: "At the moment

[1886] nature seemed to the painter to hold out promise of an imaginative revelation to be won by sheer faithfulness of sight. Thus, intense admiration for the early pictures of Millais, seen by him for the first time at the Grosvenor Gallery, prompted him to think."[40]

The Watts exhibition four years earlier also presented a comprehensive view of a long career, but one without dramatic contrast between early and late work and without the perhaps too obvious ties to eighteenth-century prototypes. Watts aimed somewhat higher than Millais, with Phidias, Michelangelo, and Titian as his main models, and allegories about eternal truths as his main subjects. Yet around 1850, when Mil-

lais was painting his early Pre-Raphaelite masterpieces, Watts painted four powerful
modern-life scenes of dislocation, distress, and
apparent suicide, which stand apart from everything else that he did and which are usually
described as "social-realist" paintings. He did
not exhibit them at the time they were painted,
probably in part because he considered their
content too raw for mid-Victorian sensibilities
and in part because they were not the sort of
works upon which he wanted to build a reputa-

tion. They were shown in a public exhibition for
the first time in the Grosvenor retrospective of
1882, and, if they did not lead to the same kind
of reassessment of the artist's career as Millais's
early pictures were to provoke four years later,
they did have an impact. The painter Hubert von
Herkomer made a special trip to London in
March 1882 to see the exhibition, and the consequences of that trip can be seen in his *Hard
Times* (fig. 35), shown at the Royal Academy
three years later, which is basically a reworking

35. Sir Hubert von Herkomer,
Hard Times, 1885. Oil on
canvas. Manchester City
Art Galleries

36. George Frederic Watts, *The Irish
Famine*, c. 1850. Oil on canvas.
Reproduced by permission
of the Trustees of the Watts Gallery,
Compton, near Guildford

of one of Watts's social-realist paintings, *The Irish Famine* (fig. 36), that he had seen.[41] Watts did not inspire Herkomer to become a social realist; *Hard Times* followed numerous related pictures that Herkomer and other artists including Fred Walker, Luke Fildes, and Frank Holl had started to paint around 1870. If anything, the public success of their work probably emboldened Watts in 1882 finally to exhibit his four paintings and, by doing so, implicitly to claim recognition as the forerunner of a thriving

school. In the timeless Michelangelesque monumentality of the starving peasants in *The Irish Famine* there are also parallels with the French peasant pictures of Jean-François Millet, for example, the exactly contemporary *Sower*, which had been praised by Comyns Carr for grandeur, simplicity, grace, and truth in an article on Corot and Millet published shortly before the Watts exhibition.[42]

If we can see affinities among the painterly handling of Watts, late Millais, Reynolds, Gains-

37. Sir Lawrence Alma-Tadema, *A Picture Gallery*, 1874. Oil on canvas. Towneley Hall Art Gallery and Museums, Burnley, Lancashire

borough, and Van Dyck, it is difficult to find a vantage point that can encompass with them the highly detailed archaeological reconstructions of the daily life of ancient Rome by Lawrence Alma-Tadema, exhibited at the gallery in 1883. Alma-Tadema seems so out of step with these other artists to raise the question if there was true consistency of vision behind the gallery's activities. Nevertheless, matters of style and handling notwithstanding, Alma-Tadema, who was ten years younger than Millais and twenty-two years younger than Watts, had a much more up-to-date outlook than was possible for them. In reviewing his exhibition, the *Art Journal* declared that the "principal intention" of the artist was "a denial of adventitious literary interest. That denial is tantamount to a declaration that painting should appeal to the eye and to the intelligence rather than to the emotions and the intellect."[43] The central "appeal to the eye" in Alma-Tadema's art was given embodiment in his numerous depictions of people looking at works of art. The two largest pictures in the retrospective of 1883 were *A Picture Gallery* (fig. 37) and *A Sculpture Gallery,* exhibited originally at the Royal Academy in 1874 and 1875 respectively. Both show groups of people gazing at art with absolute concentration, as if nothing else in life mattered. There are no stories, no incidental dramas, no references to classical myth or history. Art is the subject, and implicit in these pictures of people looking at art is the belief at the heart of Aestheticism, proclaimed by Walter Pater in the conclusion to *The Renaissance,* that life offers no higher meaning or purpose than experience. Pater's essay and the book conclude: "Of such wisdom, the poetic passion, the desire of beauty, the love of art for its own sake, has most. For art comes to you proposing frankly to give nothing but the highest quality to your moments as they pass, and simply for those moments' sake."[44]

In Alma-Tadema's pictures the aesthetes are Romans clad in togas, who gaze at works by Apelles and other classical masters, but who are also the equivalents of nineteenth-century visitors to the Grosvenor Gallery and other exhibitions. These figures belong to the London of the 1870s and 1880s every bit as much as those Victorian apostles of the beautiful who fall

painfully short of the high standards of Walter Pater in the contemporaneous *Punch* cartoon of George Du Maurier. In *A Picture Gallery,* which Alma-Tadema painted for the dealer Ernest Gambart, the man standing in the center is Gambart. The seated man in front of him staring so intently at the picture on the easel is his nephew Charles Deschamps, who at the time the picture was painted represented Paul Durand-Ruel in London, selling Impressionist pictures to the English. Five years after the picture was exhibited at the Grosvenor Gallery Deschamps came to work there. Alma-Tadema's painting does not show the Grosvenor Gallery, which did not yet exist when the picture was painted, nor is it particularly representative of the works of art shown there. Nevertheless, in its depiction of people of cultivation and sensitivity, beautifully dressed and in a tastefully sumptuous setting, engrossed in the contemplation of works of art, it represents something very close to the essence of the Grosvenor Gallery.

4

Burne-Jones and the Pre-Raphaelite Circle at the Palace of the Aesthetes

Susan P. Casteras

THE REVOLUTION IN ART engendered by the earnest Pre-Raphaelite Brotherhood, founded in 1848, did not end when its central trio of John Everett Millais, Dante Gabriel Rossetti, and William Holman Hunt went their separate ways as painters from the mid-1850s onward. The fate of later Pre-Raphaelitism, especially its transformation in the hands of Rossetti and his comrade and acolyte Edward Burne-Jones, would have been very different had Burne-Jones and the so-called second generation of other Pre-Raphaelite adherents not been so active in contributing pictures to the Grosvenor Gallery, particularly during its first decade of existence.

Pre-Raphaelitism intersected with the history of the Grosvenor Gallery on several complex levels, from the notable absence of one of the key figures, Dante Gabriel Rossetti, to the stunning prominence for several years of his friend and principal spiritual heir, Burne-Jones. The Grosvenor Gallery helped also to shape the careers and showcase the accomplishments of several artists in the circle of Burne-Jones, including various women painters. In addition, the kind of criticism leveled at Burne-Jones and his followers reflected cultural concerns and biases about the Aesthetic Movement. Taken in sum, these multiple points all make for a rich interplay of critical reception and cultural resonance in the history of the Grosvenor and of Pre-Raphaelitism as well.

DANTE GABRIEL ROSSETTI

Although he had not achieved the public accolades and commercial success of his Pre-Raphaelite comrade John Everett Millais, Rossetti was nonetheless acknowledged to be a formidable force in contemporary art. Sir Coutts Lindsay may have met him and others in the Pre-Raphaelite circle at professional or social occasions, for example, at Little Holland House, the Prinsep residence, where George Frederic Watts was a star boarder and where Millais and Holman Hunt joined Alfred Tennyson and other eminent guests. Lindsay wanted Rossetti, who was almost legendarily reluctant to exhibit his works publicly, to be part of his new venture and therefore commissioned his representatives to pursue this possibility. J. Comyns Carr (who also knew members of the Pre-Raphaelite co-terie) shared Lindsay's opinions and wrote of how "Holman Hunt, Rossetti, Burne-Jones, Ford Madox Brown . . . knew nothing at that time of academic honour, and their work, if it was sub-mitted for official judgement, was either coldly received or was treated in a spirit of active hos-tility."[1] Accordingly, in early April 1876, a year before the Grosvenor Gallery opened, Carr contacted Rossetti on this subject, saying, "I don't know whether you have heard of a plan projected by Sir Coutts Lindsay for the establish-ment of an exhibition for the higher kind of painting which the Academy has either failed to represent or has represented unfavorably and imperfectly. There is to be no attempt to serve a popular taste but rather to protest against the concessions which have been made to popu-larity at the expense and sacrifice of poetical art." To this he added Lindsay's conviction that a definite need existed to exhibit "works like yours and [Burne-]Jones's. . . . He has mentioned the scheme to Jones and to Watts, Millais, Whistler and one or two others who have promised their help and has asked me to write to you to know if you would consent to become a contributor to such an Exhibition." Carr also cited exhibition reforms, including one that "artists should contribute by invitation and that there should be no attempt to crowd the galleries."[2]

A few days later Rossetti began discussing the topic with his friends and accordingly wrote to Ford Madox Brown, "I never heard of the project you allude to 'til I got the other day the enclosed from George's friend Carr, whom I have met only three or four times. . . . I answered in a few words and quite undecisively. You do not say whether you would feel inclined to join such a scheme."[3]

In addition to Carr's involvement Charles Hallé, artist and special secretary to Lindsay, wrote to Rossetti. (In time both assistants would leave Lindsay to join forces and form their own aesthetic proving grounds at the New Gallery.) Hallé, an admirer of Burne-Jones's art, was also personally acquainted with the Pre-Raphaelite brethren. He seems to have met Burne-Jones when "he and Rossetti had seen some work of mine at the Dudley Gallery, and had sent

Simeon Solomon to look me up and ask me to come and see them."[4] He also wrote in his memoirs that, "Besides Burne-Jones and Ros-setti, I saw a great deal at this time of Millais, as I had a studio close to his, and often went in to see what he was about."[5] Hallé also attended parties at Little Holland House, where he men-tioned seeing Marie Spartali Stillman's father as a guest (and perhaps the daughter was there, too). Moreover, Hallé reported that the seeds of the Grosvenor Gallery were planted during an 1875 visit with the Lindsays and a discussion of how unsatisfactory viewing conditions were for artists like Rossetti, Hunt, Burne-Jones, and others "whose works were rarely seen."[6] The next winter Lindsay came to see Hallé in London and offered a £1,000 guarantee toward the rental of exhibition space. Hallé then spoke with Burne-Jones "and two or three other men, and they authorized me to tell Sir Coutts that they would be willing to exhibit their pictures under the conditions suggested," although they could not contribute toward the cost of the rent.[7]

In January 1877 Hallé, armed with this knowledge and support, wrote to Rossetti under the apparent impression that he might wish to send works. Hallé thus wrote, "I hear from Comyns Carr that you are willing to do so and that you have moreover expressed a wish no attempts should be made to obtain any of your works from private collections." Hallé reassured Rossetti on this point and also tried to justify (presumably to counter Rossetti's objections) why Lindsay had invited six Royal Academicians and was going to include any works by Royal Academicians, along with those by more pro-gressive artists: "Sir Coutts Lindsay felt that it would be bad policy to exclude all paintings by members of the Academy." If he were to do so, he "would not have received many admirable works by Watts and other Academicians who have never been seen or properly seen owing to the bad lighting and method of hanging at Burlington House." Hallé also explained how Lindsay would defray all expenses, send out invitations, retain "sole management of the exhibitions," and spend nearly £100,000 to erect a special building: "The principal reason that induced him to build this gallery was the fact that neither your pictures nor those of Mr.

Burne Jones, Holman Hunt, Whistler, Stanhope, Legros, and others were seen by the public for a good room to which they could be sent without all the annoyances attending upon exhibitions at the Academy." Eager to recruit Rossetti, Hallé diplomatically expressed his enthusiasm and strategically importuned: "I need hardly say . . . that it will be a great disappointment should your name not be found among the contributors—I have had instructions not to complete the collection for this year until your final decision has been ascertained." To tip the scale in favor of a positive response, Hallé also indicated he had contacted some "owners of your works [who] would be willing to let me have them, but as I said before I should never think of taking even a sketch unless I was quite sure you would have no objection."[8]

What transpired next did so partly in the pages of the London *Times.* Rossetti was upset that his name had been mentioned in an article as a future participant to the Grosvenor and thus somewhat acidly wrote to the editor in March, "Will you allow me to state that my health has nothing whatever to do with my not exhibiting at the new gallery?"[9] He then cited a letter he had sent to Hallé two months earlier about his decision not to accept an invitation to join this venture. In this letter, also published in the *Times,* Rossetti voiced his opinion that he "felt no certainty" about his possible participation "but would speak to Mr. Burne-Jones on my return to London. Since I have been here again I have seen both Mr. Carr and Mr. Burne-Jones, and expressed to them the reasons why I do not think it, on the whole, advisable for me to exhibit at the Grosvenor Gallery." However much he tried to defuse the situation, Rossetti's central objection clearly focused on Lindsay's decision to invite Royal Academicians. Despite his admiration for artists in this category like Millais and Watts, Rossetti said, "Such men must be an accession, indeed to any ranks; but a principle was put forward simultaneously with the project of building the Grosvenor Gallery which seems to me irreconcilable with the invitation of artists belonging to the Royal Academy, as I cannot myself see that they fail of due opportunity for the display of their powers on their own walls." Basically, Rossetti as a "single secluded artist"

held out hope for a "fair field for all." He ultimately chose to phrase his nonparticipation not in terms of his resentment of the Royal Academy but for personal reasons: "What holds me back is simply the lifelong feeling of dissatisfaction which I have experienced from the disparity of aim and attainment in what I have all my life produced as best I could." He ended by expressing thanks for the invitation and wishing the success of this enterprise, indicating, "Your scheme must succeed, were it but for one name associated with it—that of Burne-Jones—a name representing the loveliest art we have."[10]

Hallé, seemingly horrified at the public statement of Rossetti's annoyance, immediately attempted to assuage his pique: "On seeing your letter in *The Times* yesterday morning, I wrote to the writer of the article on the Grosvenor Gallery to which you referred to ask him if he had kept the notes he had asked me to supply him with. I have just read them and give you word for word what I wrote in answer to his query if you were to be amongst the contributors to the forthcoming Exhibition. 'Mr. Dante Gabriel Rossetti (though cordially sympathizing with the undertaking), resolved for this year at all events not to come forward.'"[11]

Thus, for all these reasons and circumstances Rossetti was not to be counted—in 1877 or ever—among the contributors to the Grosvenor Gallery. He might have agreed had Royal Academicians not been part of the scheme. Moreover, given the injection of notoriety and fame that his friend Burne-Jones ultimately gained from this enterprise, Rossetti may have fared better with critics and patrons had he chosen to participate. Perhaps this was a missed opportunity, but it was a risk that Rossetti seems to have consciously taken.

SIR JOHN EVERETT MILLAIS
Rossetti was not the only Pre-Raphaelite approached for this project. Millais and Holman Hunt were invited as well, and Millais especially took advantage of this chance and sent numerous entries over the years. Hunt's contributions were more sporadic, and both artists received critical attention but rarely extremes of approval or disapproval. It was instead Burne-Jones, whose early talents had been nurtured by

Rossetti, who received the mantle of fame as the Grosvenor devolved. Furthermore, artists perceived as Burne-Jones's "followers"—primarily John Melhuish Strudwick, John Roddam Spencer Stanhope, Marie Spartali Stillman, and Evelyn Pickering De Morgan—also benefited from this attention, both negative and positive, from the press and others.

The opening exhibition in 1877 triggered an outpouring of commentary, in part representing the poles of conservative and progressive perspectives on the new gallery and its aims. To begin with, it might have been expected that Millais, a well-established critical and financial success at this time, would be perceived as a star here, as he often was at the Royal Academy. Millais seems to have been an early supporter of Lindsay's plan, having urged him to build a permanent gallery, been present at the opening of this edifice on Bond Street, and kept his apparent promise to send numerous works over the years.[12] In the latter respect Millais was loyal, although in hindsight it might fairly be said that his contributions were not his great masterpieces and more likely portraits of varying quality than commanding subject pictures. Also, Millais participated mostly in the summer exhibitions, except for 1886, when a winter retrospective of his work was held at the Grosvenor. Overall critical reception was usually polite, sometimes enthusiastic, but there is to modern readers often a sense of forced applause, especially if one compares the succinct nods to Millais's ability registered in most journals with the paragraphs of description, analysis, and controversy generated by Burne-Jones's art. At the inaugural exhibition, for example, there were various cool remarks— from the *Spectator* (which derided Millais's three portraits as "the most soulless and degraded pieces of work by a first-rate artist which we have ever seen") to William Michael Rossetti's pronouncements in the *Academy* that Millais's *Stitch* was "a slight performance, and we might say an unlovely one . . . without being either harrowing or touching to the feelings."[13] However, there was also some enthusiasm, evident in the *Illustrated London News*'s analysis of these same portraits as constituting

"a superb series . . . of scions of the noble house of Leveson-Gower."[14]

The next year, 1878, witnessed more mixed responses to Millais's entries—from approbation by the *Saturday Review, Illustrated London News,* and *Athenaeum* of his painting entitled *Twins,* to dislike of his *Jersey Lily* portrait of Lillie Langtry.[15] In 1879 Millais's portrait of Mrs. Stibbard was admired by the *Illustrated London News* for standing "alone here in its perfectly unsophisticated fidelity to nature . . . [and its] marvellous precision . . . of the touch of light on those placid lips, the painting of the clear, candid eyes, the exquisite gradations of living colour on the cheek. The execution of the satin dress, the black kid gloves, the flowers, is no less superb."[16] Various reviewers the following year admired Millais's portrait of the artist Louise Jopling, and, as *Vanity Fair* opined, "if you prefer the real women to the dream women, well you have none of the higher culture, that's all."[17] But the *Spectator* thought his two portraits were "not worthy of him," and four illustrations Millais sent supposedly conveyed "little of his power" and lacked the distinctiveness of his early, tightly delineated phase of Pre-Raphaelitism.[18]

The French critic Théodore Duret in the *Gazette des Beaux-Arts* in 1881 predicted that Millais and Watts would be remembered as the most talented artists at the Grosvenor Gallery, although he then promptly qualified his remarks by yearning for Millais's earlier masterpieces and stating that his current works would not ultimately add much to his reputation. (Duret also lamented Rossetti's absence but correctly identified Burne-Jones as his major follower.)[19] Duret had liked Millais's portrait of Kate Dickens Perugini (fig. 38), a sentiment shared by the *Illustrated London News* and *Athenaeum,* which found it "an animated brilliant study."[20] *Art Journal* singled out the "assured handling, fine colour, and amazing richness of impasto" in *Sweetest Eyes* and furthermore speculated that "the portraits of Mr. Millais have been one of the chief agents in bringing about this revolution . . . of fine strong portraits which twenty-five years ago, were hardly looked upon as works of Fine Art at all."[21] Often Millais's depiction of children was ad-

38. Sir John Everett Millais, *Portrait of Mrs. Kate Perugini*, 1880–81, exh. 1881. Oil on canvas. Mr. and Mrs. Richard P. Mellon (pl. 14, cat. 35)

mired—his *For the Squire* (fig. 39) for its "fine and feeling" qualities of rustic daintiness and nostalgia—and other young sitters who were equally "delightful in their brightness and clearness."[22] His *Duchess of Westminster* also received positive comments as "one of the artist's greatest successes of the year."[23] In the eighties critics still referred to Millais's contributions, such as his "superb portrait of Mr. Gladstone" in 1885 and his portrait of Sir Arthur Sullivan in the 1888 exhibition, but there is a sense in all of his critical writing of attention diverted to other artists and issues.[24] By the end of this decade Millais was one of the few Pre-Raphaelite artists still contributing to the Grosvenor Gallery after the split with Hallé and Carr and the establishment of the New Gallery (to which he later gravitated). Critics seemed

rather weary in assessing his *Shelling Peas* as "not one of his happiest efforts" or, conversely, a life-size portrait of Master Rankin as "the best work of art here" in a collection of "nearly four hundred paintings . . . in every respect below the standard of its forerunners."[25]

OTHER EARLY PRE-RAPHAELITES
Also in the powerful triumvirate of Pre-Raphaelite public visibility was Holman Hunt, who contributed mostly portraits and some landscapes to the Grosvenor Gallery from 1877 to 1887. At the inaugural exhibition he was hailed by the *Spectator* as the finest colorist in England for his *Afterglow in Egypt* (fig. 40), "a wonderful piece of gorgeous colouring," and for other works. However, this critic also suggested that *Afterglow* utilized "a somewhat uninteresting subject . . . [an] Egyptian woman with her wheatsheaf on her head and pigeons at her feet."[26] William Michael Rossetti in the *Academy*, on the other hand, singled out Holman Hunt's *An Italian Child* with its face "not beau-

39. Sir John Everett Millais, *For the Squire*, 1882, exh. 1883. Oil on canvas. The FORBES Magazine Collection, New York, all rights reserved (pl. 13, cat. 34)

40. William Holman
Hunt, *Afterglow in
Egypt*, 1854–63, exh.
1877. Oil on canvas.
Southampton Art
Gallery, Civic Centre,
Southampton
(cat. 24)

tiful nor distinguished by Italian fullness."[27]
Praise was erratic, however; while one year the
Spectator liked Holman Hunt's studies of heads
and portrait of his son, *Vanity Fair* utterly

loathed the latter and called it "simply hideous
. . . one can only hope that the painter of 'The
Shadow of Death' has been temporarily color-
blind . . . not really . . . the father of this pink

demon."[28] Later portrait submissions also did not fare well, as with an 1881 portrait of Professor Owen, which was dismissed as caricatural and "a thing of horror."[29] Nearly as acid was the *Athenaeum*'s remark in 1882 that "Mr. Holman Hunt was hardly well advised when he consented to exhibit in its present state the portrait of a little girl . . . with a lamb."[30] Even Hunt's portrait of Rossetti in 1884 met with censure, the *Athenaeum* suggesting that it gave "but a weak notion of a strong and picturesque, not to say noble, face."[31]

Others in the Pre-Raphaelite circle who exhibited at the Grosvenor Gallery included Ford Madox Brown and Arthur Hughes. Brown always tended to want to be asked, at the very least, to be part of important contemporary projects (whether it was the 1857–58 exhibition of art going to America or Sir Coutts's enterprise), but he sent very little to the Grosvenor Gallery. When he did, the reviews were mixed—*Saturday Review* commented on the poor installation of Brown's work at the 1882 exhibition, a fate "which cannot have helped the artist's fame," or ego, for that matter.[32] That same year Hughes joined the Pre-Raphaelite brethren and became an exhibitor; his painting was described by *The Athenaeum* as having been rendered "with characteristic tact, sweetness of taste, [and] graceful fidelity to nature."[33] Hughes sent some other works in 1885, including *Autumn*, but the Grosvenor was not to be of central importance in his career. Henry Holiday similarly submitted some entries in the 1880s, and his interpretation of *Dante and Beatrice* in the 1883 exhibition earned him comparison with the Pre-Raphaelites, especially with Holman Hunt. His *Master Hilary*, in contrast, was deemed "overly brilliant" on the same grounds, perceived as extreme Pre-Raphaelitism for its "needlessly hard and too sharply defined" style.[34]

SIR EDWARD BURNE-JONES

The dearth of works by Rossetti accentuated a lack of transition from early, hard-edged Pre-Raphaelitism, personified to some degree at this stage by Millais and Hunt, to the more enigmatic strand embodied by Rossetti himself and translated into different realms by his friend and former acolyte Burne-Jones.[35] It was, in fact, virtually unanimous from the outset that Burne-Jones was the foremost attraction at the Grosvenor Gallery. There was effusive praise as well as condemnation, intermixed with frequent doses of aesthetic astonishment, registered in response to his offerings at the inaugural exhibition, as well as reflections on how Burne-Jones had finally earned a place of honor after a long hiatus from public view. As one critic accurately mused, "It must be nearly ten years . . . since this painter's work has been publicly exhibited. . . . It is hardly to be doubted that now the public has been allowed in to see these works side by side, that they will recognize their transcendent ability, and give this artist, whose pictures have been ridiculed and sneered down so long, their hearty recognition."[36] Sidney Colvin in the *Fortnightly Review* asserted that, while Watts's entries were strong, Burne-Jones's eight paintings constituted "an exhibition in themselves. . . . We have among us a genius, a poet in design and colour, whose like has never been seen before."[37] In echoing this evaluation, the *Illustrated London News* enthused that the show was "extremely rich in the productions of Mr. Edward Burne-Jones, a Pre-Raphaelite painter *in excelsis* and one of acknowledged power in conception in skillfulness in manipulation, but whose mannerisms are so many and so strongly pronounced that the Philistines who decline to admire—possibly because they fail to understand them—considerably outnumber the chosen people of the critics and connoisseurs who are able to comprehend and enjoy such characteristic works of this undeniably gifted master as 'The Days of Creation,' 'Venus's Mirror,' and 'The Beguiling of Merlin.' "[38]

Along with such accolades and the sense that his art embodied the highest, most esoteric, and thus most exquisite taste comprehensible only to the cognoscenti, there was also the perception that Burne-Jones's art conveyed an indefinable mood of malaise; thus, *The Days of Creation* was repeatedly singled out the next year as embodying a suspiciously "funereal sadness [that] sits on every face, as if they had all been assisting at a great melancholy blunder."[39] Similarly, Burne-Jones's *The Golden*

41. Sir Edward Coley
Burne-Jones, *The
Golden Stairs*, 1880, exh.
1880. Oil on canvas.
Tate Gallery, London

Plate 1. Sir Lawrence
Alma-Tadema, *A Garden
Altar,* 1879. Oil on panel. City
of Aberdeen Art Gallery
and Museums Collections
(cat. 2)

Plate 2. Sir Lawrence Alma-Tadema, *Ave Caesar!*
Io Saturnalia! 1880. Oil on panel. Collection of the
Akron Art Museum, Gift of Mr. Ralph Cortell (cat. 3)

Plate 3. Sir Edward Coley Burne-Jones, *Laus Veneris*, 1872–73.
Oil on canvas. Laing Art Gallery, Newcastle upon Tyne, England
(Tyne and Wear Museums) (cat. 7)

Plate 4. Blanche, Lady Lindsay of Balcarres,
Portrait of HRH the Princess Louise, c. 1878.
Watercolor. Christopher Newall (cat. 31)

Plate 5. Sir Coutts Lindsay,
Self-Portrait, c. 1864.
Oil on mahogany panel.
The Maas Gallery, Ltd.,
London (cat. 32)

Plate 6. Sir William Quiller Orchardson, *Master Baby,*
1886. Oil on canvas. National Gallery of Scotland
(cat. 43)

Plate 7. Sir George Clausen, *La Pensée,* 1880.
Oil on canvas. Glasgow Museums:
Art Gallery and Museum, Kelvingrove
(cat. 12)

Plate 8. Sir George Clausen, *Haying*, 1882. Oil on
canvas. Art Gallery of Ontario, Toronto,
purchase, 1937 (cat. 11)

Plate 9. Jules Bastien-Lepage, *Les Foins*, 1877. Oil on
canvas. Musée d'Orsay, Paris (cat. 5)

Plate 10. Valentine Cameron Prinsep,
An Unprofessional Beauty, c. 1880. Oil on canvas.
South London Gallery (cat. 45)

Plate 11. Henry Herbert La Thangue,
The Artist's Father, c. 1882. Oil on canvas.
Dunfermline District Museum, Leisure Services,
Libraries and Museums (cat. 27)

Plate 12. Edward Matthew Hale, *Three Princesses*
(Les Trois Princesses), 1881. Oil on canvas. Guildhall Art
Gallery, Corporation of London (cat. 21)

Plate 13. Sir John Everett Millais, *For the Squire,* 1882. Oil on canvas. The FORBES Magazine Collection, New York, all rights reserved (cat. 34)

Plate 14. Sir John Everett Millais, *Portrait of Mrs. Kate Perugini,* 1880–81. Oil on canvas. Mr. and Mrs. Richard P. Mellon (cat. 35)

Plate 16. George Henry and Ernest Atkinson Hornel,
The Druids: Bringing in the Mistletoe, 1890.
Oil on canvas. Glasgow Museums: Art Gallery
and Museum, Kelvingrove (cat. 23)

Stairs (fig. 41) elicited negative remarks (tempered with praise) about "the uniform pallor of the flesh tints . . . [being] neither consonant with youth, nor a gay and happy ceremony, nor with music."[40] In a kindred vein, even the spellbinding *King Cophetua and the Beggar Maid* portrayed lovers that were perplexingly "so dismal, and the beggar-maid moribund."[41] There was, moreover, the feeling that this malaise was pernicious and allied Burne-Jones and his coterie with a dangerous lack of health and with the supposed excesses of both Aestheticism and the "fleshly" poets like Rossetti and Algernon Swinburne. *Vanity Fair* elucidated this notion the most stridently, complaining that

Unless in future years he [Lindsay] . . . reduces his Swinburne school of artists, he will find that the public will not throng to his galleries. . . . If the eccentric and peculiar are to have in future exhibitions in these galleries the places of honor . . . the Grosvenor Gallery would become a *merely* artistic lounge for the wor-

shippers of the Fleshly School of Art. . . . Whether the public will fall down and worship such pictures as "Days of Creation" and Stanhope's "Love and the Maiden" remains to be seen. I can only venture to hope that a healthier feeling will prevail, and that such works will not, although placed in such a rich casket and under such high patronage, ever become popular, for if they do the English School is certain to lose all that makes it healthy and beneficial.[42]

Other critics harped on this intense self-absorption and narcissism that pervaded the atmosphere and the female protagonists in Burne-Jones's canvases. *Magazine of Art* commented on the "dreamy suggestiveness . . . the indescribable sadness in the small light of the eyes" in *The Love Song (Le Chant d'Amour)* (fig. 42) of 1878, while others branded such tendencies at the Grosvenor Gallery as eccentric. Yet even this remark was arguably a backhanded compliment in its assertion that "however much one may think that certain styles are faulty or

42. Sir Edward Coley Burne-Jones, *The Love Song (Le Chant d'Amour)*, c. 1868–77, exh. 1878. Oil on canvas. The Metropolitan Museum of Art, The Alfred N. Punnett Endowment Fund, 1947 (cat. 8)

43. Sir Edward Coley Burne-Jones, *Laus Veneris*, 1872–73, exh. 1878. Oil on canvas. Laing Art Gallery, Newcastle upon Tyne, England (Tyne and Wear Museums) (pl. 3, cat. 7)

ridiculous, one runs no danger in walking through its rooms of being brought face to face with the apotheosis of vulgar sentiment and tea-board painting."[43]

The quintessential focus and cause of furor in this vein of criticism in the second Grosvenor Gallery exhibition was Burne-Jones's *Laus Veneris* (fig. 43), a work which earned him the sobriquet of "the Magnus Apollo" to one reviewer. That same writer considered this painting "surely the finest work he has achieved. Mr. Edward Burne-Jones last season brought forward the accumulated labours of many years, and was consequently by far the most important contributor, both on account of this quantity and because of the novelty of his manner and choice of subject, which had been amply talked of but little seen." Despite Venus's enigmatic enervation—for she seems "so sad . . . tired of loving, blasé, sick of the worn-out rapture," the artist was seen to be a consummate master of feminine beauty, with Venus's attendants "all looking at themselves in a mirror with

an emotion of incurable sadness."[44] There was agreement from the *Art Journal*, which lamented in *Le Chant d'Amour* and especially *Laus Veneris* "the lubriosity with which E. Burne Jones clouds every countenance, even that of Love and the Goddess Venus." The reviewer hoped this metaphorical cloud would "lift some day when his philosophy is riper and healthier— when he has discovered that manhood, especially womanhood, do not walk about the world like hired mutes at a funeral."[45]

More virulent venom was injected, however, by Frederick Wedmore, who occasionally wrote art columns for the *Academy* and described this Venus: "The very body is unpleasant and uncomely, and the soul behind it, or through it, is ghastly. It is a soul that has known strange tortures; a body that has writhed with every impulse of sickness."[46] Henry James concurred and wittily opined in the pages of the *Nation* that Venus possessed "the face and aspect of a person who has had what the French call an 'intimate' acquaintance with life; her companions, on the other hand, though pale, sickly and wan . . . have a more innocent and vacant expression, and seem to have derived their languor chiefly from contact and sympathy."[47] In the *Spectator,* echoing and expanding upon this interpretation, a critic was dismayed that "when we do arrive at the meaning [of *Laus Veneris*], it is not one which we would care to explain . . . to child or wife. The weariness of satisfied love, and the pain of unsatisfied longing, is hardly a theme, perhaps to expend such magnificent painting upon."[48]

Similar criticism in much tamer form was also heaped upon Burne-Jones's associates, including John Roddam Spencer Stanhope, a former student of Watts's who had labored on producing what were to be ill-fated murals for the Oxford Union's debating chambers during the 1850s with Burne-Jones and Rossetti. Often his Grosvenor entries were sent from Italy, and he was probably influential in the decision to invite his niece and pupil, Evelyn Pickering (later De Morgan), to participate in Lindsay's enterprise. Although he had exhibited a dozen works at the Royal Academy prior to this avant-garde "experiment," he too benefited from his Grosvenor Gallery exposure. His paintings received mixed responses, and his *Eve Tempted* (fig. 44) provoked the common complaint that, like Burne-Jones, his figures tended to androgyny—here with a description of the serpent's "venomous vapour-breath" and "human head of indeterminate sex."[49] His 1883 entry gained some applause for its "real taste, high refinement, some lack of energy, and a most exact reflection of the inspiration and technique of Botticelli."[50] However, like all of Burne-Jones's other "followers," he was often subjected to criticism about the second generation's supposed affectations of quaintness, peculiar or pretentiously enigmatic protagonists, excessive ornamentation, awkward poses and proportions, and faulty draughtsmanship.[51]

Stylistically kindred in many ways was John Melhuish Strudwick, who had worked as a studio assistant for both Stanhope and Burne-Jones. Prior to the Grosvenor he had had only one work accepted at the Academy, although he exhibited sporadically at the Society of British Artists and elsewhere. From the outset Strud-

44. John Rodham Spencer Stanhope, *Eve Tempted,* exh. 1877. Tempera on panel. Manchester City Art Galleries

wick's Grosvenor entries were identified in mood and type with Burne-Jones, as is evident in Sidney Colvin's perception of Strudwick's 1877 contributions as depicting a "solemn and dreamy mill-stream with the lady in a boat, his tragic pair of lovers . . . his vision of Love and the maiden."[52] Frederick Wedmore certainly aligned Strudwick's mood with the "contagious" sensuousness of Burne-Jones's work and Algernon Swinburne's poetry, asserting that in

Strudwick's *Passing Days* "the conception, how-ever lovely thoughtful and suggestive, is at bottom pagan and sad, for it points at nothing, it appears more clearly than at . . . personal enjoy-ment, the folly of memories, the idleness of hopes."[53] As in the case of the other Burne-Jones affiliates, Strudwick's style was derivative yet would never have been mistaken for the "master's" or for paintings by Stanhope, Pick-ering, or Spartali Stillman. At times this was a disadvantage, as when the *Athenaeum* criticized in Strudwick's *Ten Virgins* the collective "short-comings of Messrs. E. Burne-Jones and R. S. Stanhope. It lacks both the intensity and superb romance of the former painter, and the chas-tened devotion and unflinching studies of the latter. It has none of the profound sincerity of the art of either."[54]

FEMALE ARTISTS IN THE PRE-RAPHAELITE TRADITION

While Strudwick, Stanhope, and, to a lesser extent, Brown, Hughes, and Fairfax Murray (who also sent some works to the Grosvenor) were all male adherents to the Pre-Raphaelite tradition, there was also strong representation from their female counterparts. In fact, a vital component of the Grosvenor Gallery was its inherent championing of female artists and its frequent inclusion of a wide range of practi-tioners—both amateurs and professionals as well as Pre-Raphaelites and otherwise—among its contributors. Presumably Blanche Lindsay, whose own watercolors were occasionally on display, was a factor in this development, but

45. Evelyn Pickering De Morgan, *Ariadne at Naxos*, 1877, exh. 1877. Oil on canvas. The De Morgan Foundation at Old Battersea House

the commitment to women painters continued even after the Lindsays divorced.[55] This was a somewhat revolutionary as well as exemplary achievement—infusing women (and their al-leged "feminine" painting styles) into what was formerly a male-dominated exhibition system in London. In general, the Grosvenor Gallery seemed receptive to encouraging selected women painters and treating them with greater equality. The second wave of Pre-Raphaelitism in the so-called Burne-Jones School also em-braced the participation of numerous women artists, above all Evelyn Pickering (later De Morgan) and Marie Spartali Stillman. Interest-ingly, the *Art Journal* in 1879 mentioned both women in this context and rightly observed that "among other features characteristic of the Grosvenor is the honourable place allotted to the works of female artists, and one is rejoiced to find that in every instance the ladies have proved themselves worthy of such considera-tion."[56] In addition to Pickering and Spartali Stillman, key women contributors cited included Lady Lindsay, Louisa Starr, Mrs. Val Bromley, Baroness Nathaniel de Rothschild, Mrs. Wylie, Sophie Anderson, Mrs. Edmund Gosse, Anna Lea Merritt, Louise Jopling, Miss R. L. Watson, Miss L. V. Blandy, Miss Margaret Gillies, Kate Hastings, Miss Stuart Wortley, Sarah Defries, Clara and Hilda Montalba, Lady Waterford, and Helen Allingham.

Evelyn Pickering benefited considerably from her affiliation with the Grosvenor Gallery, in part because she was just a neophyte painter when virtually her first work, *Ariadne at Naxos* (fig. 45), went on view there in her professional debut.[57] Any young artist—whether male or female—would have been fortunate to have this exposure, and in her case this was also signifi-cant. She sent more than two dozen works to the Grosvenor over the years, notably *Venus and Cupid* in 1878, *Night and Sleep* (pl. 29) in 1879, a portrait sculpture and *Mater Dolorosa* the fol-lowing year, and many other canvases throughout the 1880s. Typically she was seen as an anointed follower of Burne-Jones, as is evi-dent in a description of her 1881 entry, *The Grey Sisters* (pl. 27), which confirmed her as "the chief example of the particular school of which Mr. Burne-Jones is the head."[58]

The Grosvenor Gallery also served as a crucial showcase of Marie Spartali Stillman's talent.[59] Although her works had been displayed at the Dudley Gallery and the Royal Academy (a total of seven between 1870 and 1877), the Grosvenor provided a vital chance—almost a lifeline in her case—for maintaining visibility in the art world. This London venue was especially critical when she was living abroad owing to her husband's health problems. Letters from her mother to Dante Gabriel Rossetti reveal the latter's deep attachment to Marie as well as her mutual admiration for him, and it is not surprising that the artist continued to write to Rossetti long after her marriage.[60] On some occasions Spartali Stillman discussed her contributions to the Grosvenor Gallery, in 1878 lamenting her lack of participation (perhaps partly because of her pregnancy and Madox Brown's lack of support for her efforts): "I shall have no pictures at the Grosvenor this year, it is very unfortunate for I have had so few opportunities of having a picture well placed at any exhibition and worked so continuously since June at the picture I hoped to send, but at the last before leaving England, Mr. Brown advised me to give it up for this year and I understood this would be wisest."[61] In 1879, however, she managed to send *Gathering Orange Blossoms* and *Fiammetta Singing*. The next year she asked Rossetti to lend her an olive-green dress for a composition and said, "I am working very diligently at my picture and hope to get it finished in time for the Grosvenor and that two or three whose opinions I care for will like it *if* they happen to see it."[62] She continued to contribute art for most of the 1880s—notably *Love's Messenger* (fig. 46)—before joining the ranks of those found on the New Gallery's roster.

46. Marie Spartali Stillman, *Love's Messenger*, c. 1885, exh. 1885. Watercolor, tempera, and gold paint on paper. Delaware Art Museum, Samuel and Mary R. Bancroft Memorial (pl. 19, cat. 52)

AESTHETICISM AND ITS CRITICS

Having considered the principal artists affiliated with Pre-Raphaelitism at the Grosvenor, it is also valid to study what kinds of subjects these artists individually and collectively were seen to have created, especially in terms of the messages they generated to critics and spectators.

Burne-Jones became the preeminent spokesperson in this arena as well, enduring the criticism as well as enjoying the praise of many writers. One of the most frequent responses involved attacking the alleged sensuality of Burne-Jones's work, starting in the first exhibition with *The Beguiling of Merlin* (fig. 47) and

47. Sir Edward Coley Burne-Jones, *The Beguiling of Merlin*, 1873–77, exh. 1877. Oil on canvas. National Museums and Galleries on Merseyside, Walker Art Gallery, Liverpool

the charge that the figures' countenances embodied "passion incarnate." The same reviewer made another prescient remark that would often be raised, namely, that Burne-Jones's "faces all resemble one another and are all sorrowful. . . . It is also true that these countenances and their expressions are in their loveliness serious and yearning, or melancholy, if you will."[65] William Michael Rossetti concurred, stating that the "most marked feature of the display consists of the works by Mr. Burne-Jones . . . and his singular idiosyncrasy in art enlists the utmost curiosity, and in many cases proportionate enthusiasm" for "the sweet, serene, wistful, almost sorrowful beauty of a facial type, dreamily not barrenly monotonous, traversing the line between the humanly morbid." Rossetti went on to analyze these qualities with considerable insight, suggesting that his friend's "*welt-schmerz* or world pang belongs in that semi-abstract region where passion subsides into yearning, and to exist in bodily presence is almost to do something, and to look is to live."[64]

To some commentators the sensuality of Burne-Jones's imagery in particular was morally objectionable as well as merely vexsome or bewildering. The *Illustrated London News* in 1879 warned about latent amoral connotations and thus chastised the flaws of the supposedly "ultra-sensual school, a school which in its worst development is the morbid outcome of weakly-overwrought physique—which every man who respects his manhood and every woman who values her honour must regard with disgust, and would destroy everything of value in the national character. For our part, we see merely mawkish sentiment, not passion, in these wan, haggard faces—these limp langours, this hysterical tension."[65] The same critic went on to castigate Burne-Jones's *Pygmalion* series and in decidedly racist terms decried its alleged "supersensuousness . . . derived from Mr. Dante Rossetti's queer ideal of womankind—with hollow cheeks and square jawbones, necks like swans with goitre, hair like Topsy's, lips of the same race, 'stung' therefore swollen 'with kisses.' "[66] It was arguably epidemic lovesickness itself which was being targeted, whether in Burne-Jones's *Laus*

Veneris, Pickering's *Venus and Cupid,* or Stanhope's *Night* on view that same year. Whatever their differences, these and other works by both male and female artists were all seen as possessing intrinsically morbid and dangerous sexual and aesthetic qualities.

Indeed, some of the traits chronicled in contemporary reviews—lassitude, wan health, pallid complexion, boneless posture, passionate kisses, and unacceptable intimations of sensuality—were at the core anyway of public "suspicions" concerning the character (moral and otherwise) of the Aesthetic female both in real life and in art. The alleged lack of wholesomeness generated by Burne-Jones's figures in particular was constantly protested by reviewers. In *Vanity Fair,* a writer among those worried about the seeming contagion of weariness generated by this strand of imagery speculated that "the most notable products of the Grosvenor Gallery are the dirty men in long hair and wild women tied up in brick-dust cornsacks and sage green bedgowns."[67] Beneath the humor which would be so brilliant a part of the lampooning of aesthetes in Gilbert and Sullivan's *Patience* there was also alarm. Harry Quilter seemed genuinely agitated when he wrote in *Macmillan's Magazine* in 1880 that Pre-Raphaelitism had unleashed potentially fatal effects.

Though pre-Raphaelitism, in its pure and original form, has passed away, its dead carcase is still left with us, and is a source of corruption which cannot be too soon fully understood. The claims of the modern gospel of intensity, and the critical theories of pure sensuousness which are proclaimed so loudly just now, have their curiously unfitting root in the pre-Raphaelite movement . . . and ended in breeding phases of art and poetry which embody the lowest theory of art uselessness, and the most morbid and sickly art-results. . . . The evil is spreading from pictures and poems into private life; it has attacked . . . the decoration of our houses, and the dresses of our women. . . . If this hybrid pre-Raphaelitism has not yet erected itself into a rule of conduct, it has become in some sort effective as a standard of manners; and there may now be seen at many a social gathering young men and women whose lacklustre eyes, disheveled hair, eccentricity of attire, and general appearance of weary passion proclaim them members of the new school.[68]

Of course, the obvious partial origins of the self-centered, sirenlike, sexually powerful creature alluded to in such reviews, ideally vulnerable because of her languid melancholy and terminal ennui or enervation, were Rossetti's own "stunners." Thus, despite his absence from the Grosvenor Gallery, the legacy of this artist's haunting female icons of the 1860s and beyond lingered in the canvases of Burne-Jones and those artists affiliated with him.

Aestheticism, for all its drained female protagonists in Burne-Jones's pictures, was feared to have merged with Pre-Raphaelitism and spawned an emasculating effect on contemporary art and society. As the *Magazine of Art* critic despaired in 1881, "We have said already . . . that the moral tendency of Mr. Burne-Jones's pictures does not satisfy us. Effeminacy, even when it is associated with some aesthetic sentiment, is not a wholesome moral temper. But it is distinctly unwholesome when it is associated . . . with suggestions of a low moral tone and a very apparent pessimism. No more complete antithesis to the honourable, self-respecting and masculine character could be found than this union of pessimism and laxity."[69] Furthermore, the effete males and their Nincompoopiana behavior spoofed by George Du Maurier in countless *Punch* cartoons, along with the wan but sensuous females, had supposedly wrought an unhealthy impact on art and society that unsettled critics and viewers. Such anxiety suggests that the underlying weakness of or problem with aesthetic art, and implicitly with some of Burne-Jones's paintings, was at least in part its feminine qualities—its emphasis on decorativeness, droopy poses, androgyny, and sensuality. Anything that smacked of effeminacy was open to ridicule and loathing, and this shortcoming was attributed to the avant-garde Grosvenor and the artists it championed for public consumption. William Michael Rossetti as early as 1877 complained of these tendencies and linked Burne-Jones's proclivities in this regard to Aesthetic poets and poetry (especially by Algernon Swinburne), all of which he deemed "not masculine and progressive but reclusive and retrospective—it is art turning for ever on its own axis; and to those who find

themselves utterly out of sympathy with Mr. Jones's work we have nothing to say, beyond affirming that it is justified to itself by adequately and exquisitely fulfilling its own conditions, and that these are essentially aesthetic conditions."[70] The very next year a similar opinion was repeated in the *Magazine of Art*: "we most seriously protest . . . as unmasculine and. . . . self-consciously imitative. . . . It is fresh strenuous paganism, emasculated by false modern emotionalism."[71]

By the early and mid-twentieth century, Victorian art, especially that of Burne-Jones, would often be ridiculed for its allegedly unmasculine prettiness, its affinities with the fleshly poetic excesses of Rossetti and Swinburne, and its emphasis on decorativeness. However, despite the angst they elicited, when works by Burne-Jones and his associates no longer graced the walls of the Grosvenor Gallery after the late 1880s, critics openly regretted their loss both as artistic statements and as objects of ridicule. Even before Burne-Jones departed, there was an increasing sense that his period of primacy at the gallery was, along with Pre-Raphaelitism itself, waning. Thus, by 1883 some critics were predicting the demise of this "clique"—and its master—which had made the Grosvenor such a sensation: "Even the eccentricities that made the reputation or notoriety of the Gallery at first are disappearing or losing their piquancy with their novelty. Mr. Burne-Jones is by no means at his worst, but his followers have either deserted or are hopelessly uninteresting."[72] The *Art Journal* was in accord, indicating that this other group had otherwise accommodated to the tenor of the times: "Mr. Burne-Jones and his acolytes are but sparsely represented in the present exhibition, whilst many of the artists who first attracted public notice as adherents to his view have hoped to retain it by conforming to a more popular criterion."[73] Two years later much the same was being said, with the most "orthodox, or rigid, followers of Burne-Jones" seen as unable to hold their own as standard-bearers; therefore, "for the moment at least, their vogue seems to have passed, and until more vigorous exponents arise its return is a doubtful chance."[74] The *Spectator* expressed what had become a common assumption by 1887—namely, that the Grosvenor's quality, along with Burne-Jones's contributions, had noticeably deteriorated: "For the first time in looking at this artist's productions . . . we seem to feel an almost total lack of impulse and spontaneity. . . . We miss the feeling which has hitherto always arisen within us on contemplating his pictures, that he has painted them less because he *would* than because he *must*. . . . We are no longer transported into a pleasant world which we know has no real existence, but which we take on faith of the artist's genius; but we are enabled to look coldly and critically at the way he would have us travel, and on the whole, we decline to follow it."[75]

Thus, the erosion of Pre-Raphaelitism and of the Grosvenor Gallery were simultaneous and interrelated phenomena, perhaps inevitable given the fresh artistic developments embodied by other artists and styles both British and foreign. Along these lines William Powell Frith in a piece on "Crazes in Art" contrasted Pre-Raphaelitism with Impressionism, disliking both (especially the latter) and unequivocally maintaining that the "Pre-Raphaelite craze ran its course like a fever. . . . We have now done—long done—with the Pre-Raphaelite, and another, and far more dangerous, craze has come upon us."[76]

As a result of both the subtle as well as dramatic changes in the content and atmosphere of the gallery, to some reviewers the Grosvenor now seemed hackneyed and struggling to survive; ironically it was even described as bearing "a family likeness to the Royal Academy, which, it is assumed, was not a part of the original attention of the founders." This author continued by suggesting that Lindsay had invented, in effect, his own set of pseudo-Academicians, in which the Pre-Raphaelite contingent was the most prominent. Citing the paltry as well as problematic contributions that year of Strudwick, Pickering, Stanhope, and their leader, he pronounced the verdict: "With Mr. Jones in no great force, and with these, his most distinguished disciples, in a condition (so to speak) of collapse, it is not surprising that the Grosvenor Gallery should present, as we have said, a strong resemblance with the Royal

Academy, where, as if to complete the illusion, Mr. Jones himself is for the first time represented."[77]

The year 1888 marked the turning point; by then all the unfavorable predictions had been delivered, and Burne-Jones made his decision to exit from the Grosvenor and go over to the New Gallery. In noting the new rivalry in timing as well as content compared the Grosvenor with the New Gallery, the *Magazine of Art* astutely observed, "For years the Bond Street Gallery has been associated in the public mind with the school of art which delights in auburn-haired, lithe-limbed maidens, and lovelorn youths. . . . But all that is changed now. Miss Pickering, with Messrs. Spencer Stanhope and Fairfax Murray, alone remain to carry on the old tradition, but the canvases are unobtrusive enough. The Grosvenor, in fact, can now lay claim to no distinctive character. It is rather commonplace than eccentric." Even more damning was the oft-cited confirmation that the "general impression which it leaves . . . is that it is an epitome of the Academy. The same artists exhibit in the one as in the other."[78]

Even with these developments, however, it is significant that however much they may have attacked the Pre-Raphaelites in the past, by 1888 the critics were actively bemoaning their loss to the Grosvenor Gallery as well as noting the sense of rift and cultural redirection that resulted. *Vanity Fair* chose to interpret this as a positive development, but the *Athenaeum*'s assessment seemed closer to the truth, that "the missing works of art being those that gave the gallery its cachet, and no peculiar features having taken their places, the whole resembles, more or less closely, an ordinary London exhibition."[79] Nonetheless, *Vanity Fair,* one of many periodicals that had intermittently loved and hated Pre-Raphaelite works at the Grosvenor, complained when Burne-Jones's "alien" creatures withdrew from public sight: "Aesthetically disposed persons will . . . miss the lanky young ladies with wan faces and high cheekbones who were wont to attract crowds round them. And it must be confessed that even those who gazed on such pictures without worshipping the profane who failed to see their beauties, will regret that there is no sensational picture . . . none likely to cause discussions, if not disputes, at dinner parties and to divide Society into two camps."[80]

The Grosvenor Gallery proved to be a formidable force in shaping Burne-Jones's fate and in molding public opinion, and it must have been with real regret that the artist decided to leave this progressive but admittedly imperfect environment. He thus wrote to Hallé in late fall of 1887 that he wanted to leave the gallery because of numerous developments that rankled him: "I am troubled and anxious more than I can say by the way in which it seems to me the Gallery has been gradually slipping from its position . . . to that of a room which can be hired for evening parties. . . . The place got a character of its own, and its name has been respected, and I do seriously feel that all this is being imperilled by the innovations of the last season, and that steadily and surely the Gallery is losing caste—club rooms, concert rooms, and the rest, were not in the plans, and must and will degrade it. . . . Clubs, feasts, concerts, parties, advertisements, placards, and refreshments—how they all vex the soul."[81] These charges seemingly triggered a letter from Hallé to Lindsay about Burne-Jones's objections and prefigured Hallé's and Carr's resignation from the gallery. Lindsay remained largely resistant to their complaints, however, and was probably mortified when Carr and Hallé aired their grievances in the pages of the *Times*.[82] Burne-Jones supported Hallé and Carr and transferred his allegiance—along with Strudwick and others like Millais and Stanhope who came later—to the New Gallery after it opened in spring of 1888 until his death in 1898. (In this new setting Burne-Jones enjoyed a large solo exhibition in the winter of 1892–93, and a posthumous retrospective was also staged at the New Gallery in 1899.)

A year after Burne-Jones's departure, critics were still noting how "the higher flights of imagination are conspicuously absent" from the Grosvenor, although it was rationalized that "It must not be forgotten that, if there is less to enjoy, there is, at present, less to offend, less to startle and puzzle us."[83] While the Grosvenor had become to some "a chance-medley of styles,

unmarked by any insistent personalities," the New Gallery was perceived as "having succeeded to the cachet that was once the Grosvenor's, and is alone in presenting to us the deliberate art of the Burne-Jones school—that curious mingling of handicraft and literature which rebukes, or is rebuked by . . . the pictorial art of our younger painters."[84] Yet even the New Gallery would discover how crucial Burne-Jones's function was as a mainstay, and how vital the presence of his followers also was to many visitors: by 1890, a mere two years after the New Gallery opened, the *Art Journal* noted with distress what it saw as a decline in quality, the main reason "being that the prime mover of the already historical secession, Mr. E. Burne-Jones, is present rather in spirit than in the flesh—showing only a series of preparatory designs for the *magnum opus* at Messrs. Agnew's. . . . His followers and those of D. G. Rossetti make a last despairing attempt to recover lost ground and re-establish themselves: but in vain. . . . It is clearer than ever that their example has formed a false and unsubstantial style . . . destined to extinction."[85]

In retrospect, it is difficult to imagine the multiple histories of the Grosvenor Gallery, Pre-Raphaelitism, and Burne-Jones's fate without the integral element of his participation in this avant-garde exhibition system from 1877 through 1887. While the late 1880s marked the end of Pre-Raphaelite interaction with the radical Grosvenor, the gallery had achieved much for the careers of certain artists and had further advanced at least to some degree the cause of women painters. The lively tenure of the Pre-Raphaelite circle was to be followed by other "waves" of progressive art at the Grosvenor—above all by the contributions of younger as well as foreign artists. The Glasgow Boys and others, with their enthusiasm and fresh visions in art which were as intense as those of the early Brotherhood, in time paralleled to some extent what the Pre-Raphaelites themselves had achieved—bringing different innovations, techniques, and standards of art to Lindsay's unforgettable and continually eclectic palace of aestheticism.

5
Whistler's Decorative Darkness

John Siewert

IN THE SPRING OF 1877 James McNeill Whistler was bringing to a close his active involvement in one creative project just as he began to turn more of his attention to another enterprise, the opening of the Grosvenor Gallery's inaugural exhibition. By early March, the artist was observed applying final touches of verdigris and gold paint to complete what the periodical press already had dubbed the Peacock Room, his elaborate redecoration of the dining room in the London residence of his patron, Frederick Leyland.[1] Two months later, visitors would encounter eight oil paintings by Whistler included among the pictures hanging on the walls of the Grosvenor. What Whistler had accomplished on the interior of a private home may at first appear to have little relationship to the pictures he sent to a public venue. Yet in one significant respect, the decorative properties that define the artist's work in the Peacock Room provide a context for a consideration of the many critics who framed his paintings at the Grosvenor with a discourse of decoration.[2]

Whistler's contributions to the first Grosvenor exhibition divided evenly between characteristic examples of his portraiture and paintings he called Nocturnes, images of urban landscape cloaked in obscuring haze and darkness. The history of Whistler's association with the Grosvenor Gallery is forever linked to the fortunes of one Nocturne shown in the first exhibition. John Ruskin's critique of the 1877 event heaped scorn upon the artist's *Nocturne in Black and Gold: The Falling Rocket* (fig. 48), an image of fireworks bursting above Cremorne Gardens, a pleasure park in Victorian Chelsea.[3] For Ruskin, Whistler's apparently casual conception of painting constituted an affront to standards of well-crafted pictures and to an aesthetic hierarchy that placed intelligent substance over undisciplined demonstrations of painterly process. Whistler replied with litigation, and in 1878 the notorious libel suit brought by artist against critic played out in a London courtroom.[4]

Ruskin, however, was hardly alone in taking Whistler's Grosvenor paintings to task. While the portraits and landscapes inspired their share of appreciation, the more frequent

48. James McNeill Whistler, *Nocturne in Black and Gold: The Falling Rocket*, c. 1875, exh. 1877.
Oil on oak panel. The Detroit Institute of Arts, Gift of Dexter M. Ferry, Jr.

49. James McNeill Whistler, *Arrangement in Black
and Brown: The Fur Jacket*, 1876, exh. 1877.
Oil on canvas. Worcester Art Museum,
Worcester, Massachusetts, Museum purchase

50. James McNeill Whistler, *Portrait of Miss
Florence Leyland*, 1871–76, exh. 1877.
Oil on canvas. Portland Museum of Art, Maine,
Gift of Mr. and Mrs. Benjamin Strouse, 1968

response among critics was a decided lack of
comprehension, feigned or genuine. Why, many
writers asked, were Whistler's pictures so
difficult to see, in the most literal sense of the
word? His imagery of attenuated bodies in
danger of dissolving into dark backgrounds
prompted comparisons to wraiths: a pair of full-
length female subjects (figs. 49, 50) suggested to
one critic "a choice between materialized spirits
and figures in a London fog."[5] Another visitor to
the Grosvenor in 1877 pondered the artist's
"weird productions—enigmas so occult that

Oedipus might be puzzled to solve them."[6] And
Whistler's showing at the second Grosvenor
exhibition of 1878 changed few minds; such
pictures of figure and landscape, a critic characteristically intoned, "come like shadows and will
so depart, and it is unnecessary to disquiet one's
self about them."[7]

Critics dubious of Whistler's Grosvenor
contributions quickly established analogies
between what they perceived to be the ghostly,
"insubstantial" nature of his specific images and
a lack of substance, or seriousness, in his art as

51. James McNeill Whistler, *Arrangement in Grey and Black, No. 2: Portrait of Thomas Carlyle*, 1872–73, exh. 1877.
Oil on canvas. Glasgow Museums: Art Gallery and Museum, Kelvingrove

52. James McNeill
Whistler, *Nocturne in
Blue and Silver*, 1871–72,
exh. 1877. Oil on canvas.
Courtesy of the Fogg
Art Museum, Harvard
University Art Museums,
Bequest of
Grenville L. Winthrop

53. James McNeill
Whistler, *Thames—
Nocturne in Blue and
Silver*, 1872–78, exh.
1878. Oil on canvas. Yale
Center for British Art,
Paul Mellon Collection
(pl. 32, cat. 68)

a whole. The exception proving the point could be found in the 1877 exhibition, where *Arrangement in Grey and Black, No. 2: Portrait of Thomas Carlyle* (fig. 51) offered the "most substantial" relief from the remainder of his submitted works.[8] And, if a "choice" between spirits and fog-enshrouded figures seemed to offer a narrow range of alternatives, Whistler's Grosvenor landscape paintings could be viewed as reflexive and repetitive as well, a *Nocturne in Blue and Silver* (fig. 52) shown in 1877 echoed the following year by another picture identically

titled and depicting a similar prospect of the Battersea skyline viewed across the Thames (fig. 53).

The self-referential, suspiciously ensemble conception of Whistler's paintings led some less than sympathetic critics to conclude that such work deliberately devalued the conventional priority that pictures placed on subject matter. Whistler represented to one writer the "sort of artist in whose work the subject has no weight at all," who aims "not to represent reality, but to make a pattern," whether from the human

54. James McNeill Whistler, *Brown and Silver: Old Battersea Bridge*, 1859–63.
Oil on canvas mounted on masonite. ©Addison Gallery of American Art, Gift of Mr. Cornelius N. Bliss.
Phillips Academy, Andover, Massachusetts. All rights reserved.

figure or the world of nature.[9] In the absence of compelling attitudes toward his subjects, Whistler's paintings were approachable as exercises in form. They were, in a word frequently employed and implied by critics, "decorative," and the author of the extravagant Peacock Room could be recognized as the decorator of canvases and panels that graced the Grosvenor, a venue founded in part to elevate the concept of the decorative in exhibition art.[10] The critical rhetoric of decoration attached most readily to the Nocturnes, which accounted for nearly half of the oil paintings Whistler sent to the Grosvenor Gallery exhibitions.[11]

Two paintings by Whistler of a single landmark in his London neighborhood measure the "decorative" reconfiguration of nature that emerges in his landscapes of the 1870s. *Brown*

and Silver: Old Battersea Bridge (fig. 54), begun in 1859, appears to record the ordinary riverside scene offered in many etchings that the artist was creating at about the same time. Its contents—the wooden bridge filled with traffic between Chelsea and Battersea, the workers on and beside the Thames, the factories lined up along its opposite bank—fit together in a cohesive, matter-of-fact composition. By contrast, *Nocturne: Blue and Gold—Old Battersea Bridge* (fig. 55) looks like a world apart. A solitary bargeman poles the otherwise quiet waters past an improbably attenuated pier, a piece of the bridge that now stands in for the whole, its bold silhouette framing the vaporous distance. It is a comparatively reticent image, a picture that puzzled many of its original viewers with an idiosyncratic point of view that renders its sub-

55. James McNeill
Whistler, *Nocturne: Blue
and Gold—Old Battersea
Bridge*, c. 1872–75,
exh. 1877. Oil on canvas.
Tate Gallery, London

ject something other than clear and immediately legible.

No more than ten years separate these two paintings, a coherently panoramic display offered on the one hand, a kind of quizzical fragmentation on the other. But during that decade Whistler essentially transformed his representational concerns. Between 1863, around the time he was completing *Brown and Silver*, and 1871, when his London etchings were published and the first Nocturnes were already taking shape, Whistler virtually stopped producing prints in order to concentrate on the fundamentals of his drawing and painting. Indeed, the Nocturnes that build upon the experiences of those intervening years and constitute his principal project in landscape painting in the 1870s seem far removed from

the incisively graphic "portraiture of place" that commentators Joseph Pennell and Frederick Wedmore, among others, had applauded in the Thames etchings.[12] And Whistler himself testified in his lawsuit against Ruskin that he had not meant in the *Battersea Bridge* Nocturne "to paint a portrait of the bridge."[13] According to critics who would find Whistler's mature work fairly inconsequential, the Nocturnes failed to address their audience in the direct, meaningful ways associated with portraiture, qualities which many of those same critics readily identified in the artist's etchings of Thamesside motifs.

That capacity to engage and inform the viewer is reflected in the critical response to *Brown and Silver: Old Battersea Bridge*, which Whistler showed at the Royal Academy in 1865.

The painting caught the eye of one critic who enthusiastically pronounced it "by far the most remarkable landscape in the room" and paused before the painting long enough to praise "the skill with which the boats, the bridge, and the line of buildings on the river-side" were endowed with pictorial qualities that elevated a mundane subject to the higher order of Art.[14] If, as some writers at the time were suggesting, English landscape painting was in danger of losing its audience, here was an appealing talent who seemed to be offering fresh and promising perspectives.[15]

From the first, the *Brown and Silver* was singled out as critics took the time to focus on the very conventions of subject and style which the Nocturnes later call into question. Unlike the artist's early landscapes, Whistler's Nocturnes provoked quick dismissal far more often than prolonged contemplation. Twenty-two-year-old Oscar Wilde, already assuming the role of the insouciant critic, offered his account of the four nocturnal landscapes on display in the first Grosvenor exhibition in 1877. Noting in particular the subtle burst of fireworks at the upper right of the Battersea Bridge Nocturne and the more obvious pyrotechnics in *Nocturne in Black and Gold: The Falling Rocket* (see figs. 55 and 48), he concluded that the paintings were "certainly worth looking at for about as long as one looks at a real rocket, that is, for somewhat less than a quarter of a minute."[16] And Wilde's was only one of the wittier shots launched in what by the late 1870s had become a critical barrage: the Nocturnes appeared to many viewers to signal that Whistler's work had degenerated from the laudable to the laughable.

What had happened to remake willingness to pay close attention into such indifference and even antagonism? In the popular and popularized reaction, the severely limited palette and reductive form of the Nocturnes seemed to flaunt what even sympathetic critics earlier had called "eccentric" tendencies in the work of the younger Whistler and to declare that such eccentricities were now the defining characteristics of his art. But had his underlying approach to painting the landscape changed so much in the time between the exhibitions of 1865 and 1877 to justify the charges of frivolous subject matter, illegible style, and worse? Had he really deviated so drastically from his previous direction? Or do the Nocturnes reexamine rather more than they reject the points of view that had initially raised expectations about Whistler's work?

If the Nocturnes move away from the idea of place portraiture and its connotations of a simple, immediate relationship between representation and viewer (just as Whistler's actual portraits of the seventies and eighties often seem to be only remotely concerned with physical likeness and establishing contact with the viewer as their subjects recede into shadowy backgrounds), they also revise certain traditions of presentation that are part of the landscape genre itself. In the Nocturnes, Whistler consciously retains conventions of the landscape form—an open, horizontal composition, for example (of the thirty-two extant Nocturne oil paintings, only five are, like the Battersea Bridge Nocturne, vertically oriented), and the construction of a specific kind of vantage point from which the landscape presumably is viewed, first by the artist and then by his audience—only to work against these structures at the same time. What I am suggesting here is that various kinds of impediments—strikingly expressed by the fragment of Battersea Bridge, for instance or, more generally, in effects of darkness and mist rendered through a deliberately restrained color and composition—all but obscure landscape's conventions of display and complicate a clear reading of the imagery built upon their tenuous remains. For the Nocturnes were (and are) difficult to read. And when critics found themselves unable to apply their usual terminology of a legibly represented view of nature to these paintings, they looked at them through a different lens and discussed them with words appropriated from an alternative lexicon—especially that of "the decorative."

Whistler's own efforts in the second half of the 1860s were directed toward finding ways to make his art embrace notions of both nature and decoration in the guise of delineated form (however sublimated) and what often seemed to critics like its dissolution into formless, "decorative" color. Ultimately, the fact that so many of his contemporaries were perplexed by the apparent lack of tangible form in the Nocturnes is made particularly ironic when we realize that Whistler was preoccupied as never before with refining his drawing ability and other structural foundations of his art precisely during the years bracketed by his two very different interpretations of Battersea Bridge. The Nocturnes, I suggest, result directly from the dialogue Whistler sought to sustain between an art of engaged observation, on the one hand, and an art of decorative "arrangement," on the other. Indeed, the titles Whistler gave his paintings beginning in the early 1870s made it all but impossible for critics to ignore the principles of "arrangement" and "harmony" that informed all of his work, from his interior designs to his essays in the more conventionally "high art" genres of portraiture and landscape painting. Whistler's biographers were summing up a fairly well-established idea rather than breaking new ground when they noted in 1921 that his "genius as a decorator is seen in every picture, in every drawing he made."[17]

In order to understand more fully the nuances of the Nocturnes, it is important to consider how ideas of the "decorative" came to inflect Whistler's view of nature. For despite the predilection on the part of many critics to try to see his paintings as either objective transcriptions or essentially subjective inventions, the Nocturnes sustain a creative give-and-take between the perceptual and the conceptual or, as it might otherwise be described, the natural and the decorative. Indeed, the artist himself used the latter pair of terms to name the options he believed were available to the landscapist. William Michael Rossetti's diary records Whistler's presence at a Chelsea gathering in 1867 where there was "much discussion about Turner—W being against him as not meeting either the simply natural or the decorative requirements of landscape-art, which he regards as the only alternative."[18] But Whistler's own concern even as he made his remark was not to maintain rigid boundaries between these alternatives. Rather, he increasingly worked at uncovering nature's intrinsically decorative properties and cultivating from their interaction a hybrid pictorial form, a process of discovery

and synthesis that culminated in events and images of 1867.

This particular reference to Turner needs to be seen as part of the larger critique of his loyalties that Whistler was making at the time as he struggled to establish foundations for his own creative identity. Even heroes that would continue to play important parts in his work were brusquely, though not quite convincingly, thrust aside in the process of declaring that he had attained his aesthetic maturity. In that vein, only months after summarily dispensing with Turner—the dominant figure in the modern English landscape tradition within which he was now working to make his name—Whistler would write his friend and fellow artist Henri Fantin-Latour to renounce "that damned Realism" and to deny that Courbet's influence had followed him from France.

In his "damned Realism" letter Whistler offers a pointed assessment of his professional life and work ethic to date. He describes himself to Fantin-Latour as a formerly naive "disciple" (apôtre) of Courbet's Nature, writing about himself in the third person as if to put behind him a youthful indiscretion: "He had only to open his eyes and paint what he found in front of him! beautiful nature and what have you [tout le bataclan]! that was it!" He then proceeds to disavow that "spoiled child" (polisson) along with the works his blind faith in wide-eyed perception had produced, "the piano [picture]— The White Girl—the Thames views—the seascapes."[19] And it is especially significant that these categories correspond in each instance to the paintings—among them the Brown and Silver Thames canvas—that Whistler had sent in the spring of 1867 to Paris, where Fantin-Latour would have seen them at the Salon and the Exposition Universelle.[20]

Courbet himself made only a token appearance at those venues, preparing instead to open a large one-man show near the Exposition site two months later.[21] The tactic reprised his earlier gesture of dissent, when his Pavillon du Réalisme stood in defiance of the Exposition of 1855. That same year, Whistler had arrived in Paris from the United States to pursue his artistic training in early November, only days before the Exposition and Courbet's challenge

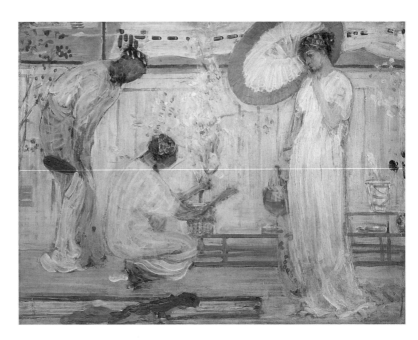

56. James McNeill
Whistler, *The White
Symphony: Three Girls*,
c. 1868. Oil on millboard
mounted on wood.
Courtesy of the Freer
Gallery of Art,
Smithsonian Institution,
Washington, D.C.

to it closed, and it is unlikely that the Pavillon's significance would have escaped the notice of the eager student and self-styled iconoclast.[22] Twelve years later, Courbet's aggressive independence must have seemed a less appealing model for a still largely unknown artist whose own pose belied his appreciation for the tangible benefits of official recognition. Indeed, the focus of Whistler's letter to Fantin-Latour quickly shifts from Courbet to Ingres, a figure whose own powerful brand of exclusivity was being smoothed over by the fine arts establishment even as Whistler wrote, so that he was seemingly as central to the French academy as Courbet was determined to remain marginal to it.

Ingres's death in January 1867 prompted the Ecole des Beaux-Arts to mount a massive memorial exhibition that opened on April 8, another oeuvre against which Whistler could reassess the values he attached to his own paintings concurrently on display in Paris. As if to counteract his conspicuous presence three years earlier in Fantin-Latour's group portrait titled *Homage to Delacroix* (Musée d'Orsay, Paris), Whistler in 1867 looks wistfully to Ingres and declares to Fantin-Latour that color without the firm foundation of drawing is "vice." In an extended though hardly unique analogy, he

calls color a seductive and capricious mistress who quickly becomes a promiscuous "whore" (*putain*) without the steadying, respectable companionship of drawing, "her lover but also her master."[23] Color, like nature, exerts a sensual appeal that must be guided by the intelligence of the strict yet responsive artist; indeed, this same dynamic of dominance and submission reappears in Whistler's "Ten O'Clock" lecture of 1885 to characterize the relationship between the artist and nature, "her son and her master—her son in that he loves her, her master in that he knows her."[24] In his letter Whistler performs something of the role he assigns to color and nature. He casts himself as a callow student whose intuitive attraction to the easy charms of color might have been better served by the stabilizing influence he identifies with Ingres's mastery of line.

This aesthetic soul-searching continues as Whistler confides to Fantin-Latour his intention to inject a new sense of discipline into his art. And, just as his 1867 letter invokes the name of Ingres in order to moderate the authority of Courbet, the most important works Whistler produced in the late 1860s deliberately engage what he had come to call the "only alternative" to the "simply natural," as he set out to modify his reliance on "beautiful nature" by nurturing

57. James McNeill Whistler, *Variations in Blue and Green*, c. 1868. Oil on millboard mounted on wood. Courtesy of the Freer Gallery of Art, Smithsonian Institution, Washington, D.C.

and testing his newfound discipline within the context of decorative painting. The pictures now known as the *Six Projects* (figs. 56, 57) are composition studies for an unrealized "scheme of decoration" intended for Frederick Leyland, for whom the artist would later create the Peacock Room, his most significant statement in decorative art.[25]

But to see this turn toward the "decorative" around 1867 simply as Whistler's way of repudiating realism would be to underestimate the essential complexity of the work he produced at that time. In the *Six Projects*, he attempted to encompass the full range of themes—nature and decoration, color and drawing, Ingres's aesthetic—that he had raised in the late sixties. These decorative paintings were at the heart of a self-prescribed, remedial course of instruction which, Whistler told Fantin-Latour, had been occupying him for over a year. While the *Projects* were virtually complete by the time the poet Algernon Swinburne described several of them in 1868, probably after a visit to the artist's studio in the spring, the letter to Fantin-Latour indicates that they were already well underway the year before.[26] With obvious excitement, Whistler recounts how he has been diligently drawing from the model ("Je passe la journée avec des modèles à dessiner!!")—in effect,

making systematic studies from nature—as a crucial part of his artistic re-education. Many of these drawings explore single figures and combinations that form the basis for the *Projects* ensemble.[27] Indeed, the minimal props and indeterminate settings of the *Six Projects* keep the focus on the human figure, that most academic of artistic subjects and the foundation of Ingres's classicizing art.

The *Six Projects* were based on precedents ranging from classical and Asian art to contemporary British figure painting, especially the work of Albert Moore, an eclecticism no doubt designed, in part, to avoid appearing too "perversely French," a phrase Whistler applied to some of the paintings in Ingres's commemorative exhibition.[28] A new preoccupation with the essentially academic *process* of piecing together pictures from his own life studies and from sources in other art suggests that Whistler was attempting to narrow the distance between "simply natural" inspirations and more conceptual "decorative requirements." That such an effort was not entirely lost on others is indicated in a review of Whistler's one-man exhibition held at London's Flemish Gallery in 1874. Writing about one of the *Six Projects*, a critic noted that "the scheme of the picture has a direct and unmistakable relation with nature, and yet belongs just as certainly to the realm of artistic invention."[29]

It was in the late sixties, at the very time that he was absorbed in creating the *Six Projects*, and extending into the next decade, that Whistler began to speak openly about his concern to inject into his art a new sense of order. He informed Fantin-Latour that the progress he was making in his work had to do mainly with what he called the "science" of color which, he believed, his thorough study had reduced to something of a system.[30] The same sort of phrasing recurs in 1873, when he urged an American friend to visit his exhibition at the Galerie Durand-Ruel in Paris, the first public display of the works he had produced during this crucial period. These were meant, Whistler wrote, "to indicate slightly to 'those whom it may concern' something of my theory in art. The *science* of color and '*picture pattern*' as I have worked it out for myself during these years."[31]

According to his brother, the artist posed his models for the *Six Projects* beside a human skeleton and a replica of the *Venus de Milo*.[32] Such studio props represent aspects of the actuality and the perfection of form that these largely experimental paintings were meant to bring together. They also provide reference points for our understanding of the significance Whistler attached to the project's relatively careful development. He had come to believe that his previous efforts at plein-air realism and other varieties of naturalist objectivity had suffered from the lack of a methodical approach. Indeed, his attraction to Moore's art may have had as much to do with his interest in the English artist's painstaking way of constructing his images as it did with a shared affinity for a figural motif.[33] Whistler's own increased attention to drawing during the late 1860s was meant to address what he perceived as a weakness, to provide a firmer anatomy for his work and a more rigorously charted path for his pursuit of "Venus" and ideal beauty.

Whistler never translated the *Six Projects* into the full-scale presentation he envisioned, and by 1870 he had largely conceded such arrangements of female figures to Albert Moore, who would make the subject and its decorative

treatment his specialty. But if the *Projects* appear to mark a fairly short-lived phase in Whistler's career, their impact on his art was lasting. The Pennells saw in them a technical basis for much of his subsequent work, especially the Nocturnes,[34] most of which have the same fluid facture that characterizes the earlier ensemble. The quality of paint in both groups of paintings is at once both restrained and purposeful, sensually responsive to the material properties of liquid pigment. And the reductive qualities of the decorative oil sketches are echoed in the typical Nocturne composition, pared, in many cases, to horizontal bands of closely related color.

But the connections between the *Six Projects* and the Nocturnes go even deeper than such surface considerations. The discipline that Whistler sought to gain from the drawing process which underlies the *Six Projects* has its corollary in the memory technique he developed to aid in making the Nocturnes.[35] In the *Projects*, single figures and groups were reiterated in numerous preparatory studies, and in the variations on poses worked out in the six oil sketches themselves. For the Nocturnes, Whistler's rehearsal, recitation, and finally his visual performance of the memorized observation constituted a similar process of gradually mastering the object of his attention. The artist equated the activity of drawing with this more indirect species of visual organization in 1878, when he testified during *Whistler v. Ruskin*: "I do not always sketch the subjects of my pictures, but I form the idea in my mind conscientiously and work it out to the best of my ability."[36] Both the *Projects* and the Nocturnes, then, establish structural principles by way of sustained, deliberate activities—the repeated tracing of graphic form on paper, in the one case, and the imprinting of form onto the memory through a process of trial and error, in the other—in order to provide a consistent frame through which "nature" itself might be appropriated, and against which a certain image of that nature could be tested, repeated, and refined.

In 1877 Sidney Colvin, Slade Professor of Fine Art at Cambridge University as Ruskin was at Oxford, published his review of the first Grosvenor Gallery exhibition in the *Fortnightly*

58. James McNeill Whistler, *Nocturne: Grey and Gold—Westminster Bridge*, 1871–72? exh. 1877. Oil on canvas. Glasgow Museums: The Burrell Collection

Review. In addition to *Falling Rocket*, the painting that had so enraged Ruskin when he saw it at the same exhibition, Whistler showed three other Nocturnes. One of these, exhibited as *Nocturne in Blue and Gold* (a painting now known as *Nocturne: Grey and Gold—Westminster Bridge*, fig. 58), gained Colvin's particular approval. Not only did it present "a lovely and satisfying sight to the eye," he wrote, but it expressed with "a perfect justice the silvery mystery of the night, the subtly varied monotony of the great glimmering river surface, the soft profundity of the sky, and that indefinable atmosphere above the houses, half duskiness, half glare, which is the effluence of the city's life." The languages of nature and art merge here into a single statement; for Colvin, the picture of Westminster Bridge successfully integrated the natural and the decorative in an image of nocturnal harmony. The other Nocturnes shown in 1877 at the Grosvenor, however, did not fare as

well. "Others of these moonlights," Colvin continued, "are spoiled by the introduction of Cremorne fireworks, or by being taken from fantastic points of view, from the foot of some incredible timber arch, or from the top of some unaccountable elevation."[37]

In addition to the Westminster Bridge painting, the Nocturnes Whistler sent to the 1877 Grosvenor exhibition were *Nocturne in Blue and Silver*, together with *Nocturne: Blue and Gold—Old Battersea Bridge* and the *Nocturne in Black and Gold: The Falling Rocket*, both of which feature the fireworks mentioned in Colvin's description. His objections to aspects of these paintings return us to the issue of the relative clarity and legibility that critics frequently appreciated in Whistler's earlier bridge compositions, such as the *Brown and Silver*. The vantage point that located the viewer and *explained* the image in these earlier pictures, the vantage that was measured, fixed, and determined, as well as determining of the entire scene that unfolded from it, was in the Nocturnes oddly "unaccountable." It fluctuated from one composition to the next, now excessively low in one picture, now inexplicably high in another. These idiosyncratic points of view, Colvin seems to be saying, called attention to their own "fantastic" quality and thus distracted from the experience of viewing the image constructed around them. Rather than providing definition, the capricious viewpoints of the Nocturnes contributed only irritation and confusion.

A similar sense of disorientation plagued the proceedings of *Whistler v. Ruskin*. As it happened, the painting that figured at the center of these aesthetic-cum-legal debates was not the object of Ruskin's ire, the *Falling Rocket*, which actually received only cursory attention during the trial. Rather, attention focused on *Nocturne: Blue and Gold—Old Battersea Bridge*, the composition Colvin characterized as taken "from the foot of some incredible timber arch." Among the courtroom strategies aimed at discrediting Whistler's art was the effort made by Ruskin's principal attorney to "read" the Battersea Bridge Nocturne, an undertaking calculated to end in bewilderment and bemusement. As the attorney wondered whether the object prominently depicted in the picture was meant to be a telescope or a fire escape, the spectators gathered in the court responded with the laughter the tactic was designed to provoke.[38] Whereas Whistler's earlier bridge paintings had provided a contextualizing point of view, the kind of outlook that the attorney seemed to expect to find in pictures where objects established legible relationships and identities, the point of view indicated in the Nocturne distorted and fragmented that context and made its visual contents strange.

If Ruskin's defense attorney emphasized what he could only conclude was the generally incoherent nature of Whistler's work, the witnesses called to testify on the critic's behalf stressed more specific kinds of insufficiency. In his own trial testimony Whistler described his Nocturnes as artistic "arrangements"; the *Falling Rocket* was "an arrangement of color," he said, and the Battersea Bridge Nocturne was painted to express "a certain harmony of color."[39] Ruskin's witnesses agreed that the paintings were distinguished particularly by their colorism, but they turned that feature against the artist and his work. The painter Edward Burne-Jones, in particular, damned the Nocturnes with faint praise when he allowed that the *Nocturne in Blue and Silver* as well as the Battersea Bridge picture were indeed both beautiful in color. But, he added, Whistler's exquisite color was without form, and his paintings were without finish. Color alone was not enough to redeem an art which, he warned, set a dangerous precedent. Such paintings might be taken as an example by others who, lacking Whistler's personal gift for color, would produce "mere mechanical work . . . and so the art of the country will sink down to mere mechanical whitewashing."[40]

Burne-Jones's intimation that Whistler's paintings could lead to a time when menial craft might masquerade as fine art was amplified in the testimony of another of Ruskin's witnesses, who found in Whistler's pictures proof that the day had already arrived. The art critic Tom Taylor readily enough granted that the Battersea Bridge Nocturne possessed a "beautiful tone of color," but, he added, "the color does not represent any more than you could get from a bit of wallpaper or silk." Quoting from his own review of an earlier exhibition that included both the *Falling Rocket* and the Westminster Nocturne that Sidney Colvin had admired, Taylor offered his judgment that such paintings "only come one step nearer pictures than delicately graduated tints on a wall paper would do."[41] If Whistler's Nocturnes had their virtues, these assessments of his color make clear, they were the merits not of serious artistic representation but of possibly pleasant, largely frivolous decoration. His paintings, difficult to read as the conventional and coherent depiction of tangible objects, registered as if they were blank, like the banal surfaces of wallpaper or a patch of whitewash.

As Burne-Jones's allusion to the school of "mechanical whitewashing" they might potentially inspire makes clear, paintings like the Nocturnes failed to measure up to the expected standards of serious *work*, in every sense of that

word. This, of course, was the message of
Ruskin's criticism of an apparently slapdash
kind of painting in relation to the value of conscientious labor—the commentary that had
precipitated the courtroom arguments of artists
and attorneys over the relative merits of aesthetic issues and objects. The charge that
Whistler's pictures did not meet the criteria of
artistic accomplishment expected of any
painting worthy of the name was a predictable
enough refrain, an attack phrased usually in the
terms of a lack of "finish" in his pictures. And in
most cases, as in Ruskin's own critique of
Whistler, that lack not only reflected Whistler's
suspect execution but also implicated the va-
cancy of his entire artistic conception. The
Nocturnes, in short, did not appear to be the
products either of labor or thought.

Writing in the aftermath of *Whistler v.
Ruskin*, Frederick Wedmore expanded upon the
disparity between considered artistic production
and trifling decoration as he saw it played out in
Whistler's work. Too often, he argued,
Whistler's art appeared to settle for too little;
"contented with decoration," he said, "it dis-
dains an idea." Such satisfaction was inadequate
in the realm of art with serious aspirations. "We
cannot accept the decorative in the place of the
thoughtful," Wedmore intoned: "accept a successful pattern where association and sentiment
have been: forego comedy and pathos, laughter
and tears, for a scientific adjustment of yellow
and of red. In the word spoken we cannot excuse the boasted absence of the message. If
there be anything new in Mr. Whistler's
theory—if there be anything to the point, it is to
implore us to take a stone for bread, and the
grammar of a language in place of its literature."[42] Wedmore's penultimate image recalls
Ruskin's reference to the "chalk and water" that
too often passed as a poor substitute for "milk,"
the sustaining diet that a proper knowledge of
nature ensured.[43] Indeed, Wedmore and Ruskin
might have concurred that the understanding of
nature expressed in Turner's paintings was the
highest form of "thoughtful" landscape art,
while Whistler's decorative pictures were of
decidedly lesser intellectual reach.

Wedmore's words would seem to anato-
mize the very categories of nature and
decoration that Whistler sought to join in many
of the works he chose to send to the Grosvenor
Gallery. Like Wedmore, Henry James visited
Grosvenor exhibitions and invariably found
himself unable to sustain an enthusiasm for
Whistler's project to interrogate the subordina-
tion of style to substance. "It may be a narrow
point of view," James allowed, writing about the
inaugural showing, "but to be interesting it
seems to me that a picture should have some

59. James McNeill Whistler, *Arrangement in Black:
La Dame au brodequin jaune—Portrait of Lady
Archibald Campbell*, 1882–84, exh. 1884. Oil
on canvas. Philadelphia Museum of Art.
Purchased with the W. P. Wilstach Fund (cat. 69)

relation to life as well as to painting. Mr. Whistler's experiments have no relation whatever to life; they have only a relation to painting."[44] The following year, James returned to the Grosvenor and couched his response to Whistler more unmistakably in terms of the decorative: "He covers a large space of wall with an array of his usual 'harmonies' and 'variations,' 'arrangements' and 'nocturnes.'" Whistler's paintings, concluded James, "are pleasant things to have about, so long as one regards them as simple objects—as incidents of furniture or decoration. The spectator's quarrel with them begins when he feels it to be expected of him to regard them as pictures."[45] This critique puts into play venerable distinctions established in the vocabulary of the conventional art theory familiar to James and his readers, a discourse that distinguished between the fully considered, high-minded aspirations embodied in the *tableau*, on the one hand, and the less exalted artistic ambition of its opposite number, the more informal, less scrupulously developed *étude* or *décor*. It is precisely such ostensibly opposite properties, alternatively expressed in the rhetorical pairing of color and line, among other, related possibilities, that Whistler aimed to bring into dialogue in the works he presented at the Grosvenor Gallery exhibitions between 1877 and 1884, paintings firmly founded upon his aesthetic efforts of the sixties.[46]

It is tempting, then, to see in his single submission to the exhibition of 1884, the last Grosvenor show in which he participated, a summary of his mature artistic objectives. In *Arrangement in Black*, a full-length portrait of Lady Archibald Campbell exhibited as a *Harmony in Brown and Black* (fig. 59), the Whistlerian figure seems simultaneously to advance and retreat, engaging the viewer with a gesture and a glance as she adjusts a glove and looks over her shoulder before disappearing into the darkness that she decorates. Presented in a posture that at once solicits attention and begins to withdraw from it, Lady Campbell embodies Whistler's search for a visual form that mediates between legible statement and veiled suggestion.

Whistler exhibited his enigmatic portrait of Lady Campbell the following year at the Paris Salon, where at least one French writer fastened onto the painting as an image of the artist's disdainful repudiation of the public.[47] By the mid-1880s, however, Whistler was already intent on extending his exposure to audiences at home and abroad. In 1884, the year of his final contribution to the Grosvenor Gallery, he sent four paintings and a selection of etchings to the first exhibition of Les XX in Brussels, and he resumed the practice of submitting to the Salon, a venue he had avoided, together with the Royal Academy, for more than a decade. That same year Whistler was elected a member of the Society of British Artists. He assumed the presidency of the institution in 1885, increasingly turning his attention to its exhibitions and influence. It was at the Grosvenor Gallery, however, that the American-born artist established his most sustained conversation with the English public and press. In his regular presentation of Nocturnes, especially, Whistler offered a London audience images of a landscape made less familiar by an intervening darkness that uncovered subtle shadings in the conventionally transparent relationships between content and style even as it revealed the implicitly pictorial, decorative possibilities in the substance of the urban subject.

6

G. F. Watts at the Grosvenor Gallery
"Poems Painted on Canvas" and the New Internationalism

Barbara Bryant

IN 1880, WITH HIS REPUTATION SECURE, George Frederic Watts published his beliefs about painting and its presentation in an essay on "The Present Conditions of Art," singling out the Royal Academy for his strongest criticism: "The highest qualities of art appeal to the finest powers of judgement, the most difficult to exercise with the conditions presented by modern exhibitions. An Academy Exhibition room is no place for a grave deliberate work of art. It is seen to no advantage there being out of place. . . . It is art that corresponds to the highest literature, both in intention and effect, which must be demanded of our artists, poems painted on canvas, judged and criticized as are the poems written on paper."[1] Watts came to call his painted poems "symbolical," a term which announced their differences from narrative painting, thereby placing them in the realm of a new, thought-provoking art.[2] Given that Watts considered the Royal Academy unsuitable for such "poems painted on canvas," what alternative opportunities were available for the exhibition of his valued works? By 1880 he could afford to speak out with confidence as he had already found his ideal venue. With the opening of the Grosvenor Gallery by Sir Coutts and Blanche, Lady Lindsay, in 1877, Watts had secured a sympathetic setting and audience. The triumphant appearance of *Love and Death* (fig. 60) at the landmark opening exhibition had been the first time Watts's "symbolical" paintings were seen as the artist intended; the event ushered in a new appreciation of his largely unseen recent output and his later "painted poems," those paintings for which he is best known today.

This chapter will consider the state of Watts's art and reputation just prior to the opening of the Grosvenor Gallery and how it flowered within that context. Watts exhibited his major works widely during the ten-year heyday of the Grosvenor, and this sustained exposure and the critical comment it generated allowed him to develop the category of painting he called "symbolical." Watts also became a player on the international stage, for through key connections with France, the Grosvenor's directors heralded a new phase in contemporary English art by placing it within a continental context.

60. George Frederic
Watts, *Love and Death*,
exh. 1877. Oil on canvas.
The Whitworth Art
Gallery, University
of Manchester

The exhibitions featuring Watts's latest work, along with the recent achievements of Edward Burne-Jones, had wide repercussions in the 1880s and opened the eyes of a European audience to this type of painting in England.

At the root of Watts's involvement with the Grosvenor Gallery lay the artist's long-standing friendship with Sir Coutts Lindsay. At the time of the opening of the gallery, the two men had been friends for more than twenty-five years, first meeting perhaps in Italy in the 1840s in a circle of mutual friends, such as Lord and Lady Holland, or later on in London after Watts's return in 1847. Although Watts and Lindsay were far from social equals, Watts had the good fortune early on in his career to be taken up by aristocratic patrons, Lindsay himself being in Italy on and off in this decade, and their paths may have crossed at this time. Lindsay began his career as an artist in earnest (after resigning a commission in the Grenadier Guards in 1850),

and in the early 1850s he probably came into contact with Watts, who was at this time using empty rooms at Dorchester House as a studio.[3] The newly built London palazzo belonged to the collector Robert Holford, who married Lindsay's sister in 1854. Lindsay himself carried out some decorative painting at Dorchester House for his brother-in-law, so he and Watts spent some time together in the 1850s. Furthermore, both men fell under the spell of the beautiful Virginia Pattle (who became Countess Somers) although, unlike Lindsay, Watts only adored her from afar.[4]

Watts and Lindsay continued their friendship from the 1850s onward, meeting at Little Holland House. A portrait study of Lindsay (fig. 61) painted by Watts around 1860 bears witness to their friendship.[5] Though unfinished, this image projects the sitter's subdued, even distant, demeanor enhanced by the historical reference in the suggestion of Van Dyck cos-

61. George Frederic Watts, *Portrait of Coutts Lindsay*, c. 1860. Oil on panel. Location unknown. Photograph courtesy the Maas Gallery Ltd., London

tume. Watts valued the portrait, retaining it for his own personal collection.

Lindsay established his career as an artist, exhibiting occasionally at the Royal Academy from 1862 onward with portraits of family and friends (few of which are known today). Given Watts's high reputation as a portrait painter in the 1860s, it is not surprising that critics saw Lindsay as an artist in relation to his professional colleague.[6] Despite his essentially amateur status, Lindsay mixed with a circle of young working artists and was attuned to the art politics of the day.

Throughout the 1860s and into the next decade, many artists, including Lindsay and Watts, became disillusioned with the Royal Academy. For Watts, the turning point had occurred in 1850, when the Academy hangers placed *The Good Samaritan* (City Art Gallery, Manchester) in a poor location; thereafter his relations with the institution cooled. He stopped exhibiting subject pictures after 1850, sending only portraits. Watts's dissatisfaction with the Academy could have threatened his livelihood, but private portrait commissions and decorative projects enabled him to do without the Royal Academy for much of the 1850s. Disillusionment with the Academy determined much of Watts's subsequent career, even after he became reconciled to showing there and was elected an Academician in 1867.[7]

Widespread dissatisfaction with the Academy among professional artists took tangible form in the growth of alternative exhibition venues. Watts took full advantage of galleries like the Dudley, the French, and the various dealers staging exhibitions of recent work by artists in London. In 1862, he began sending subject pictures to the Academy again, but by this time he was fully established independently as one of the most highly regarded portrait painters of the day and as an artist whose higher ambitions could be seen in the mural *Justice: A Hemicycle of Lawgivers* (1859) at Lincoln's Inn.

Throughout the 1860s and 1870s Watts worked on a new type of imaginative subject painting that embodied universal concepts. The first and most fully realized of these "symbolical" paintings is *Love and Death*. Initially the

work took the form of oil studies, essentially experimental in nature, which Watts often exhibited before proceeding with revised, much larger versions.[8] The artist usually exploited the more select venues for his first appearance, as, for example, when Watts exhibited the earliest version of *Love and Death* at the Dudley Gallery. Smaller venues allowed visitors a more thoughtful appreciation of such works. Only the more informed critics would give consideration to the works on view in these spaces. In the 1860s, with new patrons buying directly from Watts, exhibiting was useful but not a mainstay. Watts wrote of Burne-Jones, following that artist's defection from the Old Water-Colour Society, that he considered him "more than right in not exhibiting, and I shall follow his example in the case of all but my lighter productions."[9] However, this attitude was soon to change.

By the late 1870s, as Watts worked through several of the "symbolical" subjects, his requirements evolved. The large versions were often over life size and by definition required bigger venues in which their essential virtues could be appreciated. In addition, Watts envisioned these works as a group, so the individual components would benefit from being seen in relation to each other, like "parts of an epic poem."[10] Most important, he now began to formulate a personal goal, retaining works "destined to be public property" until he was able to present them to the nation.[11] After Watts had recognized the public dimension of his major productions, he had to rethink his habit of exhibiting only the smaller versions of such subjects as *Love and Death*. Watts now required a more systematic approach to exhibiting his work if he was to promote the paintings he valued most highly.

In his essay of 1880 Watts dismissed the Academy exhibitions as unfit for a certain category of his oeuvre, those "grave, deliberate works of art," because such paintings would "be seen to no advantage there being out of place." The vast exhibitions, crammed with thousands of competing works of art, are well illustrated in William Powell Frith's *Private View of the Royal Academy of 1881* (private collection). The twenty full Academicians were entitled to send eight works each without having them vetted by the Hanging Committee. Conventions of picture hanging also ensured that the visual cacophony of the Academy exhibition (since 1868 at Burlington House) provided no respite for poetic paintings which were more subdued in their visual impact.

Watts had realized the drawbacks of the Academy as early as 1850 and he was certainly not alone. The Academy never suited all artists all the time. An alternative tradition had grown up of artists taking matters into their own hands by staging exhibitions, to attract attention for a major painting, as had, for example, John Singleton Copley in the 1780s, Benjamin West in the 1810s, and William Holman Hunt in 1860. Some artists sought to increase their selling opportunities (usually focusing on one major work with a gathering of other paintings around it), especially if they were not in the Academy fold, such as Benjamin Robert Haydon (first in 1820), John Martin in 1822, and Ford Madox Brown in 1865, by exhibiting elsewhere. Precedents also existed for artists to open studio galleries of their own, as did West (even while he was president of the Royal Academy) and J. M. W. Turner.

James McNeill Whistler, a more recent defector from the Academy exhibitions, had stopped sending his paintings in 1872. In 1874 he staged an exhibition of his own in London, having arranged a similar grouping in Paris at Durand-Ruel the previous year. At the Flemish Gallery in Pall Mall Whistler showed a dozen oils and many more drawings and etchings. This exhibition, an accumulation of the best of his recent output, attracted the attention of the most notable critic of contemporary art, Sidney Colvin; he assessed Whistler's situation in the *Academy*: "If there is any case in which an artist is justified in opening a gallery of his own, it is when he is conscious of a distinct vocation for certain kinds of artistic combinations which it takes delicate organs to appreciate, and when experience has taught him that this kind of combination receives scanty welcome at the hands of art's official censors. And this is Mr. Whistler's case."[12] Whistler's exhibition of 1874 gave him the opportunity to control such key elements of the installation as the color of the walls and the lighting, all of which were essential to an appreciation of the delicate color harmonies of his paintings.[13] The precedent of this exhibition, as Robin Spencer has pointed out, may well have encouraged Lindsay in his plans to open a new venue[14], not only for painters outside the Academy but also for those whose paintings simply looked wrong there or, as Watts put it, "out of place."

Watts no doubt also contributed to Lindsay's thinking during the 1870s. Lindsay knew his friend's career had evolved well apart from the conventional path of exhibiting primarily at the Academy. He may well have been familiar with Watts's belief that the "best way to create interest in a more solemn and serious character of art would be to get together a sufficient number of pictures of the class, and exhibit them all together."[15] In addition, he may also have realized that by this time, in the 1870s, Watts desired an appropriate showcase for his valued "symbolical" paintings. These works required a particular forum, unlike the Academy, and a particular audience, sympathetic to their thought-provoking messages.

By 1876, Lindsay and his wife, Blanche, Lady Lindsay (a Rothschild descendant with her own fortune to contribute), were planning to open a new gallery on Bond Street.[16] The Lindsays, working together, consulted widely with artist friends while entertaining in their home at Cromwell Place, South Kensington and at Balcarres, in Scotland. Early in the planning they secured the assistance of a professional artist, Charles Edward Hallé (1846–1914), their first secretary, who took on the role of visiting artists' studios. Another early adviser, Joseph Comyns Carr (1849–1916), a young art critic for the *Pall Mall Gazette,* joined them formally by early 1879 as assistant director along with Hallé.[17] A close friend of Burne-Jones and a proponent of the advanced taste of young artists, Carr became an essential linchpin in the growth of the Grosvenor's ethos.

The principles behind the founding of the new gallery suited Watts in the many ways they differed from the practices of the Academy and how that institution treated artists. Lindsay planned to invite artists to contribute to exhibitions, so that there was no need to submit paintings to a selection process. Numbers of works on view were restricted in order to give due space to each work shown and to avoid hanging to the ceiling. An important innovation consisted in grouping works by one artist together on the same or an adjacent wall. Such hanging enhanced individual artistic vision, a notion which stemmed from a respect for the artist as artist, rather than as a producer of images. Such a view of the artist-creator, with its antecedents in the High Renaissance, suited Watts particularly well.

Lindsay publicly set out his version of this agenda along with his desire to give gallery space to artists left out of the established venues. His statement appeared in the *Art Journal*: "There are several thoughtful men in London whose ideas and methods of embodying them are strange to us; but as I do not think strangeness, or even eccentricity of method, sufficient excuse for ignoring the works of men otherwise notable, I have built the Grosvenor

62. George Frederic Watts, *Portrait of Lady Lindsay Playing the Violin*, 1876–77, exh. 1877. Oil on canvas. Private collection, on loan to the John Rylands Library (pl. 24, cat. 64)

Gallery that their pictures, and those of every other man I think worthy, may be fairly and honestly seen and judged."[18] Here he seems to be referring to Burne-Jones and his younger followers, who came under critical attack for their anatomically incorrect drawing and unusual use of color. But the aim of providing a stage for artists not otherwise well represented also applied to Watts.

Thanks to his friendship with Coutts Lindsay, all these ideas would have been known to Watts in advance of the actual opening of the gallery, particularly as he was probably painting at this time the *Portrait of Blanche, Lady Lindsay* (fig. 62). Watts was certainly writing about the Grosvenor in 1876 to his patron, Charles Rickards: "I hope to have some of my important pictures ready for exhibition next spring. When they have been shown my place will be better defined; it may be a higher or lower one but at any rate I shall no longer be able to feel that my best works have not been made public."[19] At this stage in his career, Watts needed an exhibition space like the Grosvenor for the "symbolical" *Love and Death*.

For the first exhibition of the Grosvenor Gallery, in 1877, Lindsay selected four paintings by Watts. *Love and Death* had the greatest impact, and it was the one Watts considered his most important offering. This major painting, along with the contributions of Burne-Jones and Whistler and the resulting art criticism, ensured that the first Grosvenor Gallery crystallized a key stage in nineteenth-century painting.

The three portraits also on view—*Lady Lindsay Playing the Violin*; *Edward Burne-Jones* (fig. 63); and *The Hon. Mrs. Percy Wyndham* (private collection)—made an equally important statement about the artist, confirming his reputation as the premier portrait painter in Britain. The portraits of Blanche Lindsay and Edward Burne-Jones also illustrated two of the key personalities behind the founding of the gallery. The portrait of Burne-Jones (painted some years before and exhibited at the Academy in 1870), was lent by the sitter. The thinly painted face seems to fade from life. It presents the artist as a withdrawn, shadowy figure, personifying the enigmatic creator of such paintings as *The Days of Creation* (Fogg Art Museum, Harvard Univer-

63. George Frederic
Watts, *Portrait of
Edward Burne-Jones*,
c. 1870, exh. 1877.
Oil on canvas.
Birmingham Museums
and Art Gallery

sity) and *The Beguiling of Merlin* (see fig. 47) which caused a sensation at the first Grosvenor Gallery exhibition.[20] Indeed, it was a well-orchestrated move on Lindsay's part to include such an artist's portrait as this gesture added to the cult of the artist as personality which became a feature of the Grosvenor exhibitions.

In direct contrast to *Edward Burne-Jones* was Watts's *Hon. Mrs. Percy Wyndham*, a sumptuous full-length portrait in the grand manner.[21] It nearly overwhelms the viewer with upper-class hauteur, rich textures, and luscious color. Painted more than ten years earlier, the portrait shows a close friend of the artist—a keen patron of advanced contemporary painting whose collection included works by Watts and Whistler. *The Hon. Mrs. Percy Wyndham* had not

been seen widely prior to the first exhibition of the Grosvenor Gallery. Lindsay clearly felt this painting would add not only to Watts's reputation but also to the image of the Grosvenor as a gathering place for the artistic avant-garde.

Watts's *Blanche, Lady Lindsay* hung near to *Burne-Jones* in the East Gallery, and together these two works epitomized the spirit of the whole Grosvenor venture. Blanche, in her early thirties at the time, is portrayed as the fashionable Aesthetic woman, absorbed in the creative process of music-making. A talented watercolorist, she apparently limited her efforts as an artist due to deteriorating vision and devoted herself to the violin.[22] This pursuit attracted Watts's attention in conceiving his portrait of her. The unusual three-quarter-length format allowed the artist to produce an unconventional portrait image, quite unlike the grand-manner spirit of *The Hon. Mrs. Percy Wyndham*. *Blanche, Lady Lindsay* captures a moment, as the subject turns toward her audience in her London town-house. But she also, of course, turns to welcome the artistic élite to the Grosvenor Gallery's first exhibition.

Watts's portraits provided a visual cast of characters for the Grosvenor, but *Love and Death* represented by far his most significant contribution to the exhibition. It dominated the north end of the main West Gallery, where it was paired with *The Hon. Mrs. Percy Wyndham*, which, at seven feet in height, was comparable in scale. Ample space surrounded these two large paintings. With such a position Lindsay and his colleagues declared their commitment to Watts's stature as an artist.

With *Love and Death* Watts unveiled for the first time one of his large-scale "symbolical" pictures. He had previously exhibited two smaller versions;[23] for the Grosvenor version Watts increased the scale of the subject to about eight feet in height, which further underlines its importance in his canon. The painting presents an original interpretation of the imagery of death, without adherence to traditional iconography. *Love and Death* was one of the works Watts considered among the "poems painted on canvas."[24] These symbolical paintings were suggestive rather than explicit, requiring careful scrutiny and thought. Such images carried a universal appeal, both in their visual language and their meaning. The rich, sonorous tones of this painting glowed from the crimson walls. The massive forms, sculptural in their inspiration and painted on a large scale, shone out across the large West Gallery. In the artist's own words, the painting showed "the passionate though unavailing struggle to avert the inevitable."[25] The highly serious aim of Watts, so unlike other artists at the Grosvenor Gallery or elsewhere, received acknowledgment from art critics in the forefront of new ideas in contemporary painting. Sidney Colvin referred to the "greatness of the invention" with its breadth and largeness of design.[26]

Oscar Wilde contributed an unusually perceptive review of the first Grosvenor exhibition to the *Dublin University Magazine* in which he recognized the pathos of the allegory in *Love and Death*. His opinions seem remarkably in tune with advanced art movements in London, even though he was at the time an undergraduate at Magdalen College, Oxford. Wilde declared the exhibition of *Love and Death* to be a rare opportunity to see Watts, whose "power . . . lies in his great originative and imaginative genius and . . . in the startling vividness of his conceptions."[27] Wilde's reading of *Love and Death* goes farther than other commentators in understanding the meaning of the allegory enacted by the "grey phantom," Death, and the "beautiful boy," Love. Finding no comparisons in English art, Wilde concluded: "There are perhaps few paintings to compare with this in intensity of strength and in marvel of conception."[28] His review reflects the Aesthetic theories of Walter Pater and Algernon Swinburne, both of whom were invoked in his essay.[29] It is entirely appropriate that Wilde recorded the link between the early Aesthetic writers of the 1860s and the role played by the first exhibition at the Grosvenor Gallery, which brought together the paintings that epitomized the values of "art for art's sake" and presented them to a wide audience for the first time.

Henry James, the expatriate American and another commentator on the opening exhibition of the Grosvenor Gallery,[30] turned his hand to different types of criticism, and, while not primarily involved in the art world, he wrote regularly on French and English painting and on the related matters of museums and collecting. Not having an English background, James provided an unprejudiced outsider's view of the exhibition. He dismissed the "ill-natured intimation which I heard put forth somewhere, that he [Lindsay] built the Grosvenor Gallery in order to have a place to exhibit his own productions."[31] James praised the notion of painters who "may communicate with the public more directly than under the academic dispensation, and in which the more 'peculiar' one in especial may have a chance to get popular."[32] Burne-Jones and Watts drew his attention. According to James, Watts was "the first portrait painter in England" who also had a "great longing to deal with 'subjects.' He has indulged it in one of the pictures at the Grosvenor and the result certainly justifies him. 'Love and Death' is an allegory, an uncomfortable thing in painting, but Mr. Watts's allegory is eminently pictorial. . . . The picture has a certain graceful impressiveness, and the painter has rendered with peculiar success the air of majestic fatality in the pale image which shows no features."[35] James recognized what set *Love and Death* apart: while an allegory or "symbolical" work, the painting itself also made an impressive visual statement on its own terms.

James and Wilde differ in their assessment of the Grosvenor Gallery, yet both agree that the first exhibition was a landmark occasion, notable for Lindsay's decision to display works by artists not widely seen in London. He selected just that type of work neglected by the established institutions or painted by artists intent on avoiding the Academy. The outsiders Lindsay included in his Grosvenor Gallery encompassed not only major British artists but also painters from the Continent. Lindsay's own taste may have contributed to the strong international element in the exhibition, another area in which the Grosvenor could outshine the Academy. Wealthy and well travelled, he reflected a distinctly noninsular point of view. Although the Academy contained a few honorary foreign exhibitors (especially in the years around 1870 due to a number of exiled artists fleeing the Franco-Prussian war), this group only amounted to a handful, whereas the Grosvenor had a substantial number of foreign contributors who provided a far wider context for the English artists on view. In its first few exhibitions the Grosvenor can be said to have introduced a new international spirit to the London art world of the late 1870s. The development of this European context gained wide currency in the following decades, but it first came to the fore with the opening of the Grosvenor Gallery.

Lindsay's catholic taste was significantly supported by his assistant directors at the Grosvenor, most notably Joseph Comyns Carr. The young critic's comments on the failings of the Royal Academy first recommended him, but he had also written glowing articles about Burne-Jones, who became his great friend, and

about Dante Gabriel Rossetti, whom he found "inspiring."[34] When Lindsay invited Carr to join the Grosvenor team, he must have been aware that, since 1875 (a few months after the periodical's founding), Carr had held the position of "directeur pour l'Angleterre" for *L'Art: Révue hebdomadaire illustrée*.[35] The post, more than just an editorial one (he was hired to popularize the periodical in England), provided Carr with unrivaled opportunities to forge links between the French and English art worlds; he was asked to become an adjunct editor because of "his association with French artists and men of letters."[36] Such firsthand knowledge of French art gave Carr a unique status and well suited the purposes of Lindsay in his creation of a gallery offering exhibition space to the best and most interesting artists of the day.

Lindsay seems to have thrown his own weight behind *L'Art*, for its offices at 134 New Bond Street stood immediately next door to the Grosvenor Gallery at 135–137.[37] This proximity was entirely intentional, particularly since Lindsay (in addition to his other holdings on New Bond Street)[38] can now be identified for the first time as the leaseholder for 134, as well, and Carr had official responsibility for this site.[39] In effect, Lindsay enabled the French periodical to open its London office. That Carr was *L'Art*'s director for England, in addition to being an assistant director at the Grosvenor, shows how mutually supportive these two operations were. Lindsay drew upon Carr's knowledge of the French art world to gain key exhibitors, while Carr gave the Grosvenor Gallery extensive coverage in *L'Art*.

Thanks to Carr, *L'Art* played a key role in fostering connections between artists in England and France. Although written in French, this periodical had an appeal beyond its text, for it was lavishly illustrated with original etchings and other engravings. Foremost among the engravings were many after English works of art and, in this way, *L'Art* provided an array of visual information about contemporary English painting for its primarily French audience (see fig. 68). In its fortnightly issues *L'Art* carried reports of the London art scene. The periodical eventually foundered in its English incarnation by 1883. Carr admitted that *L'Art* was "so luxuriously produced that it could not be destined ever to win a very large public."[40] Nevertheless, during the years Carr directed its activities in London, he facilitated a substantial exchange of ideas and works between London and Paris.

The venture had further ramifications: at 134 New Bond Street in addition to the offices of *L'Art* were the Librairie de L'Art, publishers of some of Carr's books as well as Grosvenor Gallery publications.[41] Also at 134 New Bond Street was the Galerie de L'Art, which seems to have been an exhibition space used primarily to display engravings seen as illustrations in *L'Art*. These prints were issued separately for purchase. At the Grosvenor Gallery in 1877, etchings, including Watts's *Portrait of Blanche, Lady Lindsay* by the French etcher Louis Monzies, were on view in the vestibule as one entered the building. The selling opportunities provided by the link between the Grosvenor and *L'Art*, had been cleverly taken into account. All these related efforts, designed to foster Anglo-French artistic relations, grew directly out of the ethos of the Grosvenor Gallery as an international forum for the best fine art, whether English or Continental.

In 1877 Comyns Carr wrote a key essay on the first Grosvenor Gallery exhibition for *L'Art*, summarizing and analyzing its aims. In particular, he stressed that the "Grosvenor Gallery should be almost exclusively devoted to the higher kinds of painting," since "the Academy has always made sure of popular success but it has never been strong on artistic qualities."[42] This essay is important for how it disseminated to the French art world a full account of the aims of the Grosvenor and the achievements of the first exhibition, all of which was given by Carr, a critic fully in tune with advanced English art of the 1870s. His discussion of Burne-Jones and Watts placed these artists in the forefront of contemporary painting, and this was his key message to the French. For Watts, in particular, Carr's essay broadcast the distinctive qualities of his work as seen in "the richly coloured monumental composition of *Love and Death*." Carr elaborated on the subject of this painting: "There are few English painters of our time who have so fine an understanding of the principles of poetic design and there is certainly none of

Mr. Watts's pictures which leave so strong an impression of his imaginative power as this noble illustration of the eternal conflict of Love and Death."[43] Carr further highlighted the qualities of "style" of Watts's paintings in, for example, *Portrait of Blanche, Lady Lindsay* (illustrated in the article by Monzies's stunning engraving), which was "marked by a suavity of line and sumptuous amplitude of form that accord very happily with the suggestion of music."[44] The musical analogy with form and color was another advanced aesthetic idea now linked with Watts's work. Carr presented Watts as an artist of imaginative power and poetic design, both notions which lay behind his "symbolical" paintings. This commentary makes clear how, in a stroke of the critic's pen, Watts's work came to feature within the French art scene. Interest in the fully realized aims of his art began to filter through from 1877 onward. Watts emerged as an imaginative artist par excellence, and this aspect of his oeuvre, as in *Love and Death*, became a potent source of inspiration to the French Symbolists of the 1880s.[45]

Through his writings in *L'Art*, Carr promoted the representation of foreign artists at the Grosvenor Gallery. His knowledge of the French art world, in addition to that of Hallé, provided the necessary expertise from which Lindsay benefitted. By including selected exhibitors from abroad and from the expatriate artistic community in the first Grosvenor, the directors further accentuated the distinctive appearance of the exhibition. Whistler and James Tissot both resided in London and made their careers in England, yet because they were foreign-born they tended to be grouped with the foreigners in the exhibition. Whistler had abandoned the Academy early in the decade and needed a showcase for his work; Tissot also never found the Academy entirely congenial. To the first Grosvenor, with Lindsay's blessing, Whistler sent six paintings and Tissot exhibited ten, one of which belonged to a projected (and thoroughly uncharacteristic) allegorical cycle, *The Triumph of the Will*.[46] The Dutch-born Lawrence Alma-Tadema exhibited at the Grosvenor as did Frenchman Alphonse Legros (a friend of Whistler and by this time a teacher in the Slade School), who sent one of his realist works and some studies for students. Giovanni Costa, an Italian friend of Frederic Leighton, exhibited a landscape, *A Winter Evening on the Sands near Ardea, Campagna di Roma* (private collection); it was lent, as was one of Watts's portraits, by the Percy Wyndhams.

But the range of foreign talent did not end with those artists resident in London who happened to have been born abroad. Along with his friend Tissot, Ferdinand Heilbuth, a German-born naturalized Frenchman, was the best represented of all the artists with eleven works, one of which *Past and Present: Excavations in Rome* (fig. 64) had already been acquired by Sir Richard Wallace, the Francophile collector.[47] His art had much in common with Tissot's vision of modern life, though Heilbuth usually set his scenes in Italy and populated them with Catholic clergy.[48] Sending his works from Charles Hallé's address, Heilbuth was obviously a favored insider with some English patronage upon which to build further.

The portrait painters Rudolf Lehmann and Victor Mottez, a friend of Hallé from Paris whose work appeared in the first exhibition, both had close ties with the English artistic community. In later exhibitions, Jules Bastien-Lepage was well-represented, particularly in 1880 when nine of his paintings could be seen. Among the Germans were Carl Schloesser, a painter of genre scenes, and Otto Weber, a naturalized Frenchman, who resided in London at the time of his death. His realist paintings in the manner of Courbet, often featuring animals,[49] attracted the patronage of Queen Victoria. The unusually large contingent of foreign sculptors indicate how valued sculpture was as a decorative adjunct to the appearance of the galleries.[50]

In the exhibition of 1877, most of these European contributions appeared in the East Gallery, the first as visitors entered. By virtue of their position, these works took precedence in the catalogue; therefore the first names in the catalogue are Weber, Costa, Lehmann, Heilbuth, and Tissot. This primacy of siting, surely intentional, heralded the international character of the exhibition. Lindsay and his colleagues specifically emphasized this aspect of their exhibition as they sought to carve out a new niche for the Grosvenor.

64. Ferdinand Heilbuth, *Past and Present: Excavations in Rome*, exh. 1877. Oil on canvas. Reproduced by permission of the Trustees of the Wallace Collection

In addition to this group of continental artists, one name calls for further comment because his work does not fall into the represented categories of portraiture, genre, or social realism. In the East Gallery, number 35 was *L'Apparition* (fig. 65) by Gustave Moreau, an artist then hardly known in London. Unlike many of the other exhibitors from abroad, Moreau had no obvious links with London nor with English artists. English collectors had not discovered his work as they had the paintings of Costa and Heilbuth, for example. This lack of familiarity with Moreau's output probably accounts for the fact that his contribution in 1877 went almost entirely unnoticed. Why then was Moreau included in this first Grosvenor Gallery exhibition?

Part of the explanation may be gathered from the address he gave in the catalogue. He lent his own painting, giving as his address "Office of *L'Art*, 135 New Bond Street."[51] This connection with *L'Art* strongly suggests that Comyns Carr may well have organized the inclusion of Moreau's large watercolor. The fact that no other artist in the exhibition gave the address of *L'Art* offices emphasized that, in this case, Carr's unique contacts with Paris gave him a key role as a conduit for ideas and images to the Grosvenor.

The inclusion of Moreau may well have become desirable due to his acclaimed return in 1876 to public exhibitions in Paris after a hiatus of some years.[52] At the Salon of 1876 he exhibited several works including *Salomé (dansant devant Hérode)* (Armand Hammer collection at UCLA), an oil, and *L'Apparition*, a large watercolor. Although clearly intended to be considered as a sequence, from the episode of Salomé's dance to her vision, after the murder, of John the Baptist's head, the two works differed in media and in size. Indeed, at the Salon, due to the differing media they did not appear in the same gallery; *L'Apparition* hung with the watercolors and *Salomé* with the oils.[53]

Moreau's much praised return to the Salon prompted *L'Art* to publish an elaborate engraving of *Salomé*, along with some large reproductions of his studies for the paintings of 1876, including some of the crayon and ink studies for *Salomé* and *L'Apparition*,[54] accompa-

nied by eulogizing articles.[55] Given that *L'Art* achieved a coup in gaining Moreau's cooperation for their coverage, with a selection of drawings provided by the artist, a logical next step after such a celebration must have been to encourage him to exhibit abroad. The opportunity of the Grosvenor Gallery's opening and the links between *L'Art* and the gallery made this possible. Only one work came to London; it is generally believed that this was the watercolor version of *L'Apparition* which appeared at the Salon. However, Moreau's work hung in the main East Gallery with oil paintings and not in the Grosvenor's separate watercolor room; it is possible that Moreau sent an oil version of the subject, rather than the watercolor, to London.[56] The watercolor version of *L'Apparition* is certainly a substantial and impressive work. The Grosvenor's organizing principle in such cases may have been less strictly the medium and more the importance of the work. Burne-Jones's watercolors also hung in the main galleries as, like *L'Apparition*, they gave the appearance of oils.

Moreau's *L'Apparition* is a richly detailed scene playing out the second part of the story of Salomé and Herod, loosely derived from the Old Testament account. After the beheading of John the Baptist, Salomé confronts the vision of the decapitated head. The setting suggests a distant Eastern palace with dark areas of shadow, lending an ominous tone to the work. With emotion suppressed, the figures are frozen in space. The surface, elaborated and encrusted with decorative color, is an accumulation of many minute touches of thick gouache. It is somewhat surprising that this work did not provoke any commentary from the many observers and critics of the first Grosvenor Gallery exhibition. As one might expect, Moreau's name appears in Carr's review, but without discussion. Similarly, William Michael Rossetti referred to Moreau in passing with no appreciation or analysis.[57] *L'Apparition*'s horrific and gory vision set in a hyperdetailed architectural fantasia peopled with bizarre creatures ultimately derived from the Bible must have looked unusual in an exhibition room in London, yet no one commented upon it. Is this because to an English audience Moreau's work looked like

65. Gustave Moreau, *L'Apparition*, c. 1876, exh. 1877.
Watercolor. Musée du Louvre, Département des Arts
Graphiques, fonds du Musée d'Orsay

another example of the established, largely
continental, genre of Oriental exotica, well
represented by Jean Léon Gérôme, whose
works were well known in London? Possibly
L'Apparition did not seem all that far removed
from excursions into Eastern genre executed by
John Frederick Lewis and Frederic Leighton.
Or did Moreau's work receive almost no published response because the eyes of the
art-going public, the élite of fashionable society,
and even the young critics, could not as yet
absorb the impact of a disturbing vision such as
L'Apparition?

Technically, the work parallels that of
Burne-Jones in the accumulation of details and
the elaboration of surface. Otherwise, Moreau's
strange, early Symbolist work found few cousins
in English art of the late 1870s. Watts's "symbolical" pictures, based on universal concepts and
simplified forms, had at first glance little in
common with Moreau's image. Yet both artists
had in common a major theme at the root of

their work: Watts in *Love and Death* and
Moreau in *L'Apparition* both delved into the
imagery of death, a concept which would become central to Symbolism in the following
decade.

After the success of the first Grosvenor
Gallery exhibition, particularly for Watts in the
triumphant appearance of *Love and Death,* the
artist regarded the Grosvenor as his primary
exhibiting venue. During the next ten years, he
sent nearly sixty paintings (while over the same
period of time sending about half that number,
mostly portraits, to the Royal Academy). Watts
unveiled a sequence of major compositions at
the Grosvenor: in 1878, he again dominated the
West Gallery with *Time and Death* (later with
the addition of *Judgment*; on loan to the Watts
Gallery), which followed upon the theme of
death. In the same year *Mischief* (fig. 66) veered
in another direction, a seemingly lighthearted
allegory. The composition evolved during the
1860s, making it one of the earliest of the "symbolical" designs.[58] It continued to preoccupy
Watts, who described it as representing "the
tyranny of Earthly Love."[59] In fact, the meaning
of the allegory was far from humorous, as it is
another example of mankind falling victim to
forces beyond his control, as here Love ensnares
the unsuspecting victim, rendering him help-
less. Although this picture was not the focus of
critical discussion in the same way as *Love and
Death,* it nonetheless belongs to the group of
"symbolical" works, of suggestive images which
Watts also described as "painted poems."

The Grosvenor Gallery in 1879 exhibited
for the first time large versions of Watts's *Paolo
and Francesca* (fig. 67) and *Orpheus and Eurydice* (pl. 28) which hung as pendants in the West
Gallery. These works, both on the theme of
doomed love, formed near companions (though
different in size), one derived from Dante and
the other from Ovid. The subjects would have
struck a chord with most educated viewers at
the exhibition, even though the images work on
a more symbolic level as well.

Paolo and Francesca, locked in a deadly
embrace, swirl through the doomed circles of
hell. In the illustrated catalogue of the
Grosvenor that year, compiled by Henry Blackburn, the quotation "These two together

66. George Frederic
Watts, *Mischief*,
exh. 1878. Oil on canvas.
National Gallery
of Scotland

67. George Frederic Watts, *Paolo and Francesca*,
c. 1872–84, exh. 1879.
Oil on canvas. Reproduced by permission
of the Trustees of the Watts Gallery,
Compton, near Guildford

coming, / That seem so light before the wind"
located the scene in the *Inferno* (V:73–75). Commenting on the visual qualities, he wrote "this
picture is remarkable for beauty of line and
harmony of low tones of color. The figures are
pale, against a background of clouds and fiery
rain, but without violent contrasts." The lack of
rich color further added to the atmosphere as
the artist sought to convey the mood of gloom
and death. In its way *Paolo and Francesca* also
represented the imagery of death which so
preoccupied Watts. For the benefit of the audience Blackburn also commented that *Paolo and
Francesca* is "one of a series of imaginative
compositions, upon which he [Watts] has been
engaged for some years."[60] Thematically, the
work had much in common with *Love and
Death.*

Orpheus and Eurydice* told the tale of loss,
as Orpheus turns to try to regain Eurydice from
the pull of the underworld. In the oil painting
the depiction of cold, colorless landscape fueled
the emotional tone of despondency, and the
subject works particularly well as an engraved
image (fig. 68), with its rich blacks adding to
that mood. Such an exercise in evoking a mood
fulfills Watts's own desire to spur his audience
to contemplate, rather than read, the image.
Critics of the time recognized what Watts's
paintings offered. Commenting upon *Orpheus
and Eurydice* and *Paolo and Francesca*, F. G.
Stephens wrote in 1879, "these designs are full
of poetry";[61] echoing these words, another
writer saw that they were "full of poetry and
passion."[62] Watts's vision of "painted poems"
filling the exhibition rooms became a reality
through the Grosvenor Gallery.

In addition to such scenes of doomed love,
Watts exhibited his ideal compositions featuring
the female nude, such as *Daphne* (unlocated)
and *Psyche* (fig. 69) conceived of as a pair and
seen in 1880. These works, while bearing
specific titles, were somewhat removed from
their mythological sources, enabling them to be
appreciated equally as decorative studies on life
scale. The literary frame of reference then provides a mood for each picture. *Psyche* conveys a
sense of loss, yet it also possesses purely decorative qualities which were (along with similar
qualities in *Daphne*) much commented upon by

68. John Watkins after George Frederic Watts,
"Orpheus and Eurydice," *L'Art*, 1879. Etching.
By permission of the British Library

critics, including Carr. The works exhibited in
1880, including *Daphne* and *Psyche,* prompted
Carr's evocative critique in his review of the
Grosvenor Gallery exhibition in *L'Art*. He drew
an essential contrast between the "spiritualisme
raffiné d'un peintre tel que M. Watts" and the
"cruelle veracité de M. [Bastien-]Lepage," who
that year exhibited *Les Foins* (pl. 9), among
other works. Watts's paintings of full-length
nudes epitomized "aspirations les plus opposées
de l'art contemporain"; Carr continued: "Pour la
première fois nous assistons à des efforts
sérieux, tendant à éxprimer par la ligne et la
couleur quelques-unes de ces grandes vérités
de l'imagination, qui n'ont jamais fait défaut à la
littérature anglaise. M. Watts occupe, dans ce
mouvement, une place éminente. Son talent,
s'est rarement présenté avec autant d'avantages

69. George Frederic
Watts, *Psyche*, c. 1880,
exh. 1880. Oil on
canvas. Tate Gallery,
London

que dans l'éxposition de cette année, à la Grosvenor Gallery."[65] For a French audience Carr thus placed Watts in the forefront of new ideas. The quality of "refined spiritualism" in his work, standing in direct contrast to the "cruel veracity" of realism, summed up Watts's achievement as a painter whose imagery and style then helped to inspire and to nourish Symbolism as a distinct movement.

By 1881, Watts's work represented one of the major attractions of the Grosvenor Gallery; that year he sent eight paintings depicting a range of subjects. To the Royal Academy he sent six portraits, but at the Grosvenor there were only two named portraits. The other works were a fancy head entitled *Reverie*; the full-length nude *Arcadia*; a landscape of the Carrara mountains; and three variations on classicism. *The Genius of Greek Poetry* (version, Watts Gallery) offered a visualization of the inspiration received by the figure symbolic of poetry. *The Wife of Pygmalion* (pl. 26), initially exhibited in 1868, transformed a noted Greek sculpture in the Ashmolean Museum into a painted portrait of the wife of the ancient sculptor. The latter calls up the same classical reference as Burne-Jones in the series *Pygmalion and the Image* (City Museum and Art Gallery, Birmingham), seen at the Grosvenor Gallery two years before but begun in 1868. Watts's version has no narrative trappings but is "a translation from the Greek," as he subtitled it in 1868 when it was seen at the Royal Academy. Thus Watts cast himself as Pygmalion, bringing to life the statue through his painting. This layering of meaning is characteristic of Watts's imaginative use of subject matter. *Endymion* (fig. 70), the third of the thematically linked classical paintings exhibited in 1881, had also had a previous showing in London. But it may well be that the artist sent these three works together to make up a loose trilogy which the Grosvenor would have hung together. This scene, based on classical mythology, dwells on the nighttime encounter of Diana, Roman goddess of the hunt, and Endymion, the shepherd she loved. As in *Orpheus and Eurydice* and *Paolo and Francesca*, there is an ill-starred couple, fated never to know true happiness, for in this case Endymion falls asleep forever. As in the earlier paintings,

one cannot read the facial expressions. Endymion is seen in shadow, while the strong light falls not on Diana's face, but on the great sweeping curve of her body as it bends toward Endymion. The strongly sculptural forms, accentuated in the figure of Diana by the thick swathes of drapery, belie the small, cabinet scale of the work. The potency and visual impact of the image result from simplifications in the composition, much as in *Love and Death*. In *Endymion* one can interpret this confrontation as a similar encounter between the forces of life and death, as the shepherd is seen in a deathlike sleep, awaiting the kiss of moonlight.

In all three works, which take classical culture as their point of departure, the resulting ruminations call out for sober contemplative thought. In such works Watts achieved his goal of "poems painted on canvas" on a less heroic scale than in *Love and Death*, in paintings which collector, connoisseur, and critic would have to unravel slowly and carefully. For Watts the Grosvenor provided ideal conditions in which to develop an appreciation of these imaginative subject paintings. Such was Watts's success as a featured artist at the Grosvenor Gallery in these first years that he rapidly ascended to a special category. Unlike Burne-Jones he spawned no group of disciples with whom his work was linked. Watts stood on his own, a full career already behind him, for by now he was well into his sixties.

An indication of his importance is that April 1880 one-man exhibition at the Royal Manchester Institution devoted to Charles Rickards's collection of paintings by Watts. Rickards, a patron of the artist since the 1860s, lent his two sculptures and all fifty-four paintings, including versions of *Love and Death* and *Time, Death, and Judgment*, along with many cabinet pictures and portraits. A one-man show for a living artist was still a relative rarity: occasional gallery shows, by definition on small scale, took place, such as those at The Fine Art Society, but the stimulus for an extensive retrospective of an artist's work ordinarily did not occur until soon after his or her death. Whistler had pioneered the idea of the "exposition particulière" in 1874, but this gathering was relatively small, despite the artist's promotional efforts.

70. George Frederic Watts, *Endymion*, c. 1870–72. Oil on canvas. Private collection

The Watts exhibition, although seen only in Manchester, was a landmark and had repercussions in London through reviews and word of mouth. When Lindsay and his wife returned from a trip to Manchester to see Rickards's collection, they had been "converted to the opinion that an artist's pictures should be seen together."[64] Although Lindsay's opinion of the exhibition in Manchester in 1880 is not recorded, it seems likely that this event prompted him to organize for the winter season at the Grosvenor Gallery a large exhibition of some two hundred paintings by Watts. This show, which opened in late December 1881 and continued into 1882, has the distinction of being the first full retrospective exhibition of a living British artist. It set a precedent which continued thereafter at the Grosvenor.[65]

This exhibition, entitled *Collection of the Works of G. F. Watts, R.A.*, contained many more works than the gathering of Rickards's collection in Manchester. Lindsay, Carr, and Hallé must have planned for at least a year to assemble such a vast gathering of works by the artist, many lent from private collections. Watts himself, keen to promote his work, cooperated, but—personally shy and wary of stepping into the limelight—he refused the lavish banquet arranged for the opening night. Although the English art world saw posthumous retrospectives of eminent artists fairly regularly, such an extensive review of a contemporary artist's work was unparalleled. Watts's long, rich career provided much material to draw upon. Early works emerged from private collections, as did portraits commissioned years earlier, some never seen in public before. For an English audience this exhibition contributed substantially to the notion of the individual artistic personality; in Watts's case the Grosvenor retrospective virtually created this idea of Watts by paying homage to the works and to the artist himself. The result, on one level celebrated Watts's work, and beyond this, a then unusual notion of the status of the painter as a creator and personality, as an artistic hero in society.

The main precedents to which Lindsay and his colleagues could have looked for such an exhibition existed in France. Connections between Carr and France may again have provided the background to the decision to mount a large exhibition of the artist's work. One-man shows had been staged by Courbet in 1855 with the Pavillon du Réalisme and in 1867 by Manet.[66] But these efforts, essentially adjuncts to the official showings of the Exposition Universelle, had more in common with Whistler's own exhibitions in that they were staged by the artists themselves in order to achieve more favorable displays and to promote their own work. Manet, in his mid-thirties, had a modest oeuvre upon which to draw for his exhibition of about fifty paintings. Courbet by 1867 had a longer career behind him; his show comprised something more akin to a personal retrospective. Even so, the comprehensive showing of Watts's work, initiated by Lindsay, represented an unusual case of an institution promoting a living artist.

After 1880, Watts's work was continually on view, as he opened his own picture gallery at his residence in Kensington. This idea of taking the presentation of his works into his own hands further enhanced his image and his reputation. As noted above, coverage in such periodicals as *L'Art* brought him into the Continental art sphere. Ironically, the consolidation of Watts's reputation, due chiefly to the Grosvenor Gallery, enabled him to fulfill some long-held goals about the power of art to reach beyond a fashionable audience. An exhibition also entitled the "Watts Collection" travelled to various cities throughout Britain during the mid-1880s. Also at this time Watts formulated plans to leave bequests of his works to Britain and other countries. He presented *Time, Death, and Judgment* to Canada in 1886 and later gave versions of *Love and Life* to the United States and France. In 1884 Watts showed a group of some thirty works at New York's new Metropolitan Museum of Art. Although not on the scale of the Grosvenor retrospective, this exhibition was representative of Watts's career and put contemporary British art on the map in the United States. It established a precedent for drawing crowds at the Metropolitan as well as being a rare example of a living artist's work displayed in a major museum outside his or her country. This exhibition further signaled Watts's international reputation as the foremost British artist in the 1880s.[67]

Even with worldwide fame and his own gallery, Watts did not desert the Grosvenor. The patronage of the Lindsays through the gallery enabled the artist to pursue new directions in the 1880s. He could be assured of a welcome reception for much of his output. His contributions to the Royal Academy declined as the Grosvenor became the favored exhibition space for his highly regarded subject paintings, including *Hope* (version, Tate Gallery), and such major portraits as *Cardinal Manning* (National Portrait Gallery, London). In 1887 when Carr and Hallé broke with Lindsay and left the Grosvenor to establish the New Gallery, Watts and Burne-Jones, among others, joined this fresh venture. Such loyalty underlines Watts's sympathy with the Carrs' contribution to the creation of a truly international exhibition venue for contemporary art, where leading painters, sculptors, collectors and critics from home and abroad could meet.

The Grosvenor Gallery's legacy to Watts was a new form of international status for a living artist, a position which successful artists now take for granted. This status, mediated by a cosmopolitan art press, meant that by 1887 Watts's paintings had achieved widespread public recognition, reaching new levels of appreciation both in England and abroad. The Grosvenor Gallery provided the original stimulus for this reinvigoration of Watts's reputation. Far from being a miscellany of paintings of diverse schools arranged around the major works of the leading artists, the Grosvenor Gallery as an institution, with its connections to Paris, its gathering of multinational talent, and its groundbreaking celebrations of living artists, can also be credited with introducing a new internationalism into London and into English art.

7
Rustic Naturalism at the Grosvenor Gallery

Kenneth McConkey

FROM ITS INCEPTION the Grosvenor Gallery was avant-garde and international. Its regular exhibitors were some of the leading secessionist artists of their day. They were painters who, for one reason or another, had been excluded by choice or design from the Royal Academy. Initially it seemed that Sir Coutts Lindsay, the gallery's director, had the ambition to demonstrate the progressive taste of some of his aristocratic friends. The tone of the first exhibitions complemented the decor of the galleries in being decidedly Italianate. Pre-Raphaelite art in this setting was, as an artist at the turn of the century put it, "having its last kick at the new Grosvenor Gallery."[1]

The early exhibitions "became historical" for reasons that were not predicted at the outset. Whistler's painting, so different from the "poetic" pictures of the followers of Dante Gabriel Rossetti and Edward Burne-Jones and so simple in its treatment of subject matter, immediately excited "scorn" and "hilarity." The rest was upstaged. D. S. MacColl in later years looked back upon his youthful visit to the first Grosvenor exhibition: "The Burne-Joneses carried me away on the spot: I looked at the Whistlers a little puzzled, as a good Ruskinian; but afterwards, when I looked at *things* again, and sketched them, found, to my surprise, that I was evoking Whistlers rather than Burne-Joneses."[2]

While the consequences of Whistler's inclusion in the first Grosvenor exhibition have often been recounted in detail, the full effect of the precedent set by Whistler—openly challenging critical dogma and, more important, daring to paint pictures that were obviously in enmity with popular standards—has not been fully explored. Young artists must have looked upon the battle as an obscure victory which somehow underscored their right to stand aside from the popular assumptions that determined public taste.

Despite his own artistic sympathies, Sir Coutts, as a gallery director, had the wit to recognize the need for a broad church in contemporary art.[3] This was signaled in the first exhibition with the works of Giovanni Costa and Ferdinand Heilbuth, which were borrowed from the aristocratic collections into which they had recently gone, and for which, in a number of cases, it is likely that Sir Coutts made use of George Howard's "Etruscan" connections.[4] The controversy which ensued over the Whistler-Ruskin trial has tended to disguise the character of the first exhibition and to obscure the degree to which the gallery in subsequent shows tried to define its position.

The general conditions—the markets in which the gallery operated—have been studied.[5] The competition for the best work of key painters who became the Grosvenor stable was intense. The degree to which Lindsay was prepared to recognize and reflect change has, however, been obscured by the myths surrounding his enterprise, generated by Gilbert and Sullivan and Oscar Wilde. He was sanguine about promoting the work of younger artists who were turning their backs upon what Whistler disparagingly referred to as "the British subject." This group eventually formed itself as a coherent avant-garde in the New English Art Club in 1886, but their debt in the first instance was to the open-minded policies of the Grosvenor. Many continued in their allegiance to the Grosvenor even after the establishment of the club. How do we uncover these new tendencies, and what made Sir Coutts's experiment an especially sympathetic venue for their cultivation?

At first the new work, outside that of a restricted clique, had little to do with the controversy around Whistler. Young would-be Grosvenor exhibitors were more preoccupied with the mundanities of craft training in the late 1870s because fine art education in England was so misguided. There was a fascination for the methods of the Paris ateliers which were growing in prestige and popularity throughout the Western world. American art students, despite the difficulties they might have with conversing in a foreign language, found it more congenial to go to Paris to complete their training than to come to London. This was, in artistic terms, not so much the Paris of the Impressionists as that of revered and commercially successful Salon painters whose work was featured in the increasingly sophisticated art journals of the period. Within this group, radical strands were pulling refined Parisian tastes

away from classicism. The lions of the Salon were painters of rustic subjects who were adopting the methods of Impressionism and plein-air painting to give circumstantial authenticity to their work.

At first, however, ruralist painting at the Grosvenor was dominated by idyllic academicism derived from the recently deceased but well-remembered Fred Walker and George Heming Mason. Walker had been widely regarded as the rising star of English painting at a time when Pre-Raphaelitism had temporarily lost its direction in the sixties. Although Mason, having spent his formative years in Italy, was seen as an "Etruscan," shortly after his death critics had no doubt that he was the painter who had conveyed "whatever remained of beauty in the rural life of England." His work contained "a passion more intense and inspired—than that of Jules Breton, conveyed by a method and manner that remind one at times of Daubigny."[6] The comparisons here are significant. Even in the 1860s the work of Mason and Walker was compared to that of the French painters of rural life, whose visual range was defined at one end by Bouguereau and at the other by Breton. The young Walker, visiting the Musée du Luxembourg in 1863, passed by the classicists and the romantics and reportedly "fastened upon the Jules Breton *La Fin de la Journée*."[7] However, these connections were not immediately apparent to the early writers on Walker and his contemporaries. Taken with the death of George Pinwell in 1875, the loss of Walker and Mason was interpreted as the fatal blow to an entire school.[8]

Sir Coutts Lindsay chose not to neglect this tendency when the Grosvenor Gallery opened two years after Pinwell's death, and to do this he had to find other young painters who were continuing the line of development first established by Walker and Mason. One of these was Philip Richard Morris, whose *The Reaper and the Flowers* (fig. 71) was shown in the first Grosvenor exhibition.[9] An aged field hand with a scythe is greeted on the roadway by a throng of joyful children "who will not stay his advance, any more than they will be able to resist the progress of time which he symbolises."[10] The children are "flowers"; the reaper will cut them

71. Philip Richard
Morris, *The Reaper and
the Flowers*, exh. 1877.
Location unknown

in mid-summer. There is an intended ambiguity; this elegy is as much about the loss of innocence as about death.[11] In later Grosvenor shows Morris played down the vague symbolism of *The Reaper and the Flowers*, although such symbolism remained an insistent feature of the representation of rural life in pictures consigned to the gallery by painters such as Fred Morgan, Alice Havers, Robert Walker Macbeth, and David Carr. For Victorian critics and artists, underwriting realistic truth with symbolic purpose provided important consolations.

Sir Coutts also had a penchant for modern landscape painting, and in 1878 he noted Cecil Lawson's *Minister's Garden,* a work which recast Pre-Raphaelite naturalism in the grand manner of Constable, and in the following year offered a place "on the line" to Lawson's *Hopgardens in Kent,* which had been badly hung at the Royal Academy. This additional exposure did not, in the mind of one reviewer, contribute to the painter's reputation, for the picture was "a tormented and spotty work, in which the effect of chaotic perspective is helped by the absence of any trustworthy horizon."[12] Nevertheless, thereafter for the remainder of his short career Lawson remained loyal to Lindsay.[13] In 1880, for instance, the gallery received his *August Moon,* a picture which came to be regarded as the high point of poetic landscape painting, recalled by one young visitor as astonishing evidence of "vigour and muscular enthusiasm

. . . amazing in a young man reputed to be so delicate."[14]

To some extent Lindsay and his fellow directors revealed their sympathy with this approach to the rural scene by including in the second Grosvenor exhibition such formidable rustic pictures as Robert Walker Macbeth's *Coming From St. Ives Market,* Morris's *Michaelmas,* G. H. Boughton's *The Rivals,* and W. J. Hennessy's *Fête Day in a Cider Orchard, Normandy* (fig. 72), which in their separate ways pointed to the essential focus of debate in the 1880s. They tackled the contemporary conditions of rural life, and they began to draw upon the stronger strand of rustic subject matter in French painting which was being re-assessed in the years of Jean-François Millet's popularity immediately following his death in 1875. They ranged from the almost anecdotal in Morris to the heroic processional in Macbeth. At the same time there was a commitment to what Courbet called "concrete" reality in the work of Alphonse Legros.

Of this group, Legros, the controversial new Slade professor, was potentially the most extreme. Initially Legros's work had not been understood in Britain.[15] When, for instance, his *L'Ex Voto* was exhibited at the Royal Academy of 1864, it was savaged by uncomprehending critics of whom the *Times* was typical: such work was not "calculated to please English eyes."[16] This justified the practice whereby the

72. William John Hennessy, *Fête Day in a Cider Orchard, Normandy*, 1878, exh. 1878. Oil on canvas.
Photograph reproduced with the kind permission of the Trustees of the Ulster Museum, Belfast

works of Legros were habitually "skied" or "floored" at the Royal Academy. In W. E. Henley's opinion, "the opening of the Grosvenor Gallery gave the painter new opportunity and a fairer field."[17] Nevertheless, when *Le Repas des Pauvres* (fig. 73) and *The Close of Day* (fig. 74) were being shown at the Grosvenor, there were similar reservations to those which had been voiced earlier. Legros's austerity, his "scorn of delight," of appealing sentiment, was "the greatest obstacle to his popularity."[18] These aspects, related to the painter's temperament, were also, in part, derived from his continued reliance upon French rather than British sources. Legros was a second-generation realist—that is, he depended on Spanish Caravaggesque methods which, although they came to be modified through the study of a broader range of old masters, were far from the mainstream of British painting during the 1870s. *Le Repas des Pauvres* was a reworking of Courbet's *L'Après-dîner à Ornans*, comparable to the "black" realism of Ribot and Bonvin. *The Close of Day*, a savagely reworked canvas, could be a page torn from Zola's later novel, *La Terre*.[19]

By the time these pictures were shown, the difference between French and British treatments of rustic subject matter was more apparent. Walker and Millet had died in the same year and in an essay on the British painter, Frederick Wedmore compared their attitudes to the representation of rural labor. Millet "saw in peasant life little beyond the hard labour of the fields," while for Walker it was a "vigour-giving, always grace-giving occupation."[20] Here was the beginning of those heroic sentiments which British painters and even some later naturalists sought to exploit. As the knowledge of French art increased, the Grosvenor Gallery encouraged change even if the nature of these changes was not fully grasped. A forerunner was found in the erstwhile Irish-American Pre-Raphaelite, William John Hennessy.[21] Having returned to Europe in 1870, Hennessy was now working in Normandy, and his large genre picture, *Fête Day in a Cider Orchard, Normandy,* was shown at the Grosvenor in 1878.

By 1880 the essential character of Grosvenor Gallery summer exhibitions was determined. The works of important regular exhibitors like Burne-Jones, George Frederic

73. Alphonse Legros,
Le Repas des Pauvres,
1878, exh. 1878.
Oil on canvas.
Tate Gallery, London

74. Alphonse Legros,
The Close of Day, 1878,
exh. 1878. Oil on canvas.
Sunderland Museum
and Art Gallery,
Sunderland, England
(Tyne and Wear
Museums)

Watts, Lawrence Alma-Tadema, and Edward Poynter attracted the most substantial critical comment. However, for the most part exhibitions were composed of reliable landscapes by the likes of Alfred Parsons, Mark Fisher, and J. W. North. Portraiture, the most popular genre, was invariably represented with examples from Val Prinsep, Charles Hallé, Hubert von Herkomer, Frank Holl, John Collier, and John Everett Millais. There were annual views of the Veneto with the distant dome of Santa Maria della Salute by Blanche Lindsay's close friend, Clara Montalba, and bombastic renditions of obscure tracts of Renaissance literature by Lindsay himself.[22]

In these early years, emboldened perhaps by the publicity of the Whistler-Ruskin trial, Lindsay and his fellow directors were prepared to take risks. Accordingly, in 1880 they invited the controversial Salon naturalist painter Jules Bastien-Lepage to stage a small retrospective of his work within the summer exhibition. The painter, an instinctive Anglophile, had been cultivating an English clientele for two years. Mixing with the players of the Comédie Française at Dieudonné's hotel in Ryder Street, London, in the summer of 1879, he had the astonishing good fortune to be summoned to Marlborough House to produce studies for a portrait of the Prince of Wales. This extraordinary costume piece was completed for the Academy summer exhibition of 1880, where it was viewed as something of a curiosity by critics.[23] In the light of the furor reverberating simultaneously in Paris following the exhibition of Bastien-Lepage's *Jeanne d'Arc Ecoutant les Voix*, Lindsay could hardly have timed his invitation better.[24] The Frenchman's naiveté about the English directly confronted British xenophobia about the French.

Bastien-Lepage's strategy for the Grosvenor show was obvious. *Les Foins* (fig. 75), his Salon painting of 1878, would introduce the viewer to a series of celebrated portraits, among them *Sarah Bernhardt*. It was a display designed to consolidate the painter's reputation and open the door to future lucrative portrait commissions. However, knives now sharpened by *The Prince of Wales* and *Jeanne d'Arc* stabbed in the direction of *Les Foins*. The uncompromising

naturalism of the picture was only hinted at in Henry Blackburn's polite description: "a young ungainly woman (worn with labour) seated in a field of new-mown hay, at rest . . . a characteristic work of the painter, unflinching in its realism, but highly finished, tenderly treated, and temperate in colour; the kind of work rarely seen in England."[25] Others were not so kind. To the writer in the *Magazine of Art* the female labourer was sitting "with her legs straight out before her, her vacant broad face looking out in an abstraction which has no thought in it, but merely the passive dreaming of an animal."[26] In an extraordinary extension of this line of attack, the *Illustrated London News* dubbed the young woman in the picture "a pure descendant of the primeval Eve as first evolved from the gorilla."[27]

The assault upon the sensibilities of British spectators was as evident in 1880 as it had been upon those of their French counterparts in 1878. Bastien-Lepage was preoccupied with the look of his models. They should appear vacant, staring and dehumanized by toil, an attitude of mind which, in the words of the perceptive American critic William Crary Brownell, was "half conscious, half ecstatic . . . [an] expression, utterly undefinable in words."[28] In a world dominated by the pretty, polite peasants of Bouguereau, pictures of this type were reaching for something more. *Les Foins* stole the show. The *Spectator* noted: "The artist holds easily this season the position wont to be filled by such painters as Messrs Burne-Jones and Holman Hunt, and round his pictures there gathers constantly a little knot of worshippers or scoffers, admiring or condemning in the most vehement manner."[29] If Bastien-Lepage had the objective of obtaining portrait commissions in mind, the strategy did not work. He realized, despite the enthusiasm for pictures like *Sarah Bernhardt*, that there was much more public interest in his rustic naturalism. Over the next three years all of his major paintings of peasants were shown in London and in a number of significant instances were purchased.[30]

In the presence of this work other rustic pictures at the Grosvenor—David Carr's *Watercress Gatherers*, Macbeth's *Landing Sardines at Low Tide*, Mark Fisher's *Coast Pastures*, J. Parker's *Field-Pea Gathering,* and Buxton

75. Jules Bastien-Lepage, *Les Foins*, 1878, exh. 1880. Oil on canvas. Musée d'Orsay, Paris (pl. 9, cat. 5)

Knight's *Breezy Uplands*—suddenly looked old-fashioned. Only one of the select group of London Scots, John Robertson Reid, could begin to measure up to the evident naturalistic truth of Bastien-Lepage's painting. It says much for the perspicacity of Coutts Lindsay and his colleagues that Reid's work now began to appear at the Grosvenor Gallery. His early exhibits, painted in Falmouth, gave a foretaste of what was to follow in the imagery of the Newlyn School. As for Reid's fellow exhibitors, fumbled technique coupled with false sentiment removed much of their appeal for young artists, many of whom were already convinced of the need for a closer engagement with French prac-

tice. Among these was Henry Herbert La Thangue, the most talented student of the Royal Academy Schools.[31] Initially La Thangue identified with Whistlerian tendencies in his Grosvenor exhibits, but these were not incompatible with visual conventions drawn from Bastien-Lepage. In this sense *A Portrait (Girl with a Skipping Rope)* (fig. 76), shown at the Grosvenor in 1883, was modern and confrontational. The accoutrements of Velázquez and the Japanese, so evident in Whistler's *Harmony in Grey and Green: Miss Cicely Alexander*, were removed from what is, in effect, a bourgeois version of Bastien-Lepage's *Pas Mèche*.[32]

76. Henry Herbert La Thangue, *A Portrait (Girl with a Skipping Rope)*, 1883, exh. 1883. Oil on canvas. Private collection, courtesy The Fine Art Society, London

The most consistent Grosvenor exhibitor whose work demonstrated an enduring attachment to the new objective naturalism of Bastien-Lepage was George Clausen. Clausen originally presented himself as a follower of the Grosvenor Gallery's French expatriate mainstay, James Tissot. In 1880 Clausen exhibited *La Pensée* (pl. 7) at the Grosvenor. The French title, the relative opulence of the interior, and the Tissot-like sophistication of handling confirm Clausen's predisposition to French painting.[33] Within two years, however, Clausen had left his Hampstead studio for the parish of Childwick Green, near St. Albans. Being in the countryside, where "one saw people doing simple things under good conditions of lighting," had an immediate effect upon his work, although "nothing was made easy for you: you had to dig out what you wanted."[34] *The Gleaners* (cat. 10) shown at the Grosvenor Gallery in 1882, was the first evidence of the transformation which had occurred. It was an extraordinary upright canvas—a shape more appropriate to full-length portraits—showing figures in a field in steep perspective. Although likened to Millet, the picture draws very little upon the more elegiac strand of French rural subject matter.[35] The plotting of the ground plan with haystooks and receding figures is a foretaste of Clausen's later more elaborately conceived spatial strategies. Like Bastien-Lepage, Clausen was anxious to achieve the effect of a real-life encounter with his figures. These are not heroic peasants seen against the sky like those of Millet and Breton; they are viewed from a standing position, as if the spectator had walked up to them in the open field. The force of this convergence should be neither dramatized nor overstated.

Haytime (pl. 8) and *Winter Work* (fig. 77), shown in 1883, extend and develop the mapping of a pictorial terrain. In the first, as in Bastien-Lepage's *Pauvre Fauvette* (Glasgow Museum and Art Gallery), there is a relationship between a prominent foreground figure and a background figure or animal. The space between the two is described by discarded clothing and equipment. In *Winter Work* there is a more complex mise-en-scène. Two field-workers, male and female, are arranged parallel to the plane of the picture, as in Millet's *L'An-*

77. Sir George Clausen,
Winter Work, 1883–84,
exh. 1883. Oil on canvas.
Tate Gallery, London

gelus. The context is nevertheless fundamentally different. In the British picture there is no backdrop of spiritual consolation, no ritual, no primitive piety. In *Winter Work* the setting is expanded to include a boy piling up the turnips in the middle distance. After the painting had been to the Grosvenor Gallery Clausen inserted a girl with a hoop on the right of the composition, turning the picture into a rural naturalist conversation piece and taking it back into the domain of John Robertson Reid. Before these later additions were made, however, it was clear that the picture mounted a serious assault upon critical sensibilities when it first appeared at the Grosvenor. One writer remarked that Clausen dared to be "thoroughly unsentimental."[36] His Grosvenor pictures were seen as "simple and earnest" and "very true in aspect, if betraying insensibility to beauty equal to Bastien-Lepage's."[37] British notions of sentiment had been discarded.

The earliest origins of *Winter Work* lay in swift notes of the figures in a small pocket sketchbook. These led to more elaborate working drawings informed by photographs, leading to a small oil, *December* (private collection, Great Britain), produced at least in part in the open air and accurately observing local tone and color but also displaying some lens-like distortions.[38] From this the artist moved to the larger Grosvenor canvas. Photographs thus informed rather than determined the process; it seemed in retrospect that the objective had been to surpass these technical processes and demonstrate the superiority of the hand and eye. "Were we ever as mad as that?" George Moore wrote in an extended criticism ten years later. "I said that he had gone further, in abject realism, than a photograph. I do not think I have exaggerated."[39]

The effect of Clausen's ruthless naturalism was immediate. In 1884 Flora MacDonald Reid, the sister of John Robertson Reid, sent *October* (fig. 78) to the Grosvenor Gallery, a solemn Clausenesque reiteration of one of Bastien-Lepage's most celebrated Salon subjects.[40] Reid himself submitted *The Rival Grandfathers* (fig. 79), a picture regarded by Henry Blackburn as "the best picture yet exhibited by the artist, note the careful drawing and study of fisherfolk."[41] William Stott of Oldham presented *L'Atelier du Grandpère* and La Thangue showed *A Poor French Family.*

78. Flora MacDonald Reid, *October (Potato Harvesters)*, 1884, exh. 1884. Oil on canvas. Photograph courtesy Sotheby's

79. John Robertson Reid, *Rival Grandfathers*, 1884, exh. 1884. Oil on canvas. National Museums and Galleries on Merseyside, Walker Art Gallery, Liverpool

Clausen's work throughout the 1880s was subject to constant revision. *The End of a Winter's Day* (fig. 80), shown at the Grosvenor Gallery in 1885, is the summation of three years' work on the subject, during which time the aged field-worker loaded with faggots had gone through various permutations.[42] The references to Millet and Walker in the final picture are fully absorbed, and the ensemble drew eloquent praise from Wilfrid Meynell, who described the picture as "the painter's most admirable work." Meynell regarded the landscape and trees as "French" and in his enthusiasm mistook English hobnail boots for sabots.[43] The confusion is, nevertheless, indicative of a powerful set of associations which surrounded Clausen's work and which were to break into a more political form with his involvement with and public

defense of the ideals of the New English Art Club.

By the mid-1880s there were serious challenges to the authority of the Grosvenor Gallery. Its strength was also its weakness. Its exhibitions now ran to a recognizable formula in which routine landscapes and conventional portraits—involving less important sitters than those at the Academy—were spiced with "Botti-chelsea" companions. Burne-Jones, the "great prop and mainstay"[44] of the Grosvenor until he defected to the New Gallery in 1888, tended to be considered by reviewers before they moved on to radical younger artists. The justification for this was that the "poetic idealism" that characterized the Grosvenor would not be seen at the Academy, where "a certain brutality, or at least vigorous ensemble of technical qualities

80. Sir George Clausen,
*The End of a Winter's
Day*, 1885. Pen and
ink on paper.
Private collection

. . . is necessary to enable a picture to hold its own . . . or give it a chance of impressing the jury both favourably and quickly."[45] Lord Henry Wotton's opinions in *The Picture of Dorian Gray* are thus confirmed.[46]

However, the prominence accorded to Burne-Jones and his followers led to a conformity in which rising standards were not enough to atone for the lack of pictures of "sensational importance."[47] These comments were made in 1886, the year in which the New English Art Club opened its doors and when the "Whistlerian dynasty" had moved into Suffolk Street to reorientate the Society of British Artists.[48] Having cleverly anticipated the need for alternative exhibition venues, Sir Coutts now found himself surrounded by them. For a decade the art market in London had been expanding

rapidly. Enterprises like the United Arts Gallery—based upon a tenuous society—briefly attracted support.[49] In addition to the watercolor societies, others including the Society of Painter-Etchers and the Institute of Painters in Oil Colours slotted themselves into the art calendar. Increasingly powerful dealers' networks were also working through Tooth's and the Fine Art Society to bring prominent Salon pictures to London. Sir Coutts may have started with the idea that he could invite contributors and hold their best work against competition, but he could not maintain it. The world was becoming more specialist and discerning.

It is true that then, as now, the Grosvenor Gallery was seen in the popular mind as the stage upon which Burne-Jones and his school achieved their apotheosis. One surely cannot

81. Henry Herbert La Thangue, *The Runaway*, illustration after painting exh. 1887 from Henry Blackburn, *Grosvenor Notes*, 1887. Location unknown

dispute the recollections of Alice Comyns Carr and Charles Hallé on the matter of Sir Coutts's commitment to the ideals of late Pre-Raphaelitism.[50] It would, however, be a serious omission not to note the strong undercurrent of modern painting which led to the Impressionists identifying Sir Coutts as a potential champion. In the winter of 1882–83, John Lewis Brown, Boudin, Cassatt, Degas, Monet, Morisot, Pissarro, Renoir, and Sisley wrote to Lindsay hoping that "so enlightened an art patron" as he would give them an exhibition at the Grosvenor Gallery, "where independent artists receive a hospitality as brilliant as it is generous."[51] The letter is a fascinating revelation of what the Impressionists thought they were about collec-

tively. They wished "to bring art back to the scrupulously exact observation of nature, applying themselves with passion to the rendering of the reality of forms in movement, as well as to the fugitive phenomena of light." These tendencies they associated with "the illustrious Turner." Possibly they had noted the fact that Lindsay had shown the work of Bastien-Lepage, and they may have thought that his sympathies would result in positive action.[52] His failure to take up the opportunity was a major loss to the Grosvenor.

The combined effect of the emergence of the New English Art Club and the re-formed Society of British Artists in removing and concentrating the avant-garde in other venues left the Grosvenor Gallery in an exposed position. When Burne-Jones abandoned it in 1888, it looked weak. There was reportedly a "new clique" in charge, but its direction was not immediately apparent. "The schools that rose with Fred Walker"[55] were not sufficiently in the forefront, although the exhibitions of the late eighties did contain a number of challenging pictures. One such was La Thangue's *Runaway* (fig. 81), shown in 1887.[54] In this two laborers discover a farm girl as she lies exhausted among the tall grasses. Living in the Norfolk fens, La Thangue was acutely aware of the massive changes occurring in the countryside. Daughters could no longer be maintained on the land and were frequently required by their families to go into service. This phenomenon, treated definitively in his *Leaving Home* in 1890, may provide the explanation for the Grosvenor picture.[55] However, in addition to the general theme of the breakup of families and the rural community, there were other visual resonances in *The Runaway*. At first glance it may have seemed like a reprise of John Robertson Reid's *Lost and Found* (unlocated), a more anecdotal treatment of the discovery of a sleeping country child. However, the painter may well have had French precedents in mind, such as James Bertrand's *Mort de Virginie* of 1869 or Alexandre Antigna's *Pauvre Femme (L'Abandonée)* of 1857. In the context of the Grosvenor Gallery it would not be inappropriate to see *The Runaway* as a modern naturalist version of Sleeping Beauty.

Vestigial innocence and purity in rural life was the central concept, worked out in themes distilled from Millet and Walker. As part of the process of distillation, the obvious features of sentiment were removed. The striking pictures at the Grosvenor Gallery in its later years were ones in which objectivity was the first criterion. Critics and commentators were left to struggle for interpretation. Clausen and La Thangue, however, argued for naturalism and objectivity for its own sake, detached from interpretation. The absence of cheap sentiment in Clausen's Grosvenor contributions in 1888, 1889, and 1890 left critics with a limited stock of conventional comments, most of which denied the background to serious, dispassionate reporting upon rural life in words and pictures. During

the eighties a distinctive rural literature emerged in the serialized and illustrated novels of Jeffries, Hardy, and others.[56] Change in the countryside was a matter of persistent concern in that it drew out issues of national identity at a time when Britain, through its empire, enjoyed unparalleled prestige. Although such rhetoric was not consonant with Sir Coutts's Italianate taste, it found a sympathetic ambience among other Grosvenor directors who wished to preserve rural values, country lore, and what they saw as the English way of life—ingredients which featured strongly in the *English Illustrated Magazine,* which Joseph Comyns Carr was invited to edit in 1883.[57] This periodical was launched by the publisher Macmillan as a rival to *Harper's, Longman's,* and *Scribner's.* During his three years as its manager, Carr commissioned articles from young, largely untested authors including Robert Louis Stevenson, Henry James, and George Bernard Shaw. Although intended as a popular publication addressing a wide audience, the magazine contained notable reports on natural history and country life within its pages. For instance, Dewey Bates, Clausen's American follower, wrote "About Market Gardens," and "The Great Fen" was celebrated in a long piece by Samuel H. Miller with illustrations from paintings by Robert Walker Macbeth, some of which had been Grosvenor exhibits.[58] Carr would only edit the *English Illustrated Magazine* so long as it contained engravings, so committed was he to the quality of the visual. He left in 1886, when his publishers installed cheaper methods of reproduction. Nevertheless, he contributed, perhaps unintentionally, to the publication of fenland lore which informed La Thangue's work.[59]

Clausen's contributions to the Grosvenor during these years underscore his role as the one artist who, with management support, could give the gallery a new direction. His work also carried trails of controversy. He had been vociferous on behalf of plein-air naturalism in face of those Academicians who saw it undermining the English school.[60] He took an uncompromising stance on Academy reform and had written eulogistically on Bastien-Lepage. For him this artist embodied the ultimate advance in

82. Sir George Clausen, *A Ploughboy*, illustration after painting exh. 1888, from Henry Blackburn, *Grosvenor Notes*, 1888. Location unknown

representation. He was completely objective: "All his [Bastien-Lepage's] personages are placed before us," Clausen wrote, "in the most satisfying completeness, without the appearance of artifice, but as they live; and without comment, as far as is possible on the author's part."[61] The painter's own words were almost paraphrased in connection with his Grosvenor exhibit of 1888. When he viewed *A Ploughboy* (fig. 82), the critic of the *Art Journal* found a picture which "contained none of those sentiments which speech and literature have woven round every subject."[62] The message was amplified in the following year when this figure was repeated in *Ploughing* (cat. 13), one of the few large pictures sent to the exhibition.[63] Again, the work triumphantly asserted literal truthfulness to critics who were attuned to the poetic depths of late Pre-Raphaelitism.

This was one of the outstanding pictures in an otherwise negligible show. Critics like that of the *Art Journal* wondered why the gallery con-

tinued to exist, so random was its selection. Sir Coutts, it seemed, had lost interest. "The Grosvenor," its critic observed, "has become a chance-medley of styles, unmarked by any insistent personalities, and unaffected by streams of tendency. If a question suggests itself as to the necessity of a Grosvenor Gallery in a city so well supplied, perhaps a mild reason for its existence is this one characteristic of unexpectedness."[64] The critic went on to praise the work of Clausen, Alfred East's *Gentle Night,* and Henry Scott Tuke's *The Fisherman* (cat. 59), but these were the works of "the good minority." It was necessary to take urgent steps to restore the popularity of the gallery.

Clausen's advice was that Lindsay should approach the members of the Glasgow School and invite them to exhibit as a group in 1890.[65] This was a daring step for two reasons. First, the Glasgow School had only recently emerged as a distinct group, at the Glasgow International Exhibition of 1888. Prior to this, its members (John Lavery, James Guthrie, Arthur Melville, George Henry, Ernest Atkinson Hornel, and others) had exhibited informally in the Glasgow Art Club and in the annual exhibitions of the Glasgow Institute of Fine Arts. The Glasgow International presented the opportunity for a retrospective survey which clearly impressed visitors. Second, enlisting the support of the Glasgow School underscored the position of the "good minority," leading the advance from naturalist to modernist tendencies. The Glasgow pictures summarized the development of painting in Scotland; they also led logically into new approaches.

Among the major works on display were rustic pictures like Guthrie's *In the Orchard,* which had been shown in Glasgow in 1887. Approving noises were made about this, even though it lacked "suggestiveness" in the eyes of one critic.[66] Melville's *Audrey and Her Goats* was, however, one of the most controversial exhibits in that it was apparently less decipherable. It was regarded by the *Saturday Review* as "needlessly huge" for a subject which was "very slight."[67] There was a debate about whether or not this work was actually exhibitable even though it had been long in the making and, as an Academy reject, had a prima facie case for

being considered by the more radical
Grosvenor.[68] Lavery's history painting *Dawn
after the Battle of Langside* was also a product of
long gestation, brought to completion for the
Glasgow International. The pathos of this composition ensured a sympathetic reception, even
though it represented a phase of Lavery's production which had long passed.[69] In the year in
which Bastien-Lepage's *Jeanne d'Arc* was re-
exhibited at the Exposition Universelle in Paris,
this poetic picture had all the pathos of a
William Quiller Orchardson canvas.

However, the Glasgow picture that presented the biggest challenge to London
sensibilities was *The Druids: Bringing in the
Mistletoe* (fig. 83), a work jointly painted by
George Henry and Ernest Atkinson Hornel and
"skied" by hangers who were evidently second-
guessing the critical response. The *Saturday
Review* was, nevertheless, impressed by the
picture, and Walter Armstrong, writing in the
Magazine of Art, positively glowed with approbation: "I am not afraid to say that *Bringing in*

the Mistletoe is a very promising production and
that its authors, or at least that member of the
partnership who is responsible for the figures,
should be looked after very carefully in
future."[70] It may be that, in this powerful clash
of crimson, green, and gold, Armstrong felt that
he had discovered the replacement for Burne-
Jones.

At any rate, in the words of the *Saturday
Review,* the gallery had, through the showing of
the Glasgow school, "asserted its right to exist
by producing a decidedly original and, in some
respects, very interesting exhibition this year.
. . . These Glasgow painters give freshness and
importance to the show, and add that element
of novelty which we have seen to be wanting at
the Royal Academy and the New Gallery."[71]
Confirmation of the preeminence of these rising
stars lay in the fact that they were head-hunted
at the Grosvenor for the forthcoming Glaspalast
exhibition in Munich and from there they regularly reappeared in international surveys
elsewhere. During the 1890s the Glasgow

83. George Henry and
Ernest Atkinson Hornel,
*The Druids: Bringing in
the Mistletoe,* 1890,
exh. 1890. Oil on canvas.
Glasgow Museums:
Art Gallery and
Museum, Kelvingrove
(pl. 16, cat. 23)

84. Sir George Clausen, *The Girl at the Gate*, 1890,
exh. 1890. Oil on canvas. Tate Gallery, London

painters were the international standardbearers of British art. Sadly, the Grosvenor Gallery, despite the strength they conferred upon it, did not survive.

Ironically, the apex of rustic naturalism also coincided with the demise of the Grosvenor Gallery. If a single picture could be chosen to stand as the final expression of this tendency in Britain it would be *The Girl at the Gate* (fig. 84), Clausen's treatment of the dilemma of the young woman of the country. This was a large and enigmatic picture, comparable in scale and ambition to Jules Bastien-Lepage's *Jeanne d'Arc Ecoutant les Voix,* which the artist had the opportunity to study afresh as he was working on his canvas. It was at this point that Clausen began to doubt the road he was on. In November 1889 he reported on the Paris Exposition to James Havard Thomas, "Lepage is good, the figure of his Joan magnificent I think—and all his work beautiful: but incomplete as pictures."[72] What did these cryptic remarks mean? Was it the case that *Jeanne d'Arc* looked overwrought by comparison to works by Courbet and Manet hanging close by? The picture, like Lavery's *Mary, Queen of Scots,* addressed issues concerning naturalistic history painting, but it was even more complicated in that it demanded handling of the problem of painting spirits. Myth, legend, and history were ultimately in opposition to contemporary visual facts. How could the artist develop what appeared to be the ultimate style, a way of working which replicated so precisely the common features of perception?[73] As he worked on *The Girl at the Gate,* Clausen became increasingly aware of the need to adopt other approaches. Like *Audrey and Her Goats* his picture had originally had a literary theme, although as it developed he evidently became uncomfortable with such a frame of reference. Initially it was to be a painting entitled *Marguerite,* a modern version

of the simple country maid in *Faust.* However he dropped this idea in favor of the present more descriptive title.[74] Objectivity worked through drawings and supporting studies was sufficient on its own. Naturalistic methods were now so thoroughly understood that they presented no challenge. With the recent staging of the London Impressionists' exhibition at the Goupil Gallery, the real challenge lay elsewhere.

Nevertheless, by comparison to the Glasgow pictures *The Girl at the Gate* was a complete statement, albeit in a French vernacular. It must have been these qualities which provoked an extraordinary departure on the part of the trustees of the Chantrey Bequest, who acquired the picture for the national collection. Approving its radicalism was one thing; departing from custom and practice in order to give recognition to the Grosvenor Gallery at the expense of the Royal Academy was another. It was, however, to be Clausen's swan song, a work which in later years he preferred not to emphasize. Nevertheless, in its own terms it was an extraordinary achievement representing the culmination of ten years of continuous striving and which was bound up with the fortunes of the Grosvenor Gallery. It stood as the last word upon a tendency which began with the followers of Fred Walker and George Heming Mason and went on into British Impressionism. This corpus, rather than confused Aestheticism or the late flowering of the Pre-Raphaelites, is the central, if unintended, achievement of the Grosvenor Gallery.

Plate 17. Albert Joseph Moore,
The End of the Story, 1877. Oil on canvas
Joey and Toby Tanenbaum,
Toronto, Canada (cat. 39)

Plate 18. Marie Spartali Stillman, *By a Clear Well,* 1883.
Watercolor and bodycolor. Julian Hartnoll (cat. 50)

Plate 19. Marie Spartali Stillman, *Love's Messenger,*
c. 1885. Watercolor, tempera, and gold paint on
paper. Delaware Art Museum, Samuel and Mary R.
Bancroft Memorial (cat. 52)

Plate 20. John Roddam Spencer Stanhope,
The Waters of Lethe by the Plains of Elysium, 1879–80.
Tempera and gold paint on canvas.
Manchester City Art Galleries (cat. 47)

Plate 21. John Melhuish Strudwick, *A Golden Thread*,
c. 1884. Oil on canvas. Tate Gallery, London (cat. 54)

Plate 22. John Melhuish Strudwick, *Isabella*, 1879.
Tempera on canvas. The De Morgan Foundation
at Old Battersea House (cat. 55)

Plate 23. George Frederic Watts, *Miss Rachel Gurney*,
1885. Oil on canvas. Reproduced by permission
of the Trustees of The Watts Gallery,
Compton, near Guildford (cat. 62)

Plate 24. George Frederic Watts, *Portrait of Lady
Lindsay Playing the Violin,* 1876–77. Oil on canvas.
Private collection, on loan to the John Rylands Library

(cat. 64)

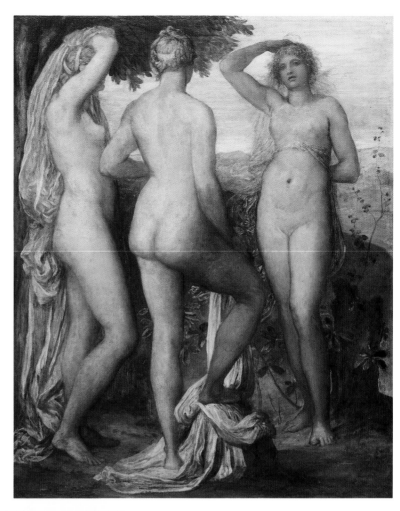

Plate 25. George
Frederic Watts,
The Judgment of Paris,
1874. Oil on canvas.
The Faringdon
Collection Trust (cat. 61)

Plate 26. George
Frederic Watts,
The Wife of Pygmalion,
1868. Oil on canvas.
The Faringdon
Collection Trust (cat. 65)

Plate 27. Evelyn Pickering De Morgan, *The Grey Sisters*,
1880–81. Oil on canvas. The De Morgan Foundation
at Old Battersea House (cat. 16)

Plate 28. George Frederic Watts,
Orpheus and Eurydice, c. 1869. Oil on canvas.
The FORBES Magazine Collection,
New York, all rights reserved (cat. 63)

Plate 29. Evelyn Pickering De Morgan, *Night and Sleep*, exh. 1879. Oil on canvas. The De Morgan Foundation at Old Battersea House (cat. 17)

Plate 30. Philip Wilson
Steer, *The Bridge,*
1887–88. Oil on canvas.
Tate Gallery, London
(cat. 48)

Plate 31. James Tissot,
*The Gallery of H.M.S.
Calcutta (Portsmouth),*
c. 1876. Oil on canvas.
Tate Gallery, London
(cat. 57)

Plate 32. James McNeill Whistler, *Thames—Nocturne
in Blue and Silver,* 1872–78. Oil on canvas.
Yale Center for British Art, Paul Mellon Fund (cat. 68)

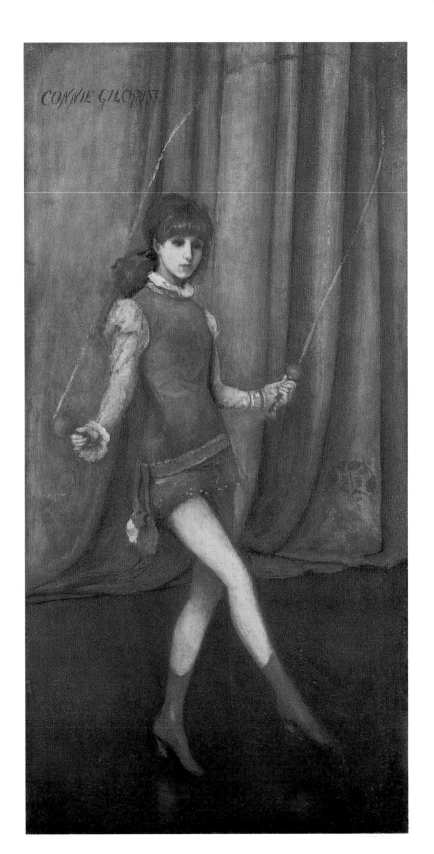

Plate 33. James McNeill Whistler, *Harmony in Yellow and Gold: The Gold Girl— Connie Gilchrist*, 1876. Oil on canvas. The Metropolitan Museum of Art, Gift of George A. Hearn, 1911 (cat. 66)

8

"Best Shop in London"
The Fine Art Society and the Victorian Art Scene

Hilarie Faberman

IN 1899, TWENTY-THREE YEARS after the establishment of The Fine Art Society Limited, the artist Walter Sickert wrote to his colleague Jacques-Emile Blanche, calling the society the "best *shop* in London."[1] Founded in 1876 (the year before the Grosvenor Gallery) and located at 148 New Bond Street (on the same fashionable thoroughfare as Sir Coutts Lindsay's enterprise), the early history of The Fine Art Society provides a case study in the diversity of the Victorian art scene and an interesting comparison with other contemporary art institutions. Between 1876 and 1890, when the Grosvenor Gallery flourished, The Fine Art Society—one of more than eighty commercial art galleries in Victorian London—enjoyed a prominent position as a publisher, printseller, dealer, exhibition organizer, and (surprisingly for a business) arts educator. Reflecting the complexity of the Victorian art scene, the society's activities paralleled the programs of the Grosvenor Gallery, the Royal Academy, and the watercolor institutions and involved many important personalities. Dedicated to the fine arts and to the differing clientele that supported them, the society was at once both traditional and progressive in outlook.

Begun in 1876 apparently for the purpose of producing engravings after well-known Victorian paintings, The Fine Art Society had issued about two hundred reproductive prints by 1890, commissioned scores of original etchings by famous and lesser-known artists, and published fine-art books and exhibition catalogues, many by distinguished authors.[2] In addition to these publications and the commissioning and selling of paintings, the society staged nearly one hundred shows of both contemporary and older (mainly British) artists in these years and was credited with virtually inventing the monographic exhibition.[3] Moreover, unlike some other art dealers and even noncommercial art institutions, the exhibitions of The Fine Art Society were distinguished by their quality and educational significance. As a reviewer in the *Art Journal* wrote about The Fine Art Society in 1881: "Commercial considerations do not appear to be the sole controlling motive of the exhibitions held . . . in this gallery. An educational purpose palpably asserts itself on every occasion, and this perhaps is the reason why this gallery has received in so large and pronounced a degree the countenance and support of the educated public. For example, with every exhibition comes an annotated catalogue, and generally a memoir of the artist whose works are gathered together, and the visitor is thus enabled on the spot to satisfy himself as to the merits of the works on view."[4]

The roster of Victorian artists and art professionals mentioned in the records of the company, the Fine Art Society Minute Books, reflects the contradictory currents and characters of the time, many of whom are familiar from the Grosvenor Gallery's history. Among the most famous were John Ruskin and Francis Seymour Haden and their adversary James McNeill Whistler, all of whom The Fine Art Society simultaneously supported. Owing to the acumen of its board of directors, its managing director Marcus Bourne Huish, and the gallery staff, The Fine Art Society also had profitable relationships with such Royal Academicians as John Everett Millais and Frederic Leighton, independent artists including William Holman Hunt, and women including the battle painter Elizabeth Thompson (later Lady Butler) and the watercolorist Helen Allingham. The society's exhibitions featured an array of artists including contemporary and old-master printmakers, illustrators, draftsmen, and watercolorists; it commissioned artists to travel abroad to create new works, and it even supported professional art institutions, such as the Society of Painter-Etchers, which had its first official exhibition on the premises of 148 New Bond Street in 1882. In the years between 1876 and 1890 the society engaged in a number of seemingly incompatible efforts which were nevertheless very successful: it offered for exhibition and sale works by British, European, and American artists of various backgrounds and approaches; it promoted reproductive and original engraving and etching; and it featured works by the old masters, Pre-Raphaelites, Victorian narrative artists, as well as those involved in social realism, battle painting, the Aesthetic Movement, and the New English Art Club. Even the society's architecture and decor—the exterior façade by E. W. Godwin with its progressive japoniste design and the

interior entrance gallery by George Faulkner Armitage with its traditional decoration—were characteristic of this breadth. It was no wonder that Sickert admired The Fine Art Society, for the gallery was recognized as a protector and promoter of all types of fine art of quality by major as well as minor artists.

Unlike the Grosvenor Gallery and some other well-known Victorian commercial art galleries owned by a principal or family (e.g., Gambart, Agnew, Colnaghi), The Fine Art Society was a limited company that belonged to its shareholders and was run by a board of directors with a managing director responsible for the daily operations of the firm. At the inaugural meeting of the board in London at 31 Ely Place on February 14, 1876, six directors comprised the board—M. B. Huish, S. H. Lofthouse, George Moger, Thomas Cope, Colonel Archibald Stuart Wortley, and chairman Arthur H. Longman. They charted the society's course, and it was their financial and personal support that made possible the company's successes.

M. B. Huish, the first managing director, was trained as a lawyer, in addition to being a scholar and a skilled businessman. Born November 25, 1843, the elder son of Marcus Huish, solicitor, of Castle Donington, Leicestershire, and his wife, Margaret Bourne, M.B. Huish attended Trinity College, Cambridge, was admitted as a student of the Inner Temple in 1864, received his LL.B. degree in 1866, and was called to the Bar in 1867. Huish's career, however, was not spent principally in the law but in art. When he joined the society in 1876 he was salaried at £400 annually plus a percentage of the profit of the firm's sales.[5] In addition to his duties at the society, he was well-known as an editor, critic, and author. He served as editor of the *Art Journal* (1881–93) and of the English-language version of *Le Japon artistique* (1888–91), as well as compiler of *The Year's Art* (1880–93), an annual compendium of facts about the contemporary British art scene. He translated Philippe Burty's memoir of Charles Méryon (1879), which was published by The Fine Art Society. He was the author of numerous art books and monographs, including two works illustrated with works by J. M. W. Turner, *The Seine and the Loire* (1886) and *The Southern*

Coast of England (1892). Among his other publications were *Birket Foster* (1890); *Greek
Terra-Cotta Statuettes* (1900); *Samplers and
Tapestry Embroideries* (1900); *Happy England
as Painted by Helen Allingham* (1903); and
British Water-Colour Art (1904). He wrote the
introductions for catalogues of the society's
shows such as *The Sea Exhibition* (1881) and
Hokusai (1890). His best-known book, *Japan
and Its Art* (1889), developed from an exhibition
at The Fine Art Society.[6] He was chairman of the
Japan Society, earned the award of Chevalier of
the Order of the Sacred Treasure from the
Japanese government for his work in the field of
Japanese art, and was honored by Italy as a
Knight of the Order of the Crown of Italy. In his
position as print publisher and lawyer, he was a
staunch advocate of the engraving trade, de-
fending it publicly against piracy and copyright
violation.[7]

The Fine Art Society managed by M. B.
Huish was situated in the heart of the Bond
Street district that had been known since the
late seventeenth century for its celebrated in-
habitants, including members of royalty, artists,
authors, and statesmen.[8] By the eighteenth
century the street had already become a commercial center, and by the nineteenth century,
as today, Bond Street was lined with elegant
shops that catered to a wealthy clientele, offering a variety of consumer items including
fine clothing, jewelry, perfume, shoes, books,
furs, tea, fruit, and furniture. Prior to its occupation by The Fine Art Society, 148 New Bond
Street was the home of Hart's Fancy Repository.
Bond Street was regarded as a prime location
for an art gallery; by 1883, in addition to the
Grosvenor Gallery, about a dozen dealers, including Thomas Agnew and Sons, Dowdeswell
and Dowdeswells, and Goupil and Company
were situated there, with other numerous firms
in nearby Piccadilly.[9]

A contemporary reporter for the *Building
News* of May 28, 1880, commented that the
façades of the buildings on New Bond Street
were a hodgepodge, containing elements of the
Italian Renaissance, Jacobean, Gothic, and
Queen Anne styles without any coherent program or distinguished frontages.[10] From the
beginning the Fine Art Society Minute Books

record that the company engaged regularly in
renovations to the building and in annexing
space periodically in the adjacent buildings at
147 and 149 New Bond Street to accommodate
its needs (the latter space was known as the
Nelson Room as the admiral had once lived
there). However, it was two particular renovations in the 1880s undertaken by E. W. Godwin
and George Faulkner Armitage that gave the
building its distinctive character and marked it
as an institution supporting both progressive
and traditional taste.

The first major project involved the re-
designing of the exterior façade (fig. 85). The
commission to "alter our front and make it
rather less of a shop front" was given in 1881 by
Huish to the architect and designer E. W.
Godwin.[11] Although modified since the 1880s,
the façade, entrance, and gates endowed the
society, then as now, with its outward identity as
a proponent of Aestheticism and remain pronounced features of the building.[12] To achieve
Huish's wishes Godwin divided the lower half of
the building's front into two large voids. The
lower half, comprising the entry and vestibule,
occupies the entire front of the building. The
entry, with two square columns *in-antis,* is
linked to an arched balcony, two-and-a-half feet
deep, above. The arch and balcony windows
may have been inspired by Godwin's earlier
japoniste experiments in furniture design, an
effect not surprising given his reputation and
his friendship with artists of the Aesthetic Movement like Whistler, who was also involved with
the society at the time.[13] This new cavernous
façade contrasted with the less architecturally
sophisticated buildings on Bond Street and
provided the society with desirable display
spaces that directly fronted the street. As John
O'Callaghan noted, Godwin was able to create
for the company a tangible expression of its
goals: the exterior entry vestibule with its exhibition cabinets encouraged the kind of
prolonged viewing outside that was equally
welcome inside, while the balcony above added
variety and a decidedly uncommercial touch, in
keeping with the upper-class domestic ambience that many of the society's clients
experienced at home.[14] Thus, the Grosvenor
Gallery and The Fine Art Society were two of the

85. T. Raffles Davison, "New Entrance Vestibule and Gallery, The Fine Art Society, E. W. Godwin, Architect," *The British Architect*, December 16, 1881. Engraving. Photograph courtesy The Fine Art Society, London

more distinguished buildings on the thoroughfare. A critic in the *Art Journal* praised the remodeling, stating that "the architect has not only given The Fine Art Society the utmost available exhibition space, but has produced also the most telling and commanding entrance in the whole of Bond Street."[15]

The second project, the redecoration of the interior entrance gallery, was undertaken by George Faulkner Armitage in 1888 (fig. 86). This project, as Rosamond Allwood noted, has been altered since, but the fireplace, library table, and chairs that remain provide an idea of Armitage's original design. The walls were divided into three sections—dado, field, and frieze. The dado protected chairs from rubbing against the wall; the field provided ample space for the display of the framed works; and the elaborately carved frieze was modeled in sinuous tendrils in high relief. Armitage seems to have deliberately

suppressed the public aspects of the commercial gallery, creating instead a domestic environment in which the society's upper-class clients would have been completely at ease.[16] In achieving this effect, both Godwin and Faulkner—although differing in their approach to design and taste—created the same result: the feeling of private spaces in a public gallery.

In April 1876, a year before the Grosvenor Gallery opened, The Fine Art Society staged its first major show and simultaneously scored a coup by exhibiting Elizabeth Thompson's picture *Balaclava* (Manchester City Art Galleries) of 1876, a work whose copyright it acquired for £3,000.[17] The painting depicts the remnants of the Light Brigade after its ill-fated charge in the Crimean War on October 24, 1854. *Balaclava* was the third in Thompson's trio of battle pieces that focused on the emotional plights of soldiers. Her preceding two works, the Crimean War

86. T. Raffles Davison, "The Fine Art Society's Gallery
Designed and Executed by George Faulkner
Armitage," *The British Architect*, January 2, 1891.
Engraving. Photograph courtesy
The Fine Art Society, London

scene, *The Roll Call* (Her Majesty the Queen) of 1874, and a Napoleonic subject, *The 28th Regiment of Quatre Bras* (National Gallery of Victoria, Melbourne) of 1875, had been exhibited at the Royal Academy in 1874 and 1875, respectively.[18] The two earlier works had earned Thompson the praise of Ruskin, who dubbed her "the Pallas of Pall Mall."[19] Although Thompson was criticized for possible financial motives in choosing to display *Balaclava* at the society rather than at the Royal Academy (possibly to increase subscriptions for the reproductive print), the artist claimed she showed it there because she could not get it ready in time for the Academy exhibition.[20] Nevertheless, subsequent to its spring showing in 1876, *Balaclava* toured the provinces (as had the other two paintings previously), further popularizing the work and gaining buyers for the engraving. Among the list of subscribers for

the three prints were Queen Victoria, the Prince of Wales, six dukes, three marquises, nine earls, three viscounts, twelve lords, and seven members of Parliament, along with numerous high-ranking military and government officials.[21]

The Fine Art Society had an enormous financial stake in the success of Thompson's paintings and in the prints published after them. For example, in 1874 the firm of J. Dickinson and Company paid £1,200 to Charles J. Galloway, who initially commissioned the painting, for the right to publish the print of *The Roll Call*.[22] Two years later, when The Fine Art Society acquired the publication rights and subscription list for *The Roll Call* from Dickinson, the society owed Dickinson the considerably larger amount of £13,500.[23] For the reproduction rights to *Quatre Bras* the society owed an additional £6,500 to Dickinson.[24] In

January 1879 the society reported that among its creditors was the engraver Frederick Stacpoole, to whom it owed £600, £1,380, and £1,580 for the plates of *The Roll Call, Quatre Bras,* and *Balaclava,* respectively.[25] Furthermore, when the society decided in 1877 that it would buy a fourth painting by Thompson, *The Return from Inkerman* (1877, Ferens Art Gallery, Hull), as well as a work by Edwin Long, *An Egyptian Feast,* also of 1877, the society issued £8,000 in debentures to cover these debts.[26] Yet while large sums were consumed in acquiring pictures and their copyrights and in touring the artworks and publishing engravings and catalogues, considerable gain could be realized in marketing reproductive prints. By December 31, 1876, The Fine Art Society's gross assets for the subscriptions for the engravings of *The Roll Call, Quatre Bras,* and *Balaclava* amounted to £34,232. Late in 1877, after the society scored another triumph by displaying the quartet of military pictures, the subscriptions for the four prints totaled £51,061; by late 1878 the figure reached £58,639.[27] So successful were these paintings and engravings that the society later published another group of prints of *The Roll Call, Quatre Bras,* and *Balaclava* in reduced versions by different printmakers.[28]

Mindful of the popularity of these battle pictures and engravings, The Fine Art Society commissioned from other artists a number of original paintings of more recent, victorious British military campaigns. These pictures were shown at the society in special exhibitions designed to arouse patriotic fervor and stimulate potential print sales.[29] For example, on May 7, 1879, the gallery paid £2,400 to the French artist Alphonse de Neuville for the copyright and picture of *The Defense of Rorke's Drift* (The Royal Regiment of Wales), a battle that had taken place in the Zulu War on January 22, 1879. The gallery featured the canvas in a special exhibition in 1880, and in 1881 it published an etching by Léopold Flameng after the painting.[30] Capitalizing on these successes with an intention of selling reproductive prints after the paintings, the society in 1883 exhibited four pictures it had specially commissioned of the Egyptian War that had been fought the preceding year. For the paintings and copyright the

society paid £800 to de Neuville for a painting of Tel-el-Kebir, £400 for two pictures of the bombardment of Alexandria by the marine painter William Lionel Wyllie, and £800 to the military illustrator Richard Caton Woodville for a picture of Kassassin (a sum that also financed Woodville's trip to Egypt to work on the subject).[31]

Nearly every major Victorian artist and art institution was affected by the critic John Ruskin, and The Fine Art Society—like the Grosvenor Gallery and the Royal Academy—was no exception. M. B. Huish and Ruskin were acquainted before the establishment of the society, and their correspondence throughout the 1870s and 1880s reveals the influence that Ruskin exerted on the society's activities.[32] Following the success of the exhibition of Elizabeth Thompson's paintings in 1877, Ruskin organized the society's next significant exhibition, an 1878 show of the work of J. M. W. Turner, for which Ruskin lent all the objects, wrote the notes for the catalogue, and even provided his own drawings illustrative of Turner. This was followed in 1879 by a second large exhibition organized by Ruskin comprised of watercolors by Samuel Prout and William Henry Hunt, a show which again was accompanied by catalogue notes by the critic.

The Turner exhibition and its catalogue, *Notes by Mr. Ruskin. Part I. On the Drawings of the Late J. M. W. Turner, R. A. Part II. On His Own Handiwork Illustrative of Turner,* featured numerous drawings which were divided into ten groups by subject and into five chronological periods. The *Notes* were published in numerous editions and reprints in 1878, with the thirteenth edition also in 1878 an illustrated quarto volume with thirty-five photogravure plates and a map.[33] The society's gallery was filled with visitors during the exhibition, and the reviewers were nearly unanimous in their praise. To understand the innovative qualities of this particular show, one needs to keep in mind the more typical Victorian exhibition, with hundreds of works hung seemingly at random and presented with the aid of a catalogue that was little more than a checklist. The Fine Art Society's Turner show offered something quite different and unique: an exhibition of works of superb quality, accompanied by an educational catalogue that elucidated the works on view as well as the artist's career. Typical of the favorable reception the show received was the *Academy* critic who praised it for illustrating Turner's progress as an artist and for the supreme taste that Ruskin exercised in forming a collection of great harmony and unity.[34] The *Times* critic summarized the society's contribution: "In these days of multiplied miscellaneous exhibitions, in which the mind and senses are bewildered by the variety of concurring and distracting appeals, an exhibition of this sort, in which we may really study in admirably chosen examples, and with the aid of the most competent of critical guides, the life's work of the greatest of English landscape painters, is a boon indeed. It should be visited again and again by all who seriously desire to cultivate in themselves the power of enjoying art as the best interpreter of nature."[35]

While the exhibition in 1879 of the work of Samuel Prout and William Hunt was "neither new enough to be fashionable nor old enough to be classic," according to the *Academy* critic, it also had the didactic purpose of illustrating works by two masters of watercolor, the former of pure draftsmanship and the latter of painting. The *Academy* critic praised the clarity of Ruskin's prose in his *Notes by Mr. Ruskin on Samuel Prout and William Hunt*, in which the critic also took a moral tone against the proponents of Aestheticism, describing "the unambitious, limited *bourgeois* buyers—genuine lovers of art . . . who met in the old rooms of the Water-Colour Society, before fashionable people had to pretend to care about art, and before artists began to think that they must pretend to be fashionable."[36]

There is no question that Ruskin occupied a prominent position in the society's activities. Huish admired him, and in the autumn of 1878, shortly after the jury decided in Whistler's favor in the *Whistler v. Ruskin* lawsuit, the managing director and others established a defense fund in the society's name at the Bank of London to help defray Ruskin's expenses.[37] The society also published a circular *Whistler v. Ruskin. Mr. Ruskin's Costs,* in order to raise funds to cover Ruskin's legal fees.[38] Even after the shows of

1878 and 1879 Ruskin continued his involvement in the society's exhibitions. For example, a large group of drawings by the recently deceased artist, John W. Bunney, a former student of Ruskin, was featured in a show of works of Venice that the Society sponsored in 1882.[39] In 1884, 1887, and 1890 the society organized exhibitions of the works of Ernest George, an architect, draftsman, and printmaker whom Ruskin admired.[40] Ruskin also contributed notes for the catalogue of an 1886 exhibition of drawings made under his tutelage by artists affiliated with the St. George's Guild, which included sketches by T. M. Rooke and Charles Fairfax Murray, both of whom were also associated with Burne-Jones and exhibited at the Grosvenor Gallery.[41]

Although Ruskin considered etching "an indolent and blundering method,"[42] The Fine Art Society clearly held an opposite view, for the company played a major role not only in publishing and supporting reproductive engraving but also in promoting original etching and printmaking. In fact, much like the winter exhibitions at the Royal Academy and the Grosvenor Gallery, The Fine Art Society interspersed its shows of contemporary artists with the works of older, deceased artists, specifically works by old-master printmakers. The first of these major old-master print shows, entitled *About Etching: A Collection by the Great Masters,* took place during 1878–79. Similar to Ruskin's Turner project, this exhibition comprised more than two hundred prints from a single lender, in this case from the collection of another famous Victorian art figure, the well-known etcher and the brother-in-law of Whistler, Francis Seymour Haden, who also provided the catalogue notes.[43] Thereafter, the society regularly offered a succession of old-master print exhibitions. In 1880 the society featured woodcuts by Thomas Bewick with notes by F. G. Stephens. In 1881 Stephens again provided the notes for a catalogue of an exhibition of drawings, paintings, and etchings by the recently deceased artist Samuel Palmer, some of whose prints the society had published. A year later the society published a book on Palmer's life and career by his son.[44] In 1885 the society sponsored a major exhibition of French eighteenth-century engravings with notes by Frederick Wedmore. In this same year the society organized an exhibition commemorating the centenary of the death of William Woollett, who was known for his reproductive prints after eighteenth-century artists like Richard Wilson and Benjamin West. In addition to the valuable catalogues by knowledgeable authors produced to accompany these exhibitions, the society published books on printmaking, including the *Complete Descriptive Catalogue of the Work of Charles Méryon* (1879); the amplification of Haden's catalogue notes *About Etching* (1879), which included comments on technique; and Frederick Wedmore's *Four Masters of Etching* (1883), to which Whistler and others contributed prints.

Moreover, through exhibitions and commissions, the society actively supported the work of both contemporary etchers and reproductive engravers. In 1880 the society featured an exhibition of etchings by Bracquemond, Herkomer, Palmer, Whistler, and others. In 1883 it offered a show of the work by Royal Academician Samuel Cousins, arguably the most famous Victorian reproductive engraver, whom the company had commissioned on numerous occasions to execute prints after the works of Millais and Leighton. More significant of this tangible support was the fact that in 1882 the society allowed its galleries to be used for the first official exhibition of the Society of Painter-Etchers, a group for which Haden served as president.[45] In fact, in addition to Haden's organizing the etching exhibition in 1879, providing notes for its catalogue, amplifying the catalogue into a longer book on the subject,[46] and supervising the exhibition of Painter-Etchers in 1882, The Fine Art Society also commissioned him to execute two original etchings, *Windsor* of 1878 and *Greenwich* of 1879–80, for which he was paid £750 per plate.[47]

That the society could engage in business with conservative figures such as Ruskin and Haden on the one hand and with such unconventional and flamboyant artists as Whistler on the other was indicative of the gallery's range. The affiliation between Whistler and the society appears to have been encouraged by Ernest G. Brown, whose employment there began in 1879 and continued for nearly twenty-five years.[48] In

1878 Brown, then employed by the publisher Seeley, Jackson, and Halliday, had become acquainted with Whistler when *Portfolio* magazine wished to publish Whistler's print *Billingsgate*, a design not included among the sixteen images in the "Thames Set."[49] Brown's support of Whistler was crucial to the artist's survival following the debacle of the infamous trial; he probably persuaded the society to purchase the "Thames Set" plates in 1879 from Ellis for £150 and to publish them in a second edition.[50] Brown also undoubtedly convinced the directors to ask Whistler to execute the Venice prints. By September 9, 1879, less than a year after Huish and the society set up the Ruskin defense fund, the society had also commissioned Whistler to travel immediately to Venice to begin to work on a new group of twelve prints, for which the artist was paid £150 and which was supposed to occupy him for three months.[51] Huish's and Brown's frustrations with Whistler and the Venice project are well-documented. Eventually, by November 1880 Whistler returned to London and printed the plates for the exhibition *Mr. Whistler's Etchings of Venice*, which opened at the society that December.[52] The exhibition of the Venetian etchings was the first of three shows of Whistler's work at the society in the next twenty-six months: *Venice Pastels*, an exhibition of fifty-three works from this trip, followed in January 1881, and *Etchings and Drypoints. Venice. Second Series*, a show of fifty-one etchings, took place in February 1883.

Whistler's involvement in the Grosvenor Gallery as artist and designer were paralleled in his activities in The Fine Art Society exhibitions. At the show of the "First Venice Set" in 1880 he decorated the walls in maroon and seems to have double-hung the prints, judging from a design of the time.[53] In the pastel exhibition most of the works were hung on a single line, similar to the Grosvenor Gallery exhibitions, and were presented in frames of green-gold and yellow-gold. According to the research of David Curry, who has explored Whistler's work as an exhibition designer, the walls in the pastel exhibition were covered in fabric, with a low skirting of yellow-gold, an olive-green fabric as the main field capped at nine feet with a molding of green or citron-gold, and a frieze of Venetian red. The frieze was crowned by a cornice of ruby gold.[54] Whistler surpassed these two efforts in his third show in 1883 in which the installation, including the livery of the attendant, was composed in white and yellow. The prints were hung on a white felt fabric, with bottom and top borders of the wall in yellow. The etchings were presented in plain white frames with simple lines as decoration. The walls were detailed with stenciled yellow lines and butterflies, Whistler's trademark. Straw matting covered the floor, and yellow and white flowers including daffodils and narcissi completed the arrangement.[55]

In addition to supporting such innovative design projects as Godwin's façade and Whistler's revolutionary installation schemes, the society in general wished to enhance the presentation of works on paper. Around 1880 it sponsored a competition, offering a first prize of five guineas for an emblematic frame for the print after de Neuville's painting *The Defense of Rorke's Drift*. A second premium, also of five guineas, was offered for a frame for a watercolor drawing; the third premium of three guineas, for a frame for an engraving or etching; and fourth premiums of two guineas each, for any frame adapted by The Fine Art Society not covered in the other categories.[56]

In addition to the shared interest in exhibition display, the Grosvenor Gallery and The Fine Art Society had several other points of contact. When the Grosvenor Gallery staged its memorial exhibition of the works of Cecil Lawson in 1883, the society published the memoir of the artist, which contained an essay by Edmund Gosse, comments by J. Comyns Carr, and illustrations by Whistler and Herkomer.[57] Moreover, many artists affiliated with the Grosvenor exhibited at The Fine Art Society. Among them were the Italian artist Giovanni Costa, an Italian associate of Leighton who had a one-person exhibition at 148 New Bond Street in 1882.[58] Another was James D. Linton, whose series of five canvases of *The Life of a Soldier in the Sixteenth Century* was shown at the society in 1884. The first painting in this set, *Victorious*, had been exhibited at the Grosvenor in 1880.[59] Members of the Ruskin

and Burne-Jones circles T. M. Rooke and Charles Fairfax Murray also showed at the society and at the Grosvenor Gallery. Furthermore, the society was similar to the Grosvenor in its policy toward women artists. It exhibited the works of female watercolorists, including Clara Montalba, and among the other women it championed in solo exhibitions were Helen Allingham (1886, 1887, and 1889); Bertha Patmore, daughter of Coventry Patmore (1889); the Dutch painter of flowers Marguerite Roosenboom (1890); and Henriette Ronner, a Belgian-Dutch animal painter (1890).[60] Like the Grosvenor, the society issued season tickets for admission, which could be obtained for five shillings—gratis to anyone who had purchased art from the firm for more than one guinea.

The exhibitions of The Fine Art Society reiterated the types of shows of British and foreign artists adopted by the Grosvenor and other galleries. For example, for many years the society offered an autumn exhibition of watercolor painting. In 1887 and 1889 the society showed watercolors by leading masters of the Dutch school, exhibitions undoubtedly similar to those offered at the Grosvenor Gallery earlier in the decade. The Grosvenor winter exhibitions of 1880 and 1881 featured sketches and drawings by contemporary artists, projects that were similar not only to The Fine Art Society's shows in general, but also to special exhibitions like *British and American Artists from the Paris Salon* (1882), *100 Paintings and Drawings by 100 Artists* (1884), and *Studies for Pictures in Various Mediums, Including Works by Burne-Jones, W. B. Richmond, A. Legros, Leighton, Watts, and Alma-Tadema* (1889). The Grosvenor Gallery may even have mimicked the society's ideas; for example, the society's exhibition in 1883 of children in contemporary Victorian art was followed in 1884 by an exhibition at the Grosvenor of Sir Joshua Reynolds's portraits of children.

The board of directors of The Fine Art Society, much like the Lindsays, maximized their professional efforts through well-placed personal contacts. For example, the society obtained permission to publish the engraving of Edward Poynter's *Atalanta's Race* because this 1876 painting (then part of a group at Wortley

Hall, Sheffield) was owned by Edward, first Earl of Wharncliffe, cousin of the photographer Colonel Archibald Stuart Wortley, who served on the board.[61] Lord Wharncliffe was also a lender to the Giovanni Costa exhibition in 1882. The society's exhibition in 1885 of William Holman Hunt's important painting *The Triumph of the Innocents* (Tate Gallery, London) was arranged by another board member, George Lillie Craik, a friend of the Pre-Raphaelite artist, who also lent several pictures to the Holman Hunt exhibition at the society in 1886, including *Strayed Sheep* (Tate Gallery, London) of 1852.[62]

One of the more interesting and profitable of the society's relationships was with John Everett Millais. Millais's brother-in-law was the society's solicitor, George Davey Stibbard, who had married Effie Millais's sister, Alice Elizabeth Gray, in 1874.[63] It was through Stibbard's efforts that the society acquired in 1878 the first of its Millais paintings, *The Princes in the Tower* (Royal Holloway College, Egham) of 1878, for which the society paid £1,000 including copyright.[64] Later that year Stibbard served as intermediary on the society's behalf in trying to obtain a picture of Lord Beaconsfield, a painting with copyright for which the society eventually paid 1,400 guineas in 1881.[65] In 1879 the society acquired for £1,000 Millais's other painting of tragic childhood, *Princess Elizabeth in Prison at St. James's* (Royal Holloway College, Egham) of 1879, which, like *The Princes in the Tower,* was also eventually sold to Thomas Holloway.[66] Among the other works that date from the early 1880s that the society bought directly from Millais were a portrait of Alfred Tennyson and the subject pictures *Caller Herrin'* (private collection) and *The Captive* (Art Gallery of New South Wales, Sydney).[67]

In addition to buying and selling Millais's paintings, the society maintained a brisk trade in publishing engravings after his well-known works. They hired Samuel Cousins to produce mezzotints after *The Princes in the Tower* (1879), *Cherry Ripe* (1881), and *Pomona* (1882). The prints of *Earl of Beaconsfield* (1882) and *Caller Herrin'* (1882) were engraved in mezzotint by Hubert Herkomer. G. H. Every made the print of *The Captive* (1885). T. O. Barlow produced mezzotints for the society of Millais's portraits of

Tennyson (1882) and the *Marquess of Salisbury* (1887). T. L. Atkinson made the plate for *Princess Elizabeth in Prison* (1881), an engraving Millais praised in a letter to the society: "The expression in the face is most charmingly given and the work throughout is carefully executed."[68] At least one of the society's prints after Millais, *Dropped from the Nest* (1884), was reproduced by Goupil in photogravure.[69]

In their tradition of monographic exhibitions of contemporary masters, The Fine Art Society organized an enormously successful exhibition of Millais's pictures in 1881, which was accompanied by a catalogue with notes by A. Lang. The exhibition, installed by Joseph Jopling (husband of the painter Louise Jopling and employee of the society), was on view at the same time as the show of Whistler's Venice pastels.[70] Although the exhibition featured fewer than twenty select works, it nevertheless attracted 42,830 visitors over several months and provided revenues of £2,141 in attendance and £273 in catalogue sales.[71] At the exhibition the society showed *The Princes in the Tower* and *Princess Elizabeth in Prison,* as well as the important painting *Isabella* (Walker Art Gallery, Liverpool) of 1848–49, which it then sold to C. A. Ionides for £1,150.[72] This Millais exhibition, held two years after the exhibition of Millais's works at Agnew's, anticipated by five years another Millais exhibition at the Grosvenor Gallery in 1886. It was indicative of the tremendous prestige the painter enjoyed and The Fine Art Society's engagement at the hub of the Victorian art scene. During the early 1880s the company did a brisk trade, its sales averaging around £25,500 annually.[73]

Through its dealings with Whistler, Millais, Ruskin, and Haden, the society demonstrated its mission to display works of the best quality with broad appeal. Thanks to this vision, the directors were able to provide innovative exhibitions, which, like those of the Grosvenor Gallery, introduced past and independent new masters to the public. In exhibiting William Holman Hunt's *Triumph of the Innocents* (Tate Gallery, London) in 1885, the society showed the work of a well-known artist who chose to separate himself from the Royal Academy and who also showed at the Grosvenor Gallery. The exhibition of *The Triumph of the Innocents,* like Elizabeth Thompson's painting *Balaclava* a decade earlier, helped to raise subscriptions for the print after the design. If there was a commercial goal to the society's exhibition of *The Triumph of the Innocents,* the critics did not see it. The critic in the *Spectator* named the painting "a great religious picture": "It is great in its actual definite achievement, its fine colour, its mastery of natural fact, its successful presentation of its subject, its originality of conception, its vigorous drawing, and in the patient, unwearied skill and thought which are evident in every line and every hue. It is great because it is a record of a man's endurance in high aims, and his conquest over numberless difficulties; it is great because it is not produced from devotion to the idols of the market, nor in deference to popular fashions."[74] Following the successful showing of the painting, the society displayed a selection of Hunt's works in 1886, at the same time that the Millais exhibition took place at the Grosvenor Gallery and Rossetti's works were auctioned at Christie's. As several reviewers noted, the three exhibitions gave testimony to the significance of the Pre-Raphaelite movement and to Hunt's place in it.[75]

The Fine Art Society dealt with many of the classicizing, archaeologically attuned artists of the late-Victorian period, including Frederic Leighton and Edwin Long. The nature of their interaction with Leighton was similar to that with Millais. The society bought pictures directly from the artist, the most famous of which was *Cymon and Iphigenia* (Art Gallery of New South Wales, Sydney) of around 1884; it acquired copyrights to his paintings; and it published reproductive prints after his compositions.[76] Leighton, like Ruskin, also promoted the works of his associates at the society. For example, Leighton was the financial supporter of and lender to the society's exhibition of the work of Giovanni Costa in 1882.[77] Leighton selected another Grosvenor exhibitor, the Italian artist Giambattista Amendola, as the sculptor to translate the painting *Wedded* (Art Gallery of New South Wales, Sydney) of around 1881–82 into a three-dimensional work of art, a commission for which the society paid the

sculptor £400, and which the society then cast and sold for various prices depending on size and media (including bronze, silvered bronze, and terra-cotta).[78] Along with prints after Leighton's work, The Fine Art Society published reproductions after the works of Edwin Long including *An Egyptian Feast* and *The Babylonian Marriage Market* (Royal Holloway College, Egham) of 1875. When the painting *The Babylonian Marriage Market* was exhibited at the society in 1889 in order to raise subscriptions for the print, the proceeds from the attendance netted the impressive amount of £5,210.[79]

Just as the Grosvenor Gallery promoted the work of decorative painters, The Fine Art Society turned its attention to a more modest class of artists—illustrators—whom it championed in one-person and group exhibitions. While there had been other London venues such as the Dudley Gallery in the 1870s that exhibited works in black and white, The Fine Art Society promoted the works of recently deceased and contemporary illustrators, much as it did for printmakers. Among its many shows were a retrospective in 1883 of the work of "Phiz," the late Hablot K. Browne, and two exhibitions in 1884 and 1887 of the work of George Du Maurier, the man who made Aestheticism famous. For the first eleven days of the Du Maurier exhibition in 1884, for which Henry James wrote the notes for the catalogue, the society netted £698 in sales; its show *One Hundred Paintings and Drawings by One Hundred Artists* held at the same time yielded a slightly larger sum, £841.[80] During these years the society showed works of literary illustration including Edwin Austin Abbey's drawings of *She Stoops to Conquer.* Before 1890 the society also featured two shows of the work of painter, printmaker, illustrator, and frequent Grosvenor exhibitor Hubert von Herkomer, *Life and Work in Bavaria's Alps* (1885) and *Around My Home* (1888).

Herkomer's shows were but two of the numerous travelogue exhibitions in which illustrations of both local haunts and exotic habitats were featured. The society's shows of British scenery, for example, included Alfred Parsons's *Drawings Illustrating Shakespeare's River* (1885), John Brett's *Three Months on the Scottish Coast* (1886), J. MacWhirter's *The Land of Burns and Scott* (1887), and E. H. Fahey's *Drawings of the Norfolk Broads & Rivers* (1887). During these early years there were three shows of John Fulleylove's scenes of England and Europe (1886, 1888, and 1890). Whistler's innovative prints of Venice, for example, were balanced by more conventional drawings of the same subject by Bunney and others in the show Ruskin organized in 1882, as well as by two exhibitions devoted exclusively to Venice by artist A. N. Roussoff (1884, 1888). From the beginning the society showed works illustrating the Orient, including H. A. Harper's *Sketches at Constantinople* (1877), Carl Haag's *Drawings of Egyptian Life* (1882), Herbert A. Olivier's *Drawings Illustrating India and Kashmir* (1885), and F. A. Bridgeman's *A Glimpse of the East: Sketches and Studies in Egypt and Algeria* (1887). As was its practice with some of these projects, the society helped to underwrite the costs of artists' travels: for example, it sent Whistler to Venice in 1879–80 and Wyllie to Egypt in 1882–83. The society also sent Alfred East to Japan for six months in 1889, a trip that resulted in an exhibition of his pictures and drawings at the society in 1890.[81]

The name of Alfred East and the subject of Japan introduces a link between British Impressionism and the early history of The Fine Art Society. Both East and David Murray, who had an exhibition at the society in 1887, were trained at the Glasgow School of Art, showed at the Grosvenor Gallery, and were allied with the complex movement known as British Impressionism.[82] A number of other artists loosely affiliated with Impressionist (i.e., non-Academy) ideals showed at The Fine Art Society, the most important of whom was Whistler, and whose pupils Mortimer Menpes and Joseph Pennell actually met him at the society's exhibitions. Among the other artists who exhibited at the society and who were later associated with British Impressionism were William Stott of Oldham, who was also a member of the New English Art Club, and John Singer Sargent. Both exhibited work at the society in 1882 in *British and American Artists from the Paris Salon*. This show featured *El Jaleo* (Isabella Stewart Gardner Museum, Boston) of 1882 by Sargent, who also exhibited in London at the Royal Academy and at the Grosvenor in this year. As Peyton Skipwith has noted, the society did not sponsor exhibitions of some of the major figures of the New English Art Club until the twentieth century. However, the society's general support for *plein-air* painting and for aspects of French art characterized some of its shows at the time.[83]

The taste for Japan was a hallmark of The Fine Art Society, not only in its patronage of Whistler, Godwin, and Alfred East, but especially in the scholarly enterprises of M. B. Huish, who organized the major loan exhibition of Japanese art in 1888 and an unprecedented one-person show of the work of Hokusai in 1890. That the society was attuned to French and Japanese taste is suggested by several tantalizingly brief entries in its records of 1888 and 1889 which concern the leasing of gallery space on its first floor to "Monsieur Bing"—a reference to Siegfried Bing, impresario par excellence of *japonisme* in Paris and elsewhere.[84]

Japan and Paris then were even farther from London culturally than they are today and are reminders of the remarkable breadth of the society's activities in the early years of its history. The society's range and prominence during these years is demonstrated clearly by its close associations with diverse and important women and men of the art world, such as Thompson, Godwin, Whistler, Haden, Ruskin, Millais, Leighton, and others. From 1876 to 1890, with its dozens of exhibitions of paintings, watercolors, drawings, and old-master and more recent prints, and its publications of reproductive engravings, modern etchings, educational exhibition catalogues, and fine-art books, The Fine Art Society (like the Grosvenor Gallery) was among the best and most interesting art institutions on Bond Street, if not in all of Victorian London.

Notes

INTRODUCTION

1   Michele Archambault, "The Grosvenor Gallery, 1877–1890" (Ph.D. diss., Courtauld Institute of Art, 1978), 142, discusses the first trip to Italy. On Lord Lindsay see Francis Haskell, *Rediscoveries in Art,* 2d ed. (Ithaca, N.Y.: Cornell University Press, 1979), 57, 71, 75, 76, and 87; and John Steegman, "Lord Lindsay's *History of Christian Art,*" *Journal of the Warburg and Courtauld Institutes* 10 (1947): 123–31.

2   Virginia Surtees, *Coutts Lindsay, 1824–1913* (Norwich, England: Michael Russell, 1993), 41, 55–56.

3   Surtees, *Coutts Lindsay,* 30.

4   Surtees, *Coutts Lindsay,* 60–63, and 82–83.

5   Mrs. Robert Henrey, *Green Leaves* (London: J. M. Dent, 1976), 27.

6   Robert Holford of Westonbirt, Gloucestershire, was married to Lindsay's youngest sister, Mary Anne. On Dorchester House see Sir George Lindsay Holford, *The Holford Collection, Dorchester House* (London: H. Millford and Oxford University Press, 1927).

7   For example, in 1880 7% of the oils, 25.7% of the watercolors, and 9.5% of the sculpture the Academy showed were by women artists, for a total of 10.4%. At the Grosvenor, 13.5% of the oils, 34.8% of the watercolors, and 25.8% of the sculpture was by women, for a total of 20.3%. See Charlotte Yeldham, *Women Artists in Nineteenth-Century France and England: Their Art Education, Exhibiting Opportunities and Membership of Exhibiting Societies and Academies, with an Assessment of the Subject Matter of Their Work and Summary Biographies,* 2 vols. (New York and London: Garland, 1984), vol. 1, tables 1 and 5.

8   Although Blanche Lindsay had fought, as had other nonmembers, to be shown at the Royal Academy (before the advent of the Grosvenor), she did become a "Lady Member" of the New Society of Painters in Water-Colours in 1879 and remained a member until 1910. She was also a member of the only group to support women exclusively, the Society of Female Artists (renamed Lady Artists and, later, Women Artists).

CHAPTER 1. THE GROSVENOR
GALLERY AS PALACE OF ART

This study was undertaken with the assistance of
the following: a University of Wyoming Arts and
Sciences Dean's Office Basic Research Grant,
summer 1991; a National Endowment for the
Humanities Planning Grant, 1992–1993; and a
Yale Center for British Art Fellowship, January
1993. I am also grateful to the University of
Wyoming for granting me a research semester in
order to complete the research and writing of this
essay.

1   "The Palace of Art (New Version), Part I," *Punch*
72 (July 7, 1877): 305.

2   "The Palace of Art (New Version), Part I," *Punch*
72 (July 14, 1877): 9.

3   On the Grosvenor Gallery see Barrie Bullen, "The
Palace of Art: Sir Coutts Lindsay and the
Grosvenor Gallery," *Apollo* 102 (1975): 352–57;
Frances Spalding, *Magnificent Dreams: Burne-
Jones and the Late Victorians* (Oxford: Phaidon;
New York: Dutton, 1978); Michele Archambault,
"The Grosvenor Gallery, 1877–1890" (Ph.D. diss.,
Courtauld Institute of Art, 1978); Colleen Denney,
"Exhibition Reforms and Systems: The Grosvenor
Gallery, 1877–1890" (Ph.D. diss., University of
Minnesota, 1990); Colleen Denney, "The Role of
Sir Coutts Lindsay and the Grosvenor Gallery in
the Reception of Pre-Raphaelitism on the Conti-
nent," in Alicia Faxon and Susan Casteras, eds.,
Pre-Raphaelitism in Its European Context (Cran-
bury, N.J.: Fairleigh Dickinson University Press,
1995); and Christopher Newall, *The Grosvenor
Gallery Exhibitions: Change and Continuity in the
Victorian Art World* (Cambridge: Cambridge
University Press, 1995).

4   Robert Holford of Westonbirt, Gloucestershire,
was married to Lindsay's youngest sister, Mary
Anne. On Dorchester House see Sir George
Lindsay Holford, *The Holford Collection, Dor-
chester House* (London: H. Millford and Oxford
University Press, 1927).

5   Walter Crane, *An Artist's Reminiscences* (London:
Methuen, 1907), 160.

6   See Tom Taylor, "Report on the Commissioners
Appointed to Inquire into the Present Position of
the Royal Academy in Relation to the Fine Arts,"
Fine Arts Quarterly Review 1 (October 1863):
275–98.

7   John Codd, "Making Distinctions," in Richard
Harker, Cheleen Mahar, and Chris Wilkes, eds.,
*An Introduction to the Work of Pierre Bourdieu:
The Practice of Theory* (New York: St. Martin's
Press, 1990), 140.

8   Codd, "Making Distinctions," 142.

9   See Charles Hallé, *Notes on a Painter's Life,
Including the Founding of Two Galleries* (London:
John Murray, 1909), 99–117, on the gallery prepa-
rations. On Mottez, see Paula Gillett, *Worlds of
Art: Painters in Victorian Society* (New Brunswick,
N.J.: Rutgers University Press, 1990), 232; and
Hallé, *Notes*, 86.

10 See Joseph Comyns Carr, *Some Eminent Victorians: Personal Recollections in the World of Art
and Letters* (London: Duckworth, 1908), 146,
266–67; and Eve Adam, ed., *Mrs. J. Comyns Carr's
Reminiscences*, 2d ed. (London: Hutchinson,
1926), 42. For an examination of Carr's promotional activities at the Grosvenor see Denney,
"Role of Sir Coutts Lindsay."

11 For a survey of this aspect of British art see Jon
Whiteley, "Exhibitions of Contemporary Painting
in London and Paris, 1760–1860," in Francis
Haskell, ed., *Salonie, Gallerie, Musei, e loro
influenza sullo sviluppo dell'arte dei secolo*
(Twenty-Fourth International Congress on the
History of Art, 1981), 69–87; Elizabeth Gilmore
Holt, *The Triumph of Art for the Public: The
Emerging Role of Exhibitions and Critics*
(Princeton, N.J.: Princeton University Press,
1982); Elizabeth Gilmore Holt, *The Expanding
World of Art, 1874–1902* (New Haven: Yale Uni-
versity Press, 1988); and Giles Waterfield, ed.,
Palaces of Art: Art Galleries in Britain, 1790–1990
(London: Dulwich Picture Gallery and the Na-
tional Gallery of Scotland, 1991).

12 See Charles Holme, ed., *The 'Old' Water-Colour
Society, 1804–1904* (London, Paris and New York:
The Studio, 1905); Charles Holme, ed., *The Royal
Institute of Painters in Water-Colours* (London:
The Studio, 1906); and Peter Fullerton,
"Patronage and Pedagogy: The British Institution
in the Early Nineteenth Century," *Art History* 5
(March 1982): 59–72. For a complete list of ex-
hibitors see Algernon Graves, *The British
Institution, 1806–1867* (Bath: Kingsmead, 1875;
reprint: facsimile edition, 1969). See also Hesketh
Hubbard, *An Outline History of the Royal Society
of British Artists*, 3 vols. (London: Royal Society of
British Artists' Art Club, 1937).

13 See Archambault, "Grosvenor Gallery," 13–14.

14 On the Egyptian Gallery see Richard Altick, *The Shows of London* (Cambridge, Mass.: Belknap Press, 1987).

15 Archambault, "Grosvenor Gallery," 16.

16 "Minor Topics," *Art Journal* 9 (1869): 258.

17 Archambault, "Grosvenor Gallery," 19.

18 Dennis Cooper, *The Courtauld Collection: A Catalogue and Introduction* (London: Athlone Press, 1954), 15.

19 Cooper, *Courtauld Collection*, 15; and G. D. Leslie, *The Inner Life of the Royal Academy* (London: John Murray, 1914), 240–42.

20 Gerald Reitlinger, *The Economics of Taste: The Rise and Fall of Picture Prices, 1760–1960*, vol. 1 (London: Barrie and Rockliff, 1961), 157–58.

21 "The Grosvenor Gallery," *Daily News* (July 21, 1877): 4.

22 On the decline of English artistic training see, for example, Cooper, *Courtauld Collection*, 16–17; and H. C. Morgan, "The Lost Opportunity of the Royal Academy: An Assessment of Its Position in the Nineteenth Century," *Journal of the Warburg and Courtauld Institutes* 32 (1969): 410–20.

23 Hallé, *Notes*, 109. Lindsay, in his toast at the inaugural dinner, claimed that he was especially grateful for the cooperation of the Academy (*Times*, May 10, 1877).

24 Hallé, *Notes*, 143–44; and see also Morgan, "Lost Opportunity," 410–20. Lord Leighton showed the following works at the 1877 Grosvenor summer exhibition: *Henry Evans Gordon, Esq.; An Italian Girl*; and *A Study* (all unlocated).

25 Experiments of this kind, where attention was being paid both to the originality of the artists and to the originality of the hanging practices, were beginning to occur simultaneously in France, particularly among the French Impressionist circle, between 1874 and 1886. See Martha Ward, "Impressionist Installations and Private Exhibitions," *Art Bulletin* 73 (December 1991): 599–622.

26 This information is advertised at the beginning of each summer exhibition catalogue, but only in the unillustrated versions (*Grosvenor Gallery Summer Exhibition* [London: Jas. Wade and Phoenix, 1877–1890], hereafter cited as *Grosvenor Summer Exhibition* followed by the appropriate year). Henry Blackburn produced illustrated guides from 1878–1890 which included engravings based on drawings by the artists themselves; Henry Blackburn, *Grosvenor Notes* (London: Chatto and Windus, 1878–1890).

27 "The Grosvenor Gallery," *Art Journal* 16 (1877): 244.

28 "The Grosvenor Gallery," *Times* (March 12, 1877): 4.

29 Adam, ed., *Mrs. Carr's Reminiscences*, 159.

30 See Virginia Surtees, *Coutts Lindsay, 1824–1913* (Norwich, England: Michael Russell, 1993), 159–60.

31 *Grosvenor Summer Exhibition* (1877), 3. Whether or not this system of members was continued after 1877 is not clear, nor is it clear who such members would be, but it is entirely possible that they were the same people who patronized the artists directly.

32 *Grosvenor Summer Exhibition* (1877), 3. On the financial side of the gallery see the comments of Hallé and Carr in "Correspondence with Sir Coutts Lindsay concerning the Resignation of Messrs. C. E. Hallé and J. Comyns Carr" (London: Victoria & Albert Museum Library [National Art Library], 1887).

33 The only information available on a possible commission taken on works of art appeared in a "Letter from Charles Hallé and Joseph Comyns Carr to the Editor of the 'Times,'" in "Correspondence with Sir Coutts Lindsay": "the gross receipts of the Gallery in entrance money, sale of catalogues and commissions on sales of pictures have averaged during the period of our management, over £7000 per annum."

34 Patricia Mainardi, *The End of the Salon: Art and the State in the Early Third Republic* (Cambridge: Cambridge University Press, 1993), 11.

35 Mainardi, *End of the Salon*, 11.

36 Mainardi, *End of the Salon*, 24.

37 See Pierre Bourdieu, *Distinction: A Social Critique of the Judgement of Taste*, trans. Richard Nice (London, Melbourne, and Henley: Routledge and Kegan Paul, 1979), where this is one of the main premises of his examination of class.

38 Waterfield, *Palaces of Art*, 17.

39 Crane, *An Artist's Reminiscences,* 150. Lindsay had acquired the doorway from George Cavendish-Bentinck. See Surtees, *Coutts Lindsay,* 147 and 200 n44, where she proposes that it actually was taken from the Church of Suola Grande di Santa Maria Della Misericordia. All other sources, however, including contemporary newspaper accounts, cite Santa Lucia as its original home.

40 Descriptions of the gallery are taken from the following 1877 newspaper sources: *Architect, Illustrated London News, Athenaeum,* and *Builder.*

41 Walter Crane held that Whistler did the decoration of the panels, a notion repeated by the contemporary newspaper accounts in 1877. However, Linda Merrill, in *A Pot of Paint: Aesthetics on Trial in Whistler v. Ruskin* (Washington, D.C., and London: Smithsonian Institution Press in collaboration with the Freer Gallery of Art, 1992), has found no evidence to support this attribution (325n5). That does not altogether exclude the possibility that Whistler painted the frieze, however. In the alterations made to the gallery in 1904 the panels were all painted over.

42 See Georgiana Burne-Jones, *Memorials of Edward Burne-Jones,* 2 vols. (London: Macmillan, 1906), 1:77; and Crane, *An Artist's Reminiscences,* 175.

43 See "Grosvenor Board Minutes," 1949/5/18, 350 (Grosvenor Estate Papers, Victoria Library Archives, Westminster City Libraries, London.)

44 Oscar Wilde, *The Portrait of Dorian Gray,* Peter Ackroyd, ed. (1891. Reprint, Harmondsworth, England: Penguin, 1985), 24.

45 Bourdieu, *Distinction,* 7.

46 Christopher Kent, respondent, "Broadside Ballads and the Grosvenor Gallery: Art and Popular Culture in Victorian England," panel, Northern American Conference on British Studies in conjunction with Western Conference on British Studies, October 1992, Boulder, Colo.

47 In large summer exhibitions, the hanging of an artist's work on one wall or in distinctive groupings was not usually the case before the advent of the Grosvenor. Simultaneously, the Impressionist painters were undertaking such experiments, paying close attention to groupings, color schemes, and framing (see note 25 above). When Whistler held exhibitions at the Flemish Gallery, 48 Pall Mall, in 1874, and later at The Fine Art Society, and during his term as president of the Society of British Artists, he demanded total control of the hanging process, display, and atmosphere. On Whistler see chapter 8 and Robin Spencer, "Whistler's First One-Man Exhibition Reconstructed," in Gabriel P. Weisberg and Laurinda Dixon, eds., *The Documented Image: Visions in Art History* (Syracuse, N.Y.: Syracuse University Press, 1987), 27–49. For Whistler's aesthetics on exhibition practices see especially David Park Curry, "Total Control: Whistler at an Exhibition," in *James McNeill Whistler: A Reexamination,* vol. 19 of *Studies in the History of Art* (Washington, D.C.: National Gallery of Art, Center for Advanced Study in the Visual Arts Symposium Papers VI), 67–82.

48 Gordon F. Fyfe, "Art Exhibitions and Power during the Nineteenth Century," in *Sociological Review Monograph 32. Power, Action and Belief: A New Sociology of Knowledge* (London, Boston, and Henley: Routledge and Kegan Paul, 1986), 37.

49 Mary S. Watts, *George Frederic Watts: The Annals of an Artist's Life,* 3 vols. (London: Macmillan, 1912), 1:323–24.

50 Fyfe, "Art Exhibitions and Power," 25–26.

51 See "The Grosvenor Gallery," *Academy* 9 (May 13, 1876): 467. On Fowke see F. H. W. Sheppard, ed., *Survey of London,* vol. 28, *The Museum Areas of South Kensington and Westminster* (London: Athlone Press for Greater London Council, 1975), 74–86.

52 Paul Greenhalgh, *Ephemeral Vistas* (Manchester: Manchester University Press, 1988), 159.

53 On Sir Charles Eastlake, see David Allan Robertson, *Sir Charles Eastlake and the Victorian Art World* (Princeton, N.J.: Princeton University Press, 1978).

54 Waterfield, *Palaces of Art,* 103.

55 For Redgrave's design efforts see Anthony Burton, "Richard Redgrave as Art Educator, Museum Official and Design Theorist," in Susan P. Casteras and Ronald Parkinson, eds., *Richard Redgrave, 1804–1888* (New Haven and London: Yale University Press in association with the Victoria & Albert Museum and the Yale Center for British Art, 1988), 60–67.

56 *Handbook of London As It Is,* rev. ed.(London: John Murray, 1879), 33, 58. For statistics on attendance see "The Grosvenor Gallery," *Architect* (1877), 41.

57 Leonore Davidoff, *The Best Circles* (London: Croom Helm, 1973), 59.

58 Thomas Heyck, personal correspondence, 1993.

59 See David Cannadine, *The Decline and Fall of the British Aristocracy* (New Haven and London: Yale University Press, 1990), 13, where he discusses an 1876 intermarriage between the aristocrat, Lord Rosebery, and Hannah Rothschild, Lady Lindsay's cousin, which linked banking families and aristocracy more closely. The Lindsays had already set the precedent.

60 See Gillett, *Worlds of Art*, 237.

61 See Chris Wilkes, "Bourdieu's Class," in Harker et al., *Introduction to the Work of Pierre Bourdieu*, 126–27.

62 Davidoff, *Best Circles*, and Hilary and Mary Evans, *The Party that Lasted One Hundred Days* (London: MacDonald and Jane's, 1976).

63 See "The Grosvenor Gallery," *Architect* 18 (July 28, 1877): 41.

64 Fyfe, "Art Exhibitions and Power," 31.

65 Agnes D. Atkinson, "The Grosvenor Gallery," *Portfolio* 8 (1877): 98.

66 Hallé, *Notes*, 109–10.

67 See Helen Smith, *Decorative Painting in the Domestic Interior in England and Wales, c. 1850–1890* (New York and London: Garland Outstanding Theses from the Courtauld Institute of Art, 1984), who lists specific sites for some of the Grosvenor paintings of this type.

68 Waterfield, *Palaces of Art*, 25–26.

69 To my knowledge, the only gallery to precede it in this careful organization was the British Institution, which had closed in 1867. The arrangement there gave students access to make copies of the old masters.

70 Waterfield, *Palaces of Art*, 28. As figure 10 shows, the original staircase was remodeled in 1904 with the addition of paneling and a new open-arcade division on the right-hand side. For the later changes see "Current Architecture," *Architectural Review* 16 (July-December 1904): 130–34.

71 See Jill Franklin, *The Gentleman's Country House and Its Plan, 1835–1914* (London, Boston and Henley: Routledge and Kegan Paul, 1981), 55–60, on which the following discussion is based; and Mark Girouard, *The Victorian Country House*, rev.

and enl. ed. (New Haven: Yale University Press, 1985), 34–35.

72 See Franklin, *Gentleman's Country House*, 59, on which the following discussion is based.

73 Girouard, *Victorian Country House*, 36.

74 For further discussion of billiard and smoking rooms see Charlotte Gere, *The Art of the Interior: Interior Decoration in the Nineteenth Century* (London: Thames and Hudson, 1992), 88; and Mark Girouard, *Life in the English Country House: A Social and Architectural History* (New Haven and London: Yale University Press, 1978), 294–97.

75 On Mudie see Richard D. Altick, *Victorian People and Ideas* (New York and London: Norton, 1973), 196.

76 Altick, *Victorian People*, 196.

77 Richard D. Altick, *The English Common Reader: A Social History of the Mass Reading Public, 1800–1900* (Chicago and London: University of Chicago Press, 1957. Reprint. Midway, 1983), 296.

78 See Grosvenor Summer Exhibition (1880–83, 1885–87,1889–90), where the library is advertised. On Lindsay's philosophy see the *Spectator* 53 (June 12, 1880): 761; and Arthur Waugh, *A Hundred Years of Publishing: Being the Story of Chapman and Hall, Ltd.* (London: Chapman and Hall, 1939), 102. The Academy included a library on its premises for members only, but it was not a circulating collection.

79 See Gervase Jackson-Stops, ed., *The Treasure Houses of Britain: Five Hundred Years of Private Patronage and Art Collecting* (Washington, D.C.: National Gallery of Art; New Haven: Yale University Press, 1985), 60.

80 Waterfield, *Palaces of Art*, 43. Only the South Kensington Museum had this advance.

81 See Waterfield, *Palaces of Art*, 42. For other examples of country houses installed with electricity at this time see Girouard, *Victorian Country House*, 25. In 1884 Lindsay formed the private firm of "Sir Coutts and Company" and built a generating station in the subbasement of the gallery (see fig. 13). A new chief engineer, Sebastian Ziani de Ferranti, was hired in 1886 and his success with the venture led to a takeover by the London Electric Supply Corporation Limited, which undertook to supply electricity to London on a vast scale. Lindsay and his brother, Lord Wantage, then became the largest share-

holders in this new company, which expanded in 1889 and again in 1890. See F. H. W. Sheppard, ed., *Survey of London*, vol. 40, *The Grosvenor Estate in Mayfair. Part II: The Buildings* (London: Athlone Press for the Greater London Council, 1980), 61. See also "Grosvenor Gallery," *Electrician* 14 (December 13, 1884): 82; "Electric Lighting Central Station," *Electrician* 14 (February 28, 1885): 324; and Robert Hudson Parsons, *The Early Days of the Power Station Industry* (Cambridge: Cambridge University Press, 1939), 23.

82   In addition to these other comforts created for the Grosvenor visitor, building alterations began in 1884 in order to include a clergyman's club on the premises, managed by Reverend Nugent Wade, father of the Grosvenor estate architect, Fairfax B. Wade; the latter was the co-manager of the venture. The 1889 plans (see figs. 9, 11) show the location of the club on the ground floor as well as on the first floor. See "Grosvenor Board Minutes," October 22, 1884, 1049/5/22, 57–58.

83   F. M. L. Thompson, *The Rise of Respectable Society: A Social History of Victorian Britain, 1830–1900* (Cambridge, Mass.: Harvard University Press, 1988), 152.

84   Fyfe, "Art Exhibitions and Power," 30.

85   Penelope Fitzgerald, *Edward Burne-Jones: A Biography* (London: Michael Joseph, 1975), 168.

86   Davidoff, *Best Circles*, 16. In 1869 the Academy moved its headquarters to Burlington House in Piccadilly, virtually around the corner from the future location of the Grosvenor, as shown in the 1879 plan of "St. James's Street, and Old and New Bond Street" (see fig. 17). Various social comforts were eventually provided, but these were not completed until 1885, and they included a refreshment room, dining room, and restaurant. Apparently the Academy saw the advantage these facilities created at the Grosvenor in attracting the public. It is clear that these features did not exist at Trafalgar Square, where the Academy was located from 1837 to 1868, since the space there was extremely cramped. See Sidney Hutchinson, *The History of the Royal Academy, 1768–1968* (London: Chapman and Hall, 1968), 103–35.

87   *Times* (May 10, 1877). The *Times* recorded the event, complete with guest list. For further discussion of the guest list, see chapter 2.

88   Lord Henry Somerset, letter to Lady Somers; quoted in Surtees, *Coutts Lindsay*, 154.

89   Louise Jopling, *Twenty Years of My Life, 1867–1887* (London: John Lane, 1925), 121–22.

90   See "The Grosvenor Gallery," *Builder* (April 28, 1877): 424; and Hallé, *Notes*, 150.

91   The author, in collaboration with Paula Gillett, is undertaking a separate study of the musical concerts and performers at the Grosvenor.

92   See Cooper, *Courtauld Collection*; and Mark Girouard, *Sweetness and Light: The Queen Anne Movement, 1860–1900* (Oxford: Clarendon Press, 1977), on which the following discussion is based.

93   Jeremy Cooper, *Victorian and Edwardian Decor: From the Gothic Revival to Art Nouveau* (New York: Abbeville Press, 1987), 137.

94   Rhoda and Agnes Garrett, *Suggestions for House Decoration in Painting, Woodwork, and Furniture*, 2d ed. (London: Macmillan, 1877, Reprint. New York: Garland, 1978), 59.

95   Mrs. H. R. Haweis, *The Art of Decoration* (London: Chatto and Windus, 1881), 10.

96   On William Morris and Company see Nicholas Pevsner, *Pioneers of Modern Design: From William Morris to Walter Gropius* (New York: Museum of Modern Art, 1949), 7–10, 20–37.

97   Smith, *Decorative Painting*, 255, 144.

98   Smith, *Decorative Painting*, 144.

99   Waterfield, *Palaces of Art*, 28. On the Academy see Hutchinson, *History of the Royal Academy*, 132.

100   "The Grosvenor Gallery," *Builder* (1877), 424.

101   See Priscilla Boniface, *Hotels and Restaurants, 1830 to the Present Day*, gen. ed. Peter Fowler (London: Royal Commission on Historical Monuments in England in conjunction with Her Majesty's Stationery Office, 1981), on which the following discussion is based.

102   *Dickens's Dictionary of London, 1879. An Unconventional Handbook* (London: Charles Dickens, "All the Year Round" Office, 26, Wellington Street, 1879), 224.

103   *Handbook of London As It Is*, 53.

104   For further discussion of this phenomenon in terms of audience, see chapter 2.

105 Hallé, *Notes,* 158.

106 Lindsay had a mistress, Kate Harriet Madley, with whom he had five children. He did not marry her until Lady Lindsay's death, by which time he and Madley were both in their sixties. Surtees suggests that the separation came about when Lindsay refused to give up Madley and his new son by her, James Lindsay, probably because he and Blanche had had only daughters, a bone of contention since he needed a son to carry on his title (Surtees, *Coutts Lindsay,* 70 and 168). He had three sons in all, including two by a previous mistress, Lizzie Chambers.

107 See Robert Henrey, *A Century Between* (New York: Longmans, Green, 1937), 228; and Surtees, *Coutts Lindsay,* 170.

108 See Sir Coutts Lindsay, letter to Anne Lindsay, November 1885, Crawford Papers, National Library of Scotland, Edinburgh.

109 Hallé, *Notes,* 152–53.

110 See for example, *Vanity Fair* 33 (May 2, 1885): 254; and "Vanities," *Vanity Fair* 41 (May 4, 1889): 317.

111 Roy T. Matthews, "Vanity Fair: The First Society Magazine," *Albion* 7 (1976): 45.

112 Burne-Jones to Charles Hallé, October 3, 1887, in "Correspondence with Sir Coutts Lindsay."

113 For further discussion of this group of artists see the introduction and chapter 7.

CHAPTER 2. ART AUDIENCES AT THE GROSVENOR GALLERY

1 For a detailed account of the trial, see Linda Merrill, *A Pot of Paint: Aesthetics on Trial in Whistler v. Ruskin* (Washington, D.C., and London: Smithsonian Institution Press in collaboration with The Freer Gallery of Art, 1992).

2 The satirical plays were *The Grasshopper,* John Hollingshead's adaptation of a French farce; Francis Burnand's *The Colonel;* and the Gilbert and Sullivan operetta *Patience.*

3 *Art Journal* 16 (1877): 244.

4 Donald L. Lawler, ed., *The Picture of Dorian Gray: Authoritative Texts, Backgrounds, Reviews, and Reactions, Criticism* (New York: Norton, 1988), 8.

5 *Illustrated London News,* May 12, 1877; Sidney C. Hutchison, *The History of the Royal Academy: 1768–1986,* 2nd ed. (London: Robert Royce, 1986), 122.

6 Hutchison, *Royal Academy,* 122.

7 The average daily attendance during the Grosvenor's opening year was 1,100. See chapter 1, note 56.

8 Virginia Surtees, *Coutts Lindsay, 1824–1913* (Norwich, England: Michael Russell, 1993), 159. According to Alice Carr, wife of art critic and Grosvenor Gallery manager Joseph Comyns Carr, the Princess of Wales sometimes accompanied her husband to Grosvenor Gallery invitational events. Eve Adam, ed., *Mrs. J. Comyns Carr's Reminiscences* (London: Hutchinson, 1926), 55.

9 *Fun* (May 9, 1877): 179. Satirists often presented upper-class speech as substituting *w* for *r.*

10 Mrs. Leyland and Graham are listed in the Grosvenor's 1877 catalogue as owners of two Whistler Nocturnes. Frederick Leyland owned two of Burne-Jones's paintings in this show, and Graham, one. Burne-Jones's patron, F. S. Ellis, a publisher and book collector, attended the opening banquet. The dispute with Leyland resulted from Whistler's unauthorized handling of a commission for work in his patron's new London house (Merrill, *Pot of Paint,* 33–35). On Ellis, see Merrill, 18. On Graham and Leyland, see Dianne Sachko Macleod, "Art Collecting and Victorian Middle-Class Taste," *Art History* 10, no. 3 (September 1987): 328–50. I am grateful to Professor Macleod for information concerning Graham's withdrawal from social life.

11 Virginia Surtees, *The Artist and the Autocrat: George and Rosalind Howard, Earl and Countess of Carlisle* (Salisbury, England: Michael Russell,

1988), 50–51; Dorothy Henley, *Rosalind Howard: Countess of Carlisle* (London: The Hogarth Press, 1959), 28, 45.

12   Jehanne Wake, *Princess Louise: Queen Victoria's Unconventional Daughter* (London: Collins, 1988), 90, 109. See also David C. Itzkowitz, "Royal Family," in Sally Mitchell, ed., *Victorian Britain* (New York: Garland, 1988), 684. On Louise's study with Parsons (and her pleasure in visiting bohemia), see *Mrs. Carr's Reminiscences*, 17–18). On Boehm, see Dennis Farr, *English Art: 1870–1940* (Oxford: Clarendon Press, 1978), 84.

13   Wake, *Princess Louise*, 92, 204–05; Lillie Langtry, *The Days I Knew* (New York: George H. Doran, 1925), 61.

14   Zachary Cope, *The Versatile Victorian, Being the Life of Sir Henry Thompson, bt., 1820–1904* (London: Harvey and Blythe, 1951), 82–83; 6–7, 102, 122–23.

15   Robert Blake, *Disraeli* (New York: St. Martin's Press, 1967), 714–16.

16   *The Gladstone Diaries*, ed. H. C. G. Matthew (Oxford: Clarendon Press, 1986), 9:217.

17   Richard Davis, *The English Rothschilds* (Chapel Hill: University of North Carolina Press, 1983), 228.

18   Arthur Jacobs, *Arthur Sullivan: A Victorian Musician* (Oxford: Oxford University Press, 1986), 181; Farr, *English Art*, 358–59.

19   *Vanity Fair*, November 4, 1876.

20   Y. Cassis, "Bankers in English Society in the Late Nineteenth Century," *Economic History Review*, 2d ser., 38 (1985): 217–29.

21   James Payn, *The Backwater of Life: or Essays of a Literary Veteran* (London: Smith, Elder, 1899), 76.

22   Virginia Cowles, *Gay Monarch: The Life and Pleasures of Edward VII* (New York: Harper, 1956), 137–40.

23   "The Rich Man," *Vanity Fair* (May 5, 1877): 279–80.

24   "Apart from the German-Jewish Sir Ernest Cassel and Baron Hirsch and the Rothschilds and Sassoons and the Portuguese Marquis de Soveral, the men and women who were intimates of the Prince of Wales came from old English families which, whether carrying titles or not, were deeply rooted in the land" (Anita Leslie, *The Marlborough House Set* [New York: Doubleday, 1973], 6). Leslie's grandmother was Leonie Jerome, sister of Jennie Jerome Churchill.

25   From *Fors Clavigera*; quoted in Stanley Weintraub, *Whistler: A Biography* (New York: Truman Talley/Dutton, 1988), 190.

26   Frances Countess of Warwick, *Afterthoughts* (London: Cassell, 1931), 40–42.

27   Paula Gillett, *Worlds of Art* (New Brunswick, N.J.: Rutgers University Press, 1990), 211–12.

28   Weintraub, *Whistler*, 164–65.

29   Jacobs, *Sullivan*, 25–26; 80–81; 98; 106.

30   Harold Perkin, *The Rise of Professional Society: England Since 1880* (London: Routledge, 1989), 90.

31   E. E. Kellett, "The Press," in G. M. Young, ed., *Early Victorian England* (London: Oxford University Press, 1951), 2:36; Joel H. Wiener, ed., *Papers for the Millions: The New Journalism in Britain, 1850s to 1914* (New York: Greenwood Press, 1988), 284–85; *Spectator*, March 19, 1881.

32   Merrill, *Pot of Paint*, 179–80.

33   Surtees, *Coutts Lindsay*, 141, 144.

34   Mrs. Robert Henrey, *Green Leaves* (London: J. M. Dent, 1976), 85.

35   Henry James, *Partial Portraits* (London: Macmillan, 1888), 366–67.

36   Leonée Ormond, *George Du Maurier* (Pittsburgh: University of Pittsburgh Press, 1969), 2.

37   *Vanity Fair*, May 18, 1878.

38   *Vanity Fair*, June 1878 (Season Number): 17.

39   George Charles Brodrick, *Memories and Impressions, 1831–1900* (London: J. Nisbet, 1900), 201.

40   Ralph Martin, *Lady Randolph Churchill* (Englewood Cliffs, N.J.: Prentice-Hall, 1969–71), 1:178.

41   Lucy C. Lillie, *Prudence: A Story of Aesthetic London* (New York: Harper, 1882), 108.

42   "The Old Grosvenor Gallery," *Times* (October 1, 1912).

43   *Vanity Fair*, May 4, 1878.

44   *Mrs. Carr's Reminiscences*, 54.

45   *The George Eliot Letters*, ed. Gordon S. Haight (New Haven: Yale University Press, 1955), 6:364–65.

46   A. M. W. Stirling, *Victorian Sidelights: From the Papers of the Late Mrs. Adams-Acton* (London: Ernest Benn, 1954), 163–64.

47   Merrill, *Pot of Paint*, 15.

48 For a fascinating account of this journal, see Peter Bailey, "Ally Sloper's Half-Holiday: Comic Art in the 1880s," *History Workshop* 16 (Autumn 1983): 4–31.

49 Ward Thoron, ed., *Letters of Mrs. Henry Adams* (Boston: Little, Brown, 1936), 153.

50 On Show Sunday, see Gillett, *Worlds of Art*, 194–96.

51 *Vanity Fair*, April 28, 1877.

52 *Vanity Fair*, April 12, 1879.

53 Quoted in Ronald Pearsall, *The Worm in the Bud* (New York: Macmillan, 1969), 37.

54 Leon Edel, *Henry James: A Life* (New York: Harper and Row, 1985), 223.

55 See John L. Sweeney, ed., *The Painter's Eye: Notes and Essays on the Pictorial Arts by Henry James* (Cambridge: Harvard University Press, 1956).

56 Edel, *James*, 223–24.

57 Thoron, *Mrs. Adams*, 159.

58 Jacobs, *Sullivan*, 85ff.

59 Frances Countess of Warwick, *Afterthoughts*, 42.

60 Thoron, *Mrs. Adams*, 154, 159.

61 John Lehmann, *Ancestors and Friends* (London: Eyre and Spottiswoode, 1962).

62 1893, MS at British Library.

63 Rudolph Chambers Lehmann, *Memories of Half a Century* (London: Smith, 1908), 5.

64 A Foreign Resident [T. H. S. Escott], *Society in London*, 2nd ed. (London: Chatto and Windus, 1885), 296.

65 Surtees, *Coutts Lindsay*, 36, 40–41, 50.

66 Michael R. Booth, *Theatre in the Victorian Age* (Cambridge: Cambridge University Press, 1991), 22–23.

67 *Vanity Fair* (Season number 1878): 5.

68 Booth, *Theatre in the Victorian Age*, 23. Henry Irving was the first actor to be knighted, in 1895; Squire Bancroft was next, in 1897. The first women were Genevieve Ward and Ellen Terry, who became Dames of the British Empire in 1921 and 1925, respectively.

69 J. M. Farrar, *Mary Anderson: The Story of Her Life and Professional Career* (London: David Bogue, 1884), 48–49; Mary Anderson, *A Few Memories* (New York: Harper, 1896), 154–55.

70 *Punch*, April 5, 1884.

71 Anderson, *A Few Memories*, 135–362.

72 Edward Aveling, in *Our Corner* (January-May 1884): 306–07.

73 Anderson, *A Few Memories*, 249; Mary Power, "Molly Bloom and Mary Anderson: The Inside Story," *European Joyce Studies 1: Modernity and Its Mediation*, 114–15.

74 "She is a charming young woman and she has done much to prove that the stage is not a hot bed of vice." *New York Saturday Evening Gazette*, 1888, quoted from Power, "Molly Bloom and Mary Anderson," 115.

75 Arthur Gold and Robert Fizdale, *The Divine Sarah* (New York: Knopf, 1991), 153.

76 Farrar, *Mary Anderson*, 48.

77 *Mrs. Carr's Reminiscences*, 58.

78 Richard Ellmann, *Oscar Wilde* (New York: Knopf, 1988), 110.

79 Ellmann, *Wilde*, 111.

80 Gower was probably the model for Lord Henry Wotton in *The Picture of Dorian Gray*. Phyllis Grosskurth, *John Addington Symonds* (New York: Arno Press, 1975), 267.

81 Ellmann, *Wilde*, 78–79.

82 Ellmann, *Wilde*, 113.

83 Margot Asquith, *More Memories* (London: Cassell, 1933), 31.

84 Thoron, *Mrs. Adams*, 158.

85 John Pye, *Patronage of British Art: An Historical Sketch* (1845; facsimile reprint, London, 1970), 172–73.

86 Several organizations formed during the late 1870s to bring classical concerts to the working classes found that to be affordable to these groups, ticket prices had to be reduced from the usual shilling minimum to sixpence or even threepence. Paula Gillett, "From Haydn to 'Home, Sweet Home': Music in Late Victorian Philanthropy," unpublished paper.

87 "London Pictures," *Painter's Eye*, 204.

88 Henry James, "The Siege of London," in *The Great Short Novels of Henry James* (New York: Dial Press, 1944), 263.

89 Pierre Bourdieu, *Distinction: A Social Critique of the Judgment of Taste*, trans. Richard Nice (Cambridge: Harvard University Press, 1984), 2.

90 *Art Journal* 16 (1877): 223.

91 Bea Howe, *Arbiter of Elegance* (London: Harvill, 1967) on Mrs. Haweis; Lucy Crane, *Art and the Formation of Taste: Six Lectures* (Boston: Chautauqua Press, 1887).

92 In 1922, at age 78, Swynnerton was elected an Associate of the Royal Academy, the first female admitted to membership since the institution's founding in 1768. For information on suffragist artists, see Deborah Cherry, *Painting Women: Victorian Women Artists* (London: Routledge, 1993), 93–94, 104.

93 *Queen*, June 30, 1877.

94 Amy Levy, "Women and Club Life" (1888), in *The Complete Novels and Selected Writings of Amy Levy: 1861–1889,* ed. Melvyn New (Gainesville: University Press of Florida, 1993), 535.

95 The Queen Anne style of the 1870s and 1880s was a picturesque mode of domestic architecture closely associated with the Aesthetic Movement. It featured red brick construction and tall sash windows, often incorporating a sunflower motif in its external decorations. Elizabeth Aslin, *The Aesthetic Movement* (New York: Excalibur Books/Simon and Schuster, 1969), 49–51. Walter Hamilton described the club as Bedford Park's most attractive feature, containing "billiard, reading and card rooms, and the prettiest of all possible ladies' drawing-rooms. . . . There is a small library, and new books are constantly supplied by the Grosvenor Gallery Library." *The Aesthetic Movement in England,* 3rd. ed. (London: Reeves and Turner, 1882), 127–28.

96 Alison Adburgham, *Shops and Shopping: 1800–1914* (London: Barrie and Jenkins, 1989), 231.

97 *Queen*, May 18, 1878.

98 *Truth*, May 9, 1878.

99 Many new clubs would follow during the 1890s. Levy, "Women and Club Life," 534–38.

100 Grosvenor catalogues were consulted at the Victoria & Albert National Art Library. In her 1888 essay Levy mentions an interesting feature of the University Club for Ladies (then located on the upper floors of a New Bond Street house): members who wanted a higher standard of food than could be obtained from the housekeeper at a moderate price could take advantage of a special arrangement "with the Grosvenor Restaurant opposite, by which more luxurious cakes can be supplied to her on the shortest notice" ("Women and Club Life," 534).

101 Brian Harrison, "Religion and Recreation in Nineteenth-Century England," in *Peaceable Kingdom: Stability and Change in Modern Britain* (Oxford: Clarendon Press, 1982), 140–41.

102 Harrison, *Peaceable Kingdom*, 141; Dunraven, "Opening National Institutions on Sunday," *Nineteenth Century* (March 1884).

103 Dunraven, "Opening National Institutions," 417.

104 *Times* (July 12, 1878).

105 *Times* (July 15, 1878).

106 *Times* (July 22, 1878).

107 *Times* (July 28, 1879).

108 *Our Corner* 4 (1884).

CHAPTER 3. "ART IS UPON THE TOWN!"

1   In this chapter, for the sake of consistency, clarity, and conciseness, I refer to all the winter exhibitions as taking place in the single year in which they were on view from January through March. Five of the exhibitions did open in the final days of the preceding December (on December 31 in at least two instances), and their catalogues are occasionally cited as publications of the earlier year.

2   The Grosvenor Gallery, *Illustrated Catalogue: Winter Exhibition of Drawings by the Old Masters and Water-colours by Deceased Artists of the British School. With Critical Introduction by J. Comyns Carr* (London, 1878), iii.

3   "The Winter Exhibitions," *Art Journal* (1879): 46.

4   Wilfrid Meynell, "The Winter Exhibition at the Grosvenor Gallery," *Magazine of Art* 4 (1881): 178.

5   Wilfrid Meynell, "The Winter Exhibition at the Grosvenor Gallery," *Magazine of Art* 3 (1880): 165.

6   See Virginia Surtees, *Coutts Lindsay, 1824–1913* (Norwich, England: Michael Russell, 1993), 99 and passim; and Wilfrid Blunt, *England's Michelangelo: A Biography of George Frederic Watts, O.M., R.A.* (London: Hamilton, 1975), passim.

7   See J. Comyns Carr, *Coasting Bohemia* (London: Macmillan, 1914), 26–41.

8   The catalogue notes were also revised by Millais. See Diana Sachko Macleod, "F. G. Stephens, Pre-Raphaelite Critic and Art Historian," *Burlington Magazine* 128 (1986): 400.

9   Lord Lindsay, *Sketches of the History of Christian Art,* 2nd ed. (London, 1885), x, from the "Advertisement to the First Edition," dated November 1, 1846.

10   Surtees, *Coutts Lindsay,* 27.

11   C. E. Hallé, *Notes from a Painter's Life* (London: J. Murray, 1909), 13–14 and 117–18.

12   Hallé, *Notes,* 4–5.

13   Hallé, *Notes,* 113.

14   J. Comyns Carr, *Essays on Art* (London, 1879), 79–173.

15   Grosvenor Gallery, *Illustrated Catalogue: Winter Exhibition of Drawings by the Old Masters and Water-colours by Deceased Artists of the British School.* No modern scholars attribute the volume to Mantegna. It is now in the British Museum and seems to be by Marco Zoppo. See Campbell

Dodgson, *A Book of Drawings Formerly Ascribed to Mantegna* (London, 1923), and Eberhard Ruhmer, *Marco Zoppo* (Vicenza: Neri Pozza, 1966), 77–81, and ills. 12, 48, 63, and 88–135.

16   J. Comyns Carr, *Papers on Art* (London, 1885), 122–95.

17   "The Winter Exhibitions," *Art Journal* (1878): 13–16, 53–56, and 90–92.

18   See Peter Fullerton, "Patronage and Pedagogy: the British Institution in the Early Nineteenth Century," *Art History* 5 (1982): 59–72.

19   Sidney C. Hutchison, *The History of the Royal Academy, 1768–1968* (London: Chapman and Hall, 1968), 241–43.

20   Marcus B. Huish, ed., *The Year's Art* (London, 1880), 88.

21   See Scott Wilcox and Christopher Newall, *Victorian Landscape Watercolors* (New York: Hudson Hills, 1992), 25 and 47.

22   Edmund W. Gosse, *Cecil Lawson: A Memoir* (London, 1883), 6.

23   *Art Journal* (1883): 132.

24   See J. Comyns Carr, *Some Eminent Victorians: Personal Recollections in the World of Arts and Letters* (London, 1908), 143ff.

25   Stanley Weintraub, ed., *Bernard Shaw on the London Art Scene, 1885–1950* (University Park: Pennsylvania State University Press, 1989), 29–30.

26   Reported by Frederic Leighton in a letter to William Michael Rossetti, quoted in Leonée and Richard Ormond, *Lord Leighton* (New Haven and London: Yale University Press, 1975), 104.

27   Pater's essay appeared in the *Fortnightly Review* in August 1870; Ruskin's main discussion of Botticelli was in lectures given in the autumn of 1872 subsequently published under the title *Ariadne Florentina.* See Gail S. Weinberg, "Ruskin, Pater, and the Rediscovery of Botticelli," *Burlington Magazine* 129 (1987): 25–27.

28   Carr, *Coasting Bohemia,* 42–43.

29   Mary Lago, ed., *Burne-Jones Talking* (Columbia: University of Missouri Press, 1981), 101 and 104.

30   Stanley Olson, *John Singer Sargent: His Portrait* (London: Macmillan, 1986), 208.

31   Charles Holmes in the *Times,* April 22, 1909; reprinted in D. S. MacColl, *Life, Work and Setting of Philip Wilson Steer* (London: Faber and Faber, 1945), 180.

32 John Ruskin, "Lectures on Landscape," 1871; reprinted in E. T. Cook and Alexander Wedderburn, eds., *The Works of John Ruskin* (London, 1903–1912), 22:58.

33 Ian Fleming-Williams and Leslie Parris, *The Discovery of Constable* (London: H. Hamilton, 1984), 88 (from the *Standard*, July 27, 1888).

34 Ibid., 89, from P. G. Hamerton, "Constable's Sketches," *Portfolio* (1890): 163.

35 "Mr. P. Wilson Steer on Impressionism in Art," Art-Worker's Guild, 1891; printed in MacColl, *Life, Work, and Setting*, 177–78.

36 See John Guille Millais, *The Life and Letters of Sir John Everett Millais* (London, 1899), 2:39–40.

37 Carr, *Coasting Bohemia*, 23.

38 Carr, *Coasting Bohemia*, 23.

39 William Holman Hunt, *Pre-Raphaelitism and the Pre-Raphaelite Brotherhood* (London: Macmillan, 1905), 2:392. I am grateful to Malcolm Warner for helpful discussion of the impact of the exhibition upon Millais.

40 R. E. D. Sketchley, *The Art of John William Waterhouse*, Christmas Supplement to the *Art Journal* (1909): 15. I am indebted to Andrew Marvick, who brought the passage to my attention. Waterhouse's *Lady of Shalott* (Tate Gallery, London) of 1888 is the prime example of this phase of his art. For Byam Shaw and Eleanor Fortescue-Brickdale, see John Christian, ed., *The Last Romantics* (London: Barbican Art Gallery, 1989), 128–31.

41 See Lee Edwards, "Hubert von Herkomer: 'Sympathy for the old and for suffering mankind,'" in Julian Treuherz, ed., *Hard Times: Social Realism in Victorian Art* (Manchester City Art Galleries, 1987), 96–99. Watts's other three social-realist paintings are *Under a Dry Arch*, *Found Drowned*, and *The Seamstress*. All four belong to the Watts Gallery, Compton, Guildford.

42 Carr, *Essays on Art*, 193.

43 "The Works of Lawrence Alma-Tadema, R.A.," *Art Journal* (1883): 33.

44 Walter Pater, *The Renaissance* (New York, 1961), 224. The conclusion, written in 1868, was included in the collection of essays first published as *Studies in the History of the Renaissance* in 1873, withdrawn from the second edition, and reinstated in subsequent editions.

CHAPTER 4. BURNE-JONES
AND THE PRE-RAPHAELITE CIRCLE
AT THE PALACE OF THE AESTHETES

1 As quoted in Colleen Denney, "Exhibition Reforms and Systems: The Grosvenor Gallery of Art, 1877–1890" (Ph.D. diss., University of Minnesota, 1990), 44–45. See also J. Comyns Carr, *Some Reminiscences in the World of Art and Letters* (London: Duckworth, 1908), for other details on the Grosvenor Gallery.

2 Letter from J. Comyns Carr to Dante Gabriel Rossetti, April 3, 1876, collection of the University of British Columbia.

3 Letter from Dante Gabriel Rossetti to Ford Madox Brown, April 7, 1876, as cited in Oswald Doughty and John R. Wahl, *Letters of Dante Gabriel Rossetti* (Oxford: Clarendon Press, 1967), 3:1422–23.

4 Charles E. Hallé, *Notes from a Painter's Life, Including the Founding of Two Galleries* (London: J. Murray, 1909), 65.

5 Hallé, *Notes*, 69–70.

6 Hallé, *Notes*, 99.

7 Hallé, *Notes*, 99.

8 Letter from Charles E. Hallé to Dante Gabriel Rossetti, January 19, 1877, collection of the University of British Columbia.

9 Letter from Dante Gabriel Rossetti to the editor of the *Times*, March 16, 1877, as quoted in Doughty and Wahl, *Letters of Dante Gabriel Rossetti*, 3:1482–83.

10 Letter from Dante Gabriel Rossetti to Charles A. Hallé, January 27, 1877, as quoted in Doughty and Wahl, *Letters of Dante Gabriel Rossetti*, 4:1469–70.

11 March 28, 1877, letter from Charles A. Hallé to Dante Gabriel Rossetti, collection of the University of British Columbia. Another letter in this collection dated February 19, 1879, to Rossetti from John W. Beer, another Grosvenor Gallery representative, suggests there may have been continued communications on this subject. Beer wrote to invite Rossetti to a meeting and to inform him that "by a resolution passed last evening your name has been added to the Committee appointed by the meeting held at the Grosvenor Gallery to bring to resolution the subject of artistic copyright to the notice of the Government."

12 Denney, "Exhibition Reforms and Systems," 29, 40.

13 "Art. The Grosvenor Gallery," *Spectator* 50 (May 19, 1877): 631, and William Michael Rossetti,

"Fine Art, The Grosvenor Gallery," *Academy* 11 (May 26, 1877): 467.

14 "The Grosvenor Gallery," *Illustrated London News* 70 (May 12, 1877): 450.

15 See, e.g., "The Picture Galleries," *Saturday Review* 45 (May 8, 1878): 561; "The Grosvenor Gallery," *Illustrated London News* 72 (May 4, 1878): 410; and "The Grosvenor Gallery," *Athenaeum* 51 (May 4, 1878): 579.

16 "The Grosvenor Gallery Exhibition," *Illustrated London News* 74 (May 3, 1879): 415.

17 "The Grosvenor Gallery," *Vanity Fair* 23 (May 15, 1880): 277.

18 "Art. The Grosvenor Gallery," *Spectator* 53 (June 2, 1880): 752, and "Art. The Grosvenor Gallery," *Spectator* 53 (January 17, 1880): 77.

19 Théodore Duret, "Expositions de la Royal Academy et de la Grosvenor Gallery," *Gazette des Beaux-Arts* 33 (1881): 551–56 passim.

20 "The Grosvenor Gallery," *Athenaeum* 54 (April 30, 1881): 599, and "The Grosvenor Gallery," *Illustrated London News* (May 7, 1881): 459.

21 "The Grosvenor Gallery," *Art Journal* 45 (1881): 189.

22 "The Grosvenor Gallery Exhibition," *Athenaeum* 56 (April 28, 1883): 547.

23 "The Grosvenor Gallery," *Art Journal* 45 (1883): 203. *Illustrated London News* said virtually the same thing.

24 "The Grosvenor Gallery," *Athenaeum* 58 (March 25, 1885): 540, and "Current Art," *Magazine of Art* 9 (1888): 347.

25 "Current Art," *Magazine of Art* 12 (1889): 291, and "The Grosvenor Gallery," *Athenaeum* 63 (May 10, 1890): 610.

26 "Art. The Grosvenor Gallery," *Spectator* 50 (May 19, 1877): 631.

27 William Michael Rossetti, "Fine Art. The Grosvenor Gallery," *Academy* 11 (May 26, 1877): 467.

28 "The Grosvenor Gallery," *Spectator* 53 (June 2, 1880): 753, and "The Grosvenor Gallery," *Vanity Fair* 23 (May 15, 1880): 277.

29 "The Grosvenor Gallery," *Vanity Fair* 27 (1882): 253.

30 "The Grosvenor Gallery," *Athenaeum* 55 (May 20, 1882): 641.

31 "The Grosvenor Gallery," *Athenaeum* 57 (May 10, 1884): 603.

32 "The Grosvenor Gallery," *Saturday Review* (December 9, 1882): 763.

33 "The Grosvenor Gallery," *Athenaeum* 55 (May, 20, 1882): 641.

34 "The Grosvenor Gallery," *Athenaeum* 56 (May 12, 1883): 609, and "The Grosvenor Gallery," *Athenaeum* 60 (May 7, 1887): 612.

35 Théodore Duret was among those who linked Burne-Jones as Rossetti's principal follower at the Grosvenor, as well as perceived the "sickly" air which allegedly permeated Burne-Jones's works.

36 "Art. The Grosvenor Gallery," *Spectator* 50 (May 19, 1877): 632. A similar point was made by Lindsay himself in his article, "On the Relationship of Fine Art to Social Science," *British Architect* 12 (October 20, 1879): 1149: "The public are only now becoming familiar with his [Burne-Jones's] works through the exhibitions of the Gallery.... He and certain others ... are advancing in the same direction."

37 Sidney Colvin, "The Grosvenor Gallery," *Fortnightly Review* 27 (1877): 825–26.

38 "The Grosvenor Gallery," *Illustrated London News* 70 (May 12, 1877): 450.

39 "The Grosvenor Gallery," *Art Journal* 39 (1877): 244.

40 "The Grosvenor Gallery," *Illustrated London News* 76 (May 5, 1880): 451.

41 "The Grosvenor Gallery," *Illustrated London News* 84 (May 3,1884): 419.

42 "The Grosvenor Gallery and the Royal Academy," *Vanity Fair* 17 (May 5, 1877): 281.

43 "The Grosvenor Gallery," *Magazine of Art* 1 (1878–79): 81–82, and "The Picture Galleries," *Saturday Review* (May 4, 1878): 561.

44 "The Grosvenor Gallery," *Athenaeum* 51 (May 4, 1878): 579.

45 "The Grosvenor Gallery," *Art Journal* 40 (1878): 155.

46 Frederick Wedmore, "Some Tendencies in Recent Painting," *Temple Bar* 53 (July 1878): 339.

47 Henry James, "The Grosvenor Gallery, 1878," as quoted in John L. Sweeney, ed., *The Painter's Eye: Notes and Essays on the Pictorial Arts by Henry James* (Cambridge: Harvard University Press, 1956), 162.

48 "Art. The Grosvenor Gallery," *Spectator* 51 (May 18, 1878): 637.

49 William Michael Rossetti, "Fine Art. The Grosvenor Gallery," *Academy* 11 (May 26, 1877): 467.

50 "The Grosvenor Gallery Exhibition," *Athenaeum* 56 (May 12, 1883): 609.

51 See, e.g., "The Grosvenor Gallery," *Athenaeum* 60 (May 7, 1887): 612.

52 Sidney Colvin, "The Grosvenor Gallery," *Fortnightly Review* 27 (1877): 829.

53 As quoted in Denney, "Exhibition Reforms and Systems," 131.

54 "The Grosvenor Gallery," *Athenaeum* 57 (May 10, 1884): 603.

55 Denney estimates (on 6) that 10–20% of all contributors to the Grosvenor were female.

56 "The Grosvenor Gallery," *Art Journal* 41 (1879): 135.

57 For additional information on Pickering, see especially Jan Marsh and Pamela Gerrish Nunn, *Women Artists and the Pre-Raphaelite Movement* (London: Virago Press, 1989), 107–13.

58 "The Grosvenor Gallery," *Art Journal* 43 (1881): 189.

59 Additional details on Spartali Stillman's career is found in Marsh and Nunn, *Women Artists*, 98–106.

60 In a February 22, 1871, letter in the collection of the University of British Columbia from Maria Spartali Stillman's mother to Rossetti, the former wrote, "She looks to you (and rightly so) as a superior being and she so admired your character, your art, and your fancy that once you had thought her worthy to be your companion in life." Spartali also was very worried about her daughter's choice of a mate and asked Rossetti not to divulge her concerns to Madox Brown. In a March 13, 1871, letter to Rossetti also in this collection, Spartali moreover voiced her opposition to W. J. Stillman, stating, "I cannot avoid deploring that she should not have chosen a more suitable man."

61 April 3, 1878, letter from Marie Spartali Stillman to Dante Gabriel Rossetti, collection of the University of British Columbia.

62 May 9, 1880, letter from Marie Spartali Stillman to Dante Gabriel Rossetti, collection of the University of British Columbia.

63 Sidney Colvin, "The Grosvenor Gallery," *Fortnightly Review* 27 (1877): 827–28.

64 "Fine Art. The Grosvenor Gallery," *Academy* 11 (May 5, 1877): 396.

65 "The Grosvenor Gallery Exhibition," *Illustrated London News* 74 (May 3, 1879): 415.

66 Ibid.

67 "The Grosvenor Gallery," *Vanity Fair* 23 (1880): 253.

68 Harry Quilter, "The New Renaissance; or, The Gospel of Intensity," *Macmillan's Magazine* 42 (September 1880): 392–93.

69 "The Winter Exhibition at the Grosvenor Gallery," *Magazine of Art* 4 (1881): 180.

70 William Michael Rossetti, "The Grosvenor Gallery," *Academy* 11 (1877): 396.

71 "The Grosvenor Gallery," *Magazine of Art* 1 (1878): 81.

72 "The Grosvenor Gallery," *Illustrated London News* 82 (May 5, 1883): 447.

73 "The Grosvenor Gallery," *Art Journal* 45 (1883): 203.

74 "The Grosvenor Gallery," *Illustrated London News* 86 (May 23, 1885): 544.

75 "Art. The Grosvenor Gallery," *Spectator* 60 (May 7, 1887): 621–22.

76 W. P. Frith, "Crazes in Art. 'Pre-Raphaelitism' and 'Impressionism,'" *Magazine of Art* 11 (1888): 190–91.

77 "Current Art," *Magazine of Art* 9 (1887): 347.

78 "Current Art," *Magazine of Art* 11 (1888): 296.

79 "The Grosvenor Exhibition," *Athenaeum* 61 (May 12, 1888): 606.

80 "The Grosvenor Gallery," *Vanity Fair* 33 (April 28, 1888): 246.

81 October 10, 1887, letter from Edward Burne-Jones to Charles A. Hallé in the collection of the National Art Library, Victoria & Albert Museum.

82 For additional details on the correspondence between Lindsay, Hallé, and Carr, see Denney, "Exhibition Reforms and Systems," 279–82.

83 "The Grosvenor Gallery," *Athenaeum* 62 (May 11, 1889): 604.

84 "The Grosvenor Gallery," *Art Journal* 51 (1889): 192.

85 "The Summer Exhibitions at Home and Abroad: The Royal Academy, The Grosvenor, and the New Gallery," *Art Journal* 52 (1890): 161.

CHAPTER 5.
WHISTLER'S DECORATIVE DARKNESS

1   See diary extracts of Alan S. Cole, March 5, 1877 (Pennell-Whistler Collection, Manuscript Division, Library of Congress; hereafter cited as PWC). For a recent account of Whistler's decorative ensemble, see Linda Merrill, "Whistler's Peacock Room Revisited," *The Magazine Antiques* 143 (June 1993): 894–901. Merrill's comprehensive forthcoming book on this subject will clarify the project's chronology and many of the assumptions that have accrued around its history.

2   Although the Grosvenor Gallery catalogue for 1877 lists seven contributions by Whistler, his portrait of Thomas Carlyle (see fig. 51), submitted too late to be noted in the catalogue, was shown in the vestibule.

3   Whistler painted and exhibited his first London Nocturnes in 1871, and he regularly submitted them to exhibitions in London and elsewhere in subsequent years.

4   The events and issues of the trial are explored fully in Linda Merrill, *A Pot of Paint: Aesthetics on Trial in Whistler v. Ruskin* (Washington, D.C., and London: Smithsonian Institution Press in collaboration with the Freer Gallery of Art, 1992).

5   [Tom Taylor], "The Grosvenor Gallery," *Times* (May 1, 1877): 10. Numerous other reviews of Whistler's contributions to the inaugural exhibition directed similar sarcasm at a full-length portrait of the actor Henry Irving (*Arrangement in Black, No. 3: Sir Henry Irving as Philip II of Spain*, Metropolitan Museum of Art, New York). For a compilation of newspaper and periodical reviews of Whistler's work that includes responses to the first three Grosvenor exhibitions, see Catherine Carter Goebel, "Arrangement in Black and White: The Making of a Whistler Legend," 2 vols. (Ph.D. diss., Northwestern University, 1988).

6   "The Grosvenor Gallery," *Daily Telegraph*, May 1, 1877, 5.

7   Julian Hawthorne, "Artists of the Future," *New York Daily Tribune*, June 4, 1878, 2.

8   Taylor, "Grosvenor Gallery," 10. Critics at the 1877 exhibition frequently pointed to the Carlyle portrait as the most comprehensible and successful work Whistler showed that year.

9   Sidney Colvin, "The Grosvenor Gallery," *Fortnightly Review* 27 (June 1877): 831.

10   On the Grosvenor and the display of the "decorative picture," see Charles Hallé's remarks cited by Colleen Denney in chapter 1.

11   Between 1877 and 1884 Whistler showed twenty-nine oil paintings at the Grosvenor, thirteen of which were Nocturnes.

12   My notion of a "portraiture of place" derives from Joseph Pennell: "In the Thames plates, it was Mr. Whistler's aim to show the river as it was in 1859, and each of them is a little portrait of a place, a perfect work of art" ("Mr. Whistler's Etchings," *Daily Chronicle*, February 22, 1895; reprint, Frederick Keppel, comp., *Concerning the Etchings of Mr. Whistler* [New York: Keppel, n.d.], 9). For earlier appreciations of what many critics deemed the penetrating veracity of Whistler's London graphics, see William Michael Rossetti, "Mr. Whistler's Etchings," *Reader* 14 (April 4, 1863): 342; "A Whistle for Whistler," *Punch* 60 (June 17, 1871): 224–25; "Mr. Whistler's Etchings," *Saturday Review* 32 (August 12, 1871); and Frederick Wedmore, "Mr. Whistler's Theories and Mr. Whistler's Art," *Nineteenth Century* 6 (August 1879): 334.

13   Merrill, *Pot of Paint*, 151. In his own, published version of this remark, Whistler stated that the picture was not intended as a "'correct' portrait of the bridge," but as "only a moonlight scene" in which things may not appear "as you know them in broad daylight" (Whistler, *The Gentle Art of Making Enemies*, 2nd ed. [1892; reprint, New York: Dover, 1967], 8). Later in the trial he applied the idea to another Nocturne, which, he said, was "not painted to offer the portrait of a particular place" (Merrill, *Pot of Paint*, 154).

14   "Royal Academy Exhibition: Middle Room," *Daily Telegraph*, May 11, 1865, 5. The painting, commissioned in 1859 and completed in the early 1860s, was originally shown at the Academy simply as *Old Battersea Bridge*.

15   Referring to the same Royal Academy exhibition of 1865, one observer of the British art scene lamented: "While figure pictures have still the chance of being hung according to their merits, landscapes are being gradually excluded or placed in positions so unfavorable as to render them invisible" (*Cornhill Magazine*, quoted in Ann Bermingham, *Landscape and Ideology: The English Rustic Tradition, 1740–1860* [Berkeley: University of California Press, 1986], 157).

16   Oscar Wilde, "The Grosvenor Gallery," *Dublin University Magazine*, 90 (July 1877): 124.

17   E. R. Pennell and J. Pennell, "Appendix I: Whistler as a Decorator," in *The Whistler Journal* (Philadelphia: J. B. Lippincott, 1921), 299. Whistler's musical nomenclature of "symphony," "harmony," "arrangement," and "nocturne" further encouraged reviewers to respond to his

pictures as if they constituted a category apart from the conventional art of painting.

18 William Michael Rossetti, *Rossetti Papers, 1862–1870* (New York: Scribner's, 1903), 233–34; entry dated May 29 [1867]. My approach here to issues of "decoration" owes a great deal to Steven Levine, "Décor/Decorative/Decoration in Claude Monet's Art," *Arts Magazine* 51 (February 1977): 136–39; and to Robert Herbert, "The Decorative and the Natural in Monet's Cathedrals," in John Rewald and Frances Weitzenhoffer, eds., *Aspects of Monet* (New York: Abrams, 1984), 162–79. By *decorative* I mean, in accordance with Herbert's succinct definition, an aesthetic concentration on surface effects, such as color and pattern, that seem to attach as much to architectural ornamentation as to traditional conceptions of easel painting (162–63).

19 Whistler to Fantin-Latour, n.d. [September 1867], PWC 1. Subsequent references to the "1867 letter" are to this document. For the complete text of the letter in a somewhat different translation, see Robin Spencer, ed., *Whistler: A Retrospective* (New York: Hugh Lauter Levin Associates, 1989), 82–84.

20 Whistler showed *At the Piano* (1858–59, Taft Museum, Cincinnati) and *The Thames in Ice* (1860; Freer Gallery of Art, Washington, D.C.) at the Salon (April 15–June 5, 1867). His submissions to the Exposition Universelle (April 1–October 1, 1867), in addition to *Brown and Silver*, were *Symphony in White, No. 1: The White Girl* (1862, National Gallery of Art, Washington, D.C.), *Wapping* (1860–64, National Gallery of Art, Washington, D.C.), and the seascape *Crepuscule in Flesh Colour and Green: Valparaiso* (1866, Tate Gallery, London).

21 Courbet had submitted only four paintings to the Exposition Universelle and nothing at all to the Salon. *Exposition des oeuvres de M. G. Courbet* opened in a purpose-built pavilion on May 29, 1867, with 115 paintings, including 20 of the seascapes Courbet had painted in 1865 while at Trouville with Whistler, and *La Jo, femme d'Irlande*, a portrait of Whistler's former mistress, Joanna Hiffernan, who had accompanied the American artist to Normandy.

22 The Exposition Universelle ended on November 15. Courbet took down his exhibition in early December; see his letter to Alfred Bruyas, dated December 9, 1855, in *Letters of Gustave Courbet*, ed. and trans. Petra ten-Doesschate Chu (Chicago: University of Chicago Press, 1992), 147.

23 Among similar expressions of this well-established distinction in French academic discourse, Charles Blanc's *Le Grammaire des arts du dessin*,

coincidentally published in 1867, equates the aggressive, organizational male principle with line, and the passive, instinctual female with color. See Richard Shiff, *Cézanne and the End of Impressionism* (Chicago: University of Chicago Press, 1984), 82–83.

24 *Mr. Whistler's "Ten O'Clock"* (London: Chatto and Windus, 1888), 15. Whistler first presented his "Ten O'Clock" lecture, the codification of his mature aesthetic views, to a fashionable invited London audience in March 1885, repeating it later that year in Cambridge and Oxford. The connection between the phrase in Whistler's letter to Fantin-Latour and its reappearance in the lecture is also made in E. R. Pennell and J. Pennell, *The Life of James McNeill Whistler*, 2 vols. (Philadelphia: J. B. Lippincott, 1908), 1:147.

25 Like the Peacock Room itself, the *Six Projects* are now in the collection of the Freer Gallery of Art, Washington, D.C. The remaining four pictures include a nude *Venus* and three groups of women in diaphanous drapery—*Symphony in Blue and Pink, Symphony in White and Red,* and *Symphony in Green and Violet*—complementing those represented in figs. 56 and 57.

26 William Michael Rossetti and Algernon C. Swinburne, *Notes on the Royal Academy Exhibition, 1868* (London: Hotten, 1868), 44–45. Here Swinburne digressed from his subject; the *Projects* were never shown at the Academy.

27 For figural studies connected with the oil sketches that comprise the *Six Projects*, see Margaret F. MacDonald, *James McNeill Whistler: Drawings, Pastels, and Watercolours, A Catalogue Raisonné* (New Haven: Yale University Press, 1995), M341–350.

28 For a discussion of these influences, see Robin Spencer, "Whistler and Japan: Work in Progress," in *Japonisme in Art: An International Symposium*, ed. for the Society for the Study of Japonisme (Tokyo: Committee for the Year 2001, 1980), 66; David Park Curry, *James McNeill Whistler at the Freer Gallery of Art*, exh. cat. (New York: Norton, in association with the Freer Gallery of Art, 1984), 107–10; Toshio Watanabe, "Eishi Prints in Whistler's Studio? Eighteenth-Century Japanese Prints in the West Before 1870," *Burlington Magazine* 128 (December 1986): 878; and, on the *Six Projects* in general and Moore's particular relevance to them, John Sandberg, "Whistler Studies," *Art Bulletin* 50 (March 1968): 59–64.

29 "Exhibition of Mr. Whistler's Paintings and Drawings," *Pall Mall Gazette*, June 13, 1874, 11.

30 Whistler to Fantin-Latour, PWC 1: "Si j'ai fait des progrès c'est dans la science de la couleur que je

crois avoir presque entièrement aprofondi [*sic*] et réduite à un système." The precise date of this letter is uncertain. Whistler gives his address as 2 Lindsey Row, where he moved following his Valparaiso interlude. That fact, together with the discussion of certain of Fantin's recent paintings, would suggest that the letter itself dates from the first half of 1867.

31 Whistler to George A. Lucas, letter postmarked January 18, 1873 (John A. Mahey, ed., "The Letters of James McNeill Whistler to George A. Lucas," *Art Bulletin* 49 [September 1867]: 252–53).

32 T. R. Way, *Memories of James McNeill Whistler, the Artist* (London: John Lane, 1912), 27.

33 For an account of Moore's exacting, exhaustive methods, which involved successive studies of the nude and clothed model, separate drawings of the drapery, and variations on his color schemes, see Alfred Lys Baldry, *Albert Moore: His Life and Works* (London: George Bell, 1894), 69–87.

34 Pennell and Pennell, *Life of Whistler*, 1:150.

35 Although he occasionally produced rough sketches of nocturnal images executed on site and in the dark, Whistler more systematically committed such motifs to memory without the aid of drawing, turning his back on the scene that attracted his attention and reciting its essential elements to a companion who would check the artist's accuracy. For eyewitness accounts of the process, see Way, *Memories of Whistler*, 67–68; Mortimer Menpes, *Whistler as I Knew Him* (London: Adam and Charles Black, 1904), 11; and Bernhard Sickert, *Whistler* (London: Duckworth; New York: E. P. Dutton, n.d. [1908]), 111–12.

36 Merrill, *Pot of Paint*, 152.

37 Colvin, "The Grosvenor Gallery," 831–32.

38 See Merrill, *Pot of Paint*, 166.

39 Merrill, *Pot of Paint*, 145, 155.

40 Merrill, *Pot of Paint*, 172–75.

41 Merrill, *Pot of Paint*, 177, 179. Taylor's self-citation was taken from "Winter Exhibitions: The Dudley," *Times* (December 2, 1875): 4.

42 Wedmore, "Mr. Whistler's Theories," 336.

43 *The Correspondence of John Ruskin and Charles Eliot Norton*, ed. John Lewis Bradley and Ian Ousby (Cambridge: Cambridge University Press, 1987), 105; letter dated August 8, 1867.

44 Henry James, "The Picture Season in London" (1877), in John L. Sweeney, ed., *The Painter's Eye: Notes and Essays on the Pictorial Arts by Henry James* (1956; reprint, Madison: University of Wisconsin Press, 1989), 143.

45 Henry James, "The Grosvenor Gallery, 1878," in Sweeney, ed., *Painter's Eye*, 164–65.

46 During this period Whistler contributed to all but the Grosvenor exhibition of 1880, when he was at work in Venice under the auspices of the Fine Art Society (see chapter 8).

47 See Joris-Karl Huysmans, "Wisthler" [*sic*], in *Certains* (Paris: Tresse & Stock, 1889), 70.

CHAPTER 6. G. F. WATTS
AT THE GROSVENOR GALLERY

1 G. F. Watts, "The Present Conditions of Art," *Nineteenth Century* (February 1880): 250; for this reference see the reprint in M. S. Watts, *George Frederic Watts: The Annals of an Artist's Life* (London, 1912), 3:180. Appropriately, in Henry James's review of the first Grosvenor Gallery exhibition, there is a characterization of the *Nineteenth Century* vis-à-vis the Gallery itself: "Sir Coutts Lindsay is his own counsel, his own jury, and his ambition, I believe, is to make of the Grosvenor Gallery a sort of *Fortnightly Review,* or more correctly, *Nineteenth Century,* among exhibitions. He plays the same part as the thoroughly 'catholic' editor of the latter periodical, who invites the lion and the lamb to lie down together, allows an equal space in his pages to Cardinal Manning and Mr. Huxley." See "The Picture Season in London," in John L. Sweeney, ed., *The Painter's Eye: Notes and Essays on the Pictorial Arts by Henry James* (London: Rupert Hart-Davis, 1956), 139.

2 For a discussion of Watts's "symbolical" paintings, see Barbara Bryant, "The Origins of G. F. Watts's 'Symbolical' Paintings: A Lost Study Identified," *Porticus: Journal of the Memorial Art Gallery* (University of Rochester, N.Y.) 10/11 (1987–88): 52–59.

3 Virginia Surtees, *Coutts Lindsay, 1824–1913* (Norwich, England: Michael Russell, 1993), 52.

4 On the intimate friendship between Virginia, Countess Somers, and Lindsay, see Surtees, *Coutts Lindsay,* 6off.

5 Watts's portrait of Lindsay (once in the collection of the Watts Gallery, Compton, Surrey) was sold by the Maas Gallery, London, in 1968 to a collector in the United States and is now unlocated. Surtees (*Coutts Lindsay,* 89 and 198n16) suggests that Lindsay sat for Watts for the head of Edward I in the mural at Lincoln's Inn, with this study as the result. It is, however, known that the head of Edward I was taken from Watts's close friend, Charles Newton, not Lindsay. It seems more likely the portrait study was conceived as a work in its own right that never reached completion.

6 William Michael Rossetti identified Lindsay's portraits as "evidently based upon study of Mr. Watts" (*Fraser's Magazine* [1862]: 74).

7 In 1867, Watts had the unusual distinction of being elected an Associate and a full member of the Royal Academy in the same year without putting his name forward; he was elected solely on the basis of this reputation. Although he stopped exhibiting major subjects in 1851, by the early 1860s Watts again showed regularly.

8 This practice is discussed in my article on the evolution of the "symbolical" design for *Mischief* (Bryant, "Origins of G. F. Watts's 'Symbolical' Paintings," 55–57).

9 Letter from Watts to Rickards (Watts, *George Frederic Watts,* 1:302).

10 Letter from Watts to Rickards, ibid., 262.

11 Ibid.

12 Sidney Colvin, "Exhibition of Mr. Whistler's Pictures," *Academy* 13 (June 1874): 672–73.

13 David Park Curry, "Total Control: Whistler at an Exhibition," in Ruth E. Fine, ed., *Studies in the History of Art,* vol. 19, *James McNeill Whistler: A Reexamination,* Center for Advanced Study in the Visual Arts, Symposium Papers VI (Washington, D.C.: National Gallery of Art, 1987), 67–80, esp. 68–70.

14 Robin Spencer, "Whistler's First One-Man Exhibition Reconstructed," in Gabriel P. Weisberg and Laurinda S. Dixon, eds., *The Documented Image: Visions in Art History* (Syracuse, N.Y.: Syracuse University Press, 1987), 44.

15 Letter from Watts to Rickards (Watts, *George Frederic Watts,* 2:3–4).

16 The modern sources on the Grosvenor Gallery are Barrie Bullen, "The Palace of Art: Sir Coutts Lindsay and the Grosvenor Gallery," *Apollo* 102 (1975): 352–57; Michele Archambault, "The Grosvenor Gallery, 1877–1890" (Ph.D. diss., Courtauld Institute of Art, 1978); Colleen Denney, "Exhibition Reforms and Systems: The Grosvenor Gallery, 1877–1890" (Ph.D. diss., University of Minnesota, 1990); Surtees, *Coutts Lindsay,* 42ff.; and Christopher Newall, *The Grosvenor Gallery Exhibitions: Change and Continuity in the Victorian Art World* (Cambridge: Cambridge University Press, 1995), which consists chiefly of a list of exhibitors and works.

17 Carr was closely involved with the earliest stages of planning for the new gallery; he wrote Dante Gabriel Rossetti by early April 1876 asking him to participate; see Rossetti's reference to this in a letter to Ford Madox Brown, April 7, 1876, in *Letters of Dante Gabriel Rossetti,* ed. Oswald Doughty and John Robert Wahl (Oxford; Oxford University Press, 1967), 3:1422–23. In the autumn of 1876 Carr and his wife, Alice, travelled to Balcarres on the invitation of the Lindsays to discuss plans for the Gallery; see Alice Comyns Carr, *J. Comyns Carr: Stray Memories,* by his wife, Alice Comyns Carr (London: Macmillan, 1920), 76. He was not listed officially as an assis-

tant director (along with Hallé) until 1879, Hallé having previously been listed as secretary.

18 "The Grosvenor Gallery," *Art Journal* (1877): 244.

19 Letter from Watts to Rickards, Watts Papers (formerly Watts Gallery).

20 On the reception of Burne-Jones's *Beguiling of Merlin* at the first Grosvenor Gallery, see Edward Morris, *Victorian and Edwardian Painting in the Lady Lever Art Gallery: British Artists Born after 1810 Excluding the Early Pre-Raphaelites* (London: HMSO, 1994), 7–11.

21 See illustration in Caroline Dakers, *Clouds: The Biography of a Country House* (New Haven and London: Yale University Press, 1993), facing 94, and color plate VIII.

22 Surtees, *Coutts Lindsay*, 133.

23 Smaller versions of *Love and Death* appeared at the Dudley Gallery in 1870 and at the annual exhibition of the Manchester Institution in 1874.

24 See note 1.

25 M. S. Watts, *George Frederic Watts*, 1:283.

26 Sidney Colvin, "The Grosvenor Gallery," *Fortnightly Review* 27 (June 1877): 823.

27 Oscar Wilde, "The Grosvenor Gallery," *Dublin University Magazine* (July 1877): 119.

28 Ibid.

29 Ibid. 119, 126.

30 "The Picture Season in London, 1877," *Galaxy* (August 1877), reprinted in Sweeney, ed., *Painter's Eye*, 139–47.

31 Ibid., 139.

32 Ibid.

33 Ibid., 142.

34 J. Comyns Carr, *Some Eminent Victorians: Personal Recollections in the World of Art and Letters* (London, 1908), 64.

35 *L'Art* was first published in April 1875 from offices in Paris with Charles Tardieu as its editor.

36 A. Carr, *J. Comyns Carr*, 143n17.

37 F. H. W. Sheppard, general ed., *Survey of London*, vol. 40, *The Grosvenor Estate in Mayfair. Part II: The Buildings* (London: Athlone Press for Greater London Council, 1980), 60–61. The numbers on New Bond Street ran consecutively.

38 From a reading of Lindsay's correspondence with his mother, Archambault notes that in 1878 he had let two of the shops and was to sign a lease for 132 New Bond Street. He was obliged to purchase the leases to preserve "ancient lights" ("The Grosvenor Gallery, 1877–1890," 283, 284–85; Denney, "Exhibition Reforms and Systems," 30; Surtees, *Coutts Lindsay*, 146–47). The two shops were probably those which flanked the main entrance (no. 136) to the Grosvenor Gallery, i.e., 135 and 137. At the time of the opening of the gallery, these two shops were still being built, according to the *Builder* (April 28, 1877): 424. By 1878 both were finished and ready to let.

39 None of the literature on the Grosvenor Gallery has taken into account the Westminster Rate books for New Bond Street. This source gives new information and confirms an interesting link between Lindsay and the magazine *L'Art*. The rate books for 1878 (Parish of St. George, Hanover Square) make it clear that 136 was the main entrance of the Grosvenor, since it was rated ten times more than the shop fronts to either side (135 and 137). An adjacent shop, 134, which became the offices of *L'Art*, was rated even lower. It seems that this was one of the additional sites Lindsay obtained (ibid.). More important, while Lindsay is listed as leaseholder and ratepayer for 134, a further note is written into the rate book with other remarks naming "James [*sic*] Comyns Carr" as the person who actually paid the rates for 134. This reference shows that Lindsay had given Carr official responsibility for the property which served as the English editorial outpost of *L'Art*.

40 Carr, *Some Eminent Victorians*, 140. Alice Carr was less charitable in her assessment of *L'Art* as "too pretentious and expensive a production" that failed partly because French was "little appreciated in this country"; see Eve Adam, ed., *Mrs. J. Comyns Carr's Reminiscences* (London: Hutchinson, 1926), 90. J. Comyns Carr went on to edit other periodicals in London.

41 In 1878, Librairie de L'Art published Carr's *Examples of Contemporary Art* (London, 1878), "with etchings from representative works by living English and foreign artists." *L'Art* was an important forum for etchers; according to one writer, "*L'Art* has done more than any other English periodical in making known to the public the modern masters of etching." For the Grosvenor Gallery, it copublished the *Illustrated Catalogue of the Winter Exhibitions and Old Master and Water-Colour Drawings* (1877–78).

42 Joseph Comyns Carr, "La Grosvenor Gallery," *L'Art* 10 (1877): 265; an English translation appears in Carr, *Examples of Contemporary Art*.

43 *Examples of Contemporary Art*, 3–4.

44 Ibid., 4.

45 This subject will be examined further in my essay for the catalogue of the forthcoming Symbolism in Britain exhibition at the Tate Gallery in 1997.

46 Tissot's bizarre allegory, *The Challenge*, the first work in a planned though unexecuted series entitled *The Triumph of the Will*, appeared at auction (Sotheby's, London, June 8, 1993, lot 25).

47 See in John Ingamells, *The Wallace Collection: Catalogue of Pictures*, vol. 2, *French Nineteenth Century* (London: Trustees of the Wallace Collection, 1986), 132–33, no. P.342, ill. on 133.

48 For his oil painting of a woman by a river, *Rêverie*, which is akin to Tissot's studies of Mrs. Newton, see *Musée d'Orsay: Catalogue sommaire illustré des peintures* (Paris: Réunion des musées nationaux, 1990), 1:227 (RF 642).

49 For an example of Weber's work see *Musée d'Orsay*, 2:483 (RF 441, *La curée du chevreuil*, bought for the French State in 1868).

50 Foreign-born sculptors included Henri Chapu (1833–1891), Eugène Delaplanche (1836–1891), Paul Dubois (1829–1905), Count Gleichen (1833–1891), and Girolamo Massini (listed as "Professor"). Auguste Rodin showed at later Grosvenor Gallery exhibitions, as did Augustus Saint-Gaudens. For the contributions of French sculptors to the Grosvenor Gallery, see Benedict Read, *Victorian Sculpture* (New Haven and London: Yale University Press, 1982), 301, with illustrations of works by Dubois and Delaplanche.

51 In the catalogue the street number for the office of *L'Art* is given as 136, rather than 134, a confusion which only underlines the close connection between the Grosvenor Gallery and *L'Art*'s English operation.

52 Pierre Mathieu, *Gustave Moreau: Sa vie, son oeuvre, catalogue raisonné de l'oeuvre achevé* (Fribourg, Switzerland: Office du Livre, 1976), 14, 128–29.

53 Salon catalogue, *Explication des ouvrages de peinture, sculpture . . . au palais des Champs-Elysées* (Paris, 1876): *Salomé*, no. 1506, with "peintures," and *L'Apparition*, aquarelle, no. 2774, with "dessins, cartoons, etc."

54 *L'Art* 5 (1876): 121ff., 207ff.; see *L'Art* 13 (1878): opp. 320 for an etching of *L'Apparition* published at the time of its showing at the Exposition Universelle in Paris.

55 Paul Leroi, "Vade-mecum du Salon de 1876," *L'Art* 5 (1876): 158.

56 The oil version of *L'Apparition* in the Fogg Art Museum, Harvard University, is often overlooked in discussions of the versions of the subject. As a finished and signed work, dating from approximately 1876, it may well be the work shown at the Grosvenor. While smaller in size compared to the Louvre watercolor, it is clearly not as late as some of the other oil versions of the subject, such as the one at the Musée Moreau (no. 222). However, a strong argument in favor of the Louvre watercolor as the picture exhibited at the Grosvenor is that it is thickly painted and not dissimilar to an oil painting in appearance. It would also seem to be a fairly straightforward matter to send on an already exhibited work from Paris to London. Mathieu gives no reference to the exhibition of this subject at the Grosvenor in his account of the versions of *L'Apparition* and *Salomé*; see Mathieu, *Gustave Moreau*, 315, nos. 157–61.

57 William Michael Rossetti, *Academy* (May 5, 1877): 396.

58 See Bryant, "Origins of G. F. Watts's 'Symbolical' Paintings," 59.

59 Explanatory text for the catalogue of the Grosvenor Gallery's *Collection of Work by G. F. Watts, R.A., 1881–82*, no. 35; see Bryant, "Origins of G. F. Watts's 'Symbolical' Paintings," 56.

60 Henry Blackburn, ed., *Grosvenor Notes: With Facsimiles of Sketches by the Artists* (London: Chatto and Windus, 1879), 28.

61 F. G. Stephens, "The Grosvenor Gallery Exhibition," *Athenaeum* (May 10, 1879): 607.

62 "The Picture Galleries," *Saturday Review* (May 17, 1879): 619.

63 "For the first time we are witnessing serious efforts, expressing by line and color some of the greatest truths of the imagination, which we never lacked in English literature. Mr Watts occupies, in this movement, an eminent place. His talent has rarely been presented to such advantage as in the exhibition of this year at the Grosvenor Gallery." J. Comyns Carr, "La Royal Academy et la Grosvenor Gallery," *L'Art* 22 (1880): 172, 173–74.

64 Watts, *George Frederic Watts*, 2:4.

65 Several retrospectives followed the successful showing of Watts's work: in 1882–83, Lawrence Alma-Tadema (along with a large group of works by Cecil Lawson, who had died in 1882) and in 1886 John Everett Millais. In 1887 the Grosvenor Gallery staged an exhibition of the recent work of Vassili Vereschagin, the Russian realist painter whose primary subject matter was war. Although Vereschagin provides an interesting parallel to Watts's international reputation, the exhibition at

the Grosvenor Gallery was not a retrospective but a collection of his recent work.

66 On Courbet's and Manet's exhibitions, see Patricia Mainardi, *Art and Politics of the Second Empire: The Universal Expositions of 1855 and 1867* (New Haven and London: Yale University Press, 1987), 57–61, 138ff.

67 Watts's exhibition in New York in 1884–85 was first discussed as the Metropolitan's first "blockbuster" by the author at a symposium at Leighton House, London, in 1993, and her findings will be published in due course.

CHAPTER 7. RUSTIC NATURALISM AT THE GROSVENOR GALLERY

1 Albert Ludovici jun., "The Whistlerian Dynasty of Suffolk Street," *Art Journal* (1906), 193.

2 D. S. MacColl, "Confessions of a Keeper," in *What Is Art?* (Harmondsworth: Penguin, 1940), 269.

3 For a discussion of the decor and fittings of the Grosvenor Gallery, see chapter 1 and Colleen Denney, "Exhibition Reforms and Systems: The Grosvenor Gallery, 1877–1890" (Ph.D. diss., University of Minnesota, 1990). Denney quotes a number of reviews and first impressions of the gallery to which may be added that of Julia Cartwright, who noted in her diary, "a Grand Palazzo entrance with vases and marble scattered about. Ceilings and walls are gorgeous with gilding of stars and crescents—the pictures are so well arranged in groups and only two rooms so one does it easily. The Whistlers are very mad" (entry for May 16, 1877, in Angela Emanuel, ed., *A Bright Remembrance: The Diaries of Julia Cartwright* [London: Weidenfeld and Nicholson, 1989], 91).

4 Lindsay borrowed extensively for the first Grosvenor exhibition, his Heilbuths coming from Sir Richard Wallace, his Doyles coming from the Duke of Buccleuch, and his Costas from the Howard family.

5 See, for instance, Paula Gillett, *The Victorian Painter's World* (New Brunswick, N.J.: Rutgers University Press, 1990).

6 Frederick Wedmore, *Studies in English Art* (London, 1876), 216.

7 H. S. Marks, *Frederick Walker, ARA,* 1896, 37; For a fuller account of the relationship between French and British paintings of rural subject matter, see Kenneth McConkey, "Rustic Naturalism in Britain," in Gabriel P. Weisberg, ed., *The European Realist Tradition* (Bloomington: Indiana University Press, 1983), 215–28.

8 Claude Phillips, *Frederick Walker and His Works* (London, 1905), 6.

9 This picture remains unlocated. It was originally acquired by Captain Henry Hill of Brighton, whose collection also contained works by Degas and Monet. For further reference see Alice Meynell, "Pictures from the Hill Collection," *Magazine of Art* (1882): 1–7, 80–84, 116–21. Meynell wrote of the picture: "The merry children link hands and form a chain before the old man on the road, but they will not stay his advance, any more than they will be able to resist the progress of Time, which he symbolizes, and which will bring them to be as decrepit as the old

woman walking up the hill, and will finally cut them down with the scythe" (2–3).

10 For further reference to this work see Wilfrid Meynell, ed., *The Modern School of Art* (London: Cassell, 1886–88), 2:106.

11 Overt references to *La Mort et les Jeunes Filles* treated as a classical subject by Puvis de Chavannes are suppressed. The scene is set in the English countryside. Diverting naturalistic details draw the eye and diffuse the effect. The concentration of purpose in Henry Herbert La Thangue's much later *The Man with the Scythe*, a Chantrey purchase of 1896, is blunted.

12 "Pictures of the Year III," *Magazine of Art* 2 (1879): 164.

13 Meynell, *Modern School of Art*, 4:124.

14 Walter Shaw Sparrow, *Memories of Life and Art* (London: Bodley Head, 1925), 117; Lawson died in 1882; *The August Moon* is at the Tate Gallery, London.

15 For a discussion of the critical responses to Legros's early work, see Alexander Seltzer, "Alphonse Legros: The Development of an Archaic Visual Vocabulary in Nineteenth Century Art" (Ph.D. diss., State University of New York at Binghamton, 1980); Musée des Beaux-Arts, Dijon, *Alphonse Legros* (catalogue of an exhibition by Timothy J. Wilcox, 1988).

16 *Times* (May 5, 1864): 8; see also *Art Journal* (1864): 166.

17 W. E. Henley, "Alphonse Legros," *Art Journal* (1881): 295.

18 *Some Modern Artists and Their Work* (1883), 178.

19 For reference to *Close of Day* see Newcastle upon Tyne Polytechnic Art Gallery, *Peasantries* (catalogue of an exhibition by Kenneth McConkey, with Jack Dawson and Ysanne Holt, 1981), 25–26.

20 Wedmore, *Studies in English Art*, 234.

21 For further reference see Linda S. Ferber and William H. Gerdts, *The New Path: Ruskin and the American Pre-Raphaelites* (catalogue of an exhibition at the Brooklyn Museum, 1985), 267–69 (entry by Barbara Dayer Gallati).

22 Herein lay the seeds of the eventual collapse of confidence in the gallery. Too many of its contributing artists were, by the second half of the 1880s, seen as old-fashioned time-servers. For a discussion of the aesthetic decline of the Grosvenor see Denney, "Exhibition Reforms and Systems."

23 Kenneth McConkey, "After Holbein: Jules Bastien-Lepage's 'Portrait of the Prince of Wales," *Arts Magazine* (October 1984): 103–07; see also Kenneth McConkey, *Edwardian Portraits* (Woodbridge, England: Antique Collectors' Club, 1987), 64–66.

24 For a discussion of British responses to this picture see Kenneth McConkey, "Listening to the Voices: A study of Jules Bastien-Lepage's 'Joan of Arc Listening to the Voices,'" *Arts Magazine* (January 1982): 154–60.

25 Henry Blackburn, ed., *Grosvenor Notes* (London: Chatto & Windus, 1880), 8.

26 "Pictures of the Year IV," *Magazine of Art* (1880): 400. Similar approaches were taken in the *Art Journal* (1880): 188, and *Athenaeum* (1880): 605. For further reference see Marie-Madeleine Aubrun, *Jules Bastien-Lepage, 1848–1884: Catalogue raisonné de l'oeuvre* (Paris, 1985), 172–75.

27 *Illustrated London News* (May 8, 1880): 451.

28 W. C. Brownell, "Bastien-Lepage, Painter and Psychologist," *Magazine of Art* (1883): 271.

29 *Spectator* (June 12, 1880): 751.

30 For further reference see Kenneth McConkey, "The Bouguereau of the Naturalists: Bastien-Lepage and British Art," *Art History* 1, no. 3 (1978): 371–82; see also James Thompson, ed., *The Peasant in French Nineteenth-Century Art* (catalogue of an exhibition at Trinity College, Dublin, 1980), 99–102.

31 Such was La Thangue's precocity that he was given a letter of introduction by Frederic Leighton to enable him to secure immediate entry into the Ecole des Beaux-Arts under Gérôme; see Oldham Art Gallery, *A Painter's Harvest: Works by Henry Herbert La Thangue, 1859–1929* (catalogue of an exhibition by Kenneth McConkey, 1978), 7.

32 For further reference to *A Portrait (Girl with a Skipping Rope)* see McConkey, *Edwardian Portraits*, 77; Bastien-Lepage's influence can be seen elsewhere in La Thangue's early work, most notably in *Portrait of a Girl: The Striped Blouse* (cat. 29). La Thangue's Grosvenor exhibits during these years are (with gallery catalogue numbers in parentheses): 1882, *Study in a Boat-building Yard on the French Coast* (46), *A Study* (176), *A Portrait* (333); 1883, *Spring in Brittany* (139), *A Portrait* (266); 1884, *A Poor French Family* (262). In the context of the present discussion, it should be noted that Whistler's *Harmony in Grey and Green: Miss Cicely Alexander* was re-exhibited at the Grosvenor in 1881 (113).

33 This tendency is confirmed by contemporary reviewers; see, for instance, *Magazine of Art* (1880): 398, quoted in Bradford Art Galleries and Tyne and Wear County Council Museums, *Sir George Clausen, R.A., 1852–1944* (catalogue of an exhibition by Kenneth McConkey, 1980), 27, and underscored by the print of Henri Gervex's *Retour du Bal* (Salon of 1879) hanging on the wall in the background.

34 Sir George Clausen, R.A., "Autobiographical Notes," *Artwork* 25 (Spring 1931): 19, quoted in Bradford Art Galleries, *Sir George Clausen*, 29.

35 Bradford Art Galleries, *Sir George Clausen*, 35.

36 *Academy* (May 5, 1883): 317.

37 *Magazine of Art* (1883): 352; *Illustrated London News* (May 5, 1883): 438.

38 For further reference to this sequence of works see Bradford Art Galleries, *Sir George Clausen*, 38–39; see also Kenneth McConkey, "Figures in a Field—*Winter Work* by Sir George Clausen," *Art at Auction 1982–83* (1983): 72–77. Bruce Laughton, prior to the discovery of Clausen's glass-plate negatives, first speculated upon the use of photography in Clausen's work of this period; see Fine Art Society, *Channel Packet: Paris-London, 1880–1920* (exhibition catalogue, 1969), n.p. In *Beyond Impressionism: The Naturalist Impulse* (New York: Abrams, 1992), 111, Gabriel P. Weisberg rightly sees Clausen's accumulation of documentary evidence informing the picture as a European naturalist strategy. The picture is also, however, a single image drawn from the connected processes of sheep husbandry seen elsewhere in Clausen's work, in which turnips, mistaken by Weisberg as sugar beets, are prepared as sheep fodder.

39 George Moore, *Modern Painting* (London, 1893), 117–20.

40 Sold at Sotheby's, New York, October 27, 1988, lot 146, as *The Potato Harvesters.*

41 Walker Art Gallery, Liverpool; Henry Blackburn, ed., *Grosvenor Notes* (London: Chatto & Windus, 1884), 9.

42 For a discussion of the derivation of this work see: Bradford Art Galleries, *Sir George Clausen*, 35–37; Newcastle upon Tyne Polytechnic Art Gallery, *Peasantries*, 49–50; Kenneth McConkey, "Dejection's Portrait: Naturalist Images of Woodcutters in Late Nineteenth-Century Art," *Arts Magazine* (April 1986): 86–87.

43 Meynell, *Modern School of Art* 4:131–33. Meynell, several years before Monet's efforts to preserve the poplars on the banks of the Epte, uses Clausen's picture as an opportunity to commend the study of French poplars to artists for the "quaint but lovely compositions" to be derived from "the effects of series and perspective" (133).

44 *Art Journal* (1887): 283.

45 Ibid.

46 Oscar Wilde, *The Picture of Dorian Gray* (1891; Harmondsworth: Penguin, 1966), 8: "The Academy is too large and too vulgar. Whenever I've gone there, there have been either so many people that I have not been able to see the pictures, which was dreadful, or so many pictures that I have not been able to see the people, which was worse. The Grosvenor is really the only place."

47 *Art Journal* (1886): 188; see also *Magazine of Art* (1886): 296.

48 For a fuller discussion see Kenneth McConkey, *Impressionism in Britain* (catalogue of an exhibition at the Barbican Art Gallery, London: Yale University Press, 1995), 30–41.

49 The organizing body in this case was the London International Exhibition Society, which enlisted the support of important foreign artists. Bastien-Lepage, for instance, exhibited *Pauvre Fauvette* and *La Petite Coquette* at the third exhibition in April 1882.

50 Eve Adam, ed., *Mrs. J. Comyns Carr's Reminiscences* (London: Hutchinson, 1926), 42, 54; Charles Hallé, *Notes from a Painter's Life, Including the Founding of Two Galleries* (London: John Murray, 1909), 66–67.

51 This letter was reproduced in full in the catalogue of the *Exhibition of Nineteenth-Century French Painters*, held at M. Knoedler and Co., London, June-July 1923. Douglas Cooper does not explicitly refer to this letter in his seminal study of the contacts between the French Impressionists and the English art establishment in *The Courtauld Collection: A Catalogue and Introduction* (London: Athlone, 1954). In a subsequent article in the *Times Literary Supplement* (June 4, 1954: 368), however, he quotes the letter in full. This letter is referred to in D. S. MacColl, *Life, Work and Setting of Philip Wilson Steer* (London: Faber and Faber, 1945), 35.

52 Cooper (*Courtauld Collection*) suggests that they were prompted to write to Lindsay by Durand-Ruel and that the reference to Turner was merely a ploy to ensure his sympathy. For a fuller discussion of the relationship between French Impressionists and English art, see McConkey, *Impressionism in Britain.*

53 *Art Journal* (1888): 187.

54 *Runaway* remains untraced. A related canvas depicting only the background field-workers, entitled *Returning from the Fields,* was sold at Phillips, London, November 14, 1989, lot 28.

55 *Leaving Home* (Forbes Magazine Collection) was exhibited at the New Gallery. For further reference see Oldham Art Gallery, *A Painter's Harvest,* 24.

56 For a fuller discussion of the cultural significance of rural life in late Victorian England see: Raymond Williams, *The Country and the City* (New York: Oxford University Press, 1973); Martin J. Weiner, *English Culture and the Decline of the Industrial Spirit* (Cambridge: Cambridge University Press, 1981); Howard Newby, *Country Life: A Social History of Rural England* (Totowa, N.J.: Barnes and Noble, 1987).

57 Adam, ed., *Mrs. Carr's Reminiscences,* 68–73.

58 *English Illustrated Magazine* (1885): 551–59; 805–17.

59 In this regard it is necessary also to cite the early albums of photographs by P. H. Emerson and T. F. Goodall, which first appeared in 1886. For a fuller discussion see N. MacWilliam and V. Sekules, eds., *Life and Landscape: P. H. Emerson, Art and Photography in East Anglia, 1885–1900* (catalogue of an exhibition at the Sainsbury Centre, University of East Anglia, 1986).

60 For a fuller discussion of these issues see Mc-Conkey, *Impressionism in Britain.*

61 George Clausen, "Bastien-Lepage and Modern Realism," *Scottish Art Review* 1 (1888): 114, quoted in Bradford Art Galleries, *Sir George Clausen,* 31.

62 *Art Journal* (1888): 188. Throughout the 1880s Clausen had produced a series of half-length "portrait" studies of country types that included woodcutters, shepherds, field-workers, and the miller's man. These had the same quasi-documentary intention as Bastien-Lepage's paintings of the barge-boy and the *fauvette.* The Grosvenor version of *A Ploughboy* was re-exhibited at the Exposition Universelle, Paris, in 1889 and remains untraced. A second version of *A Ploughboy* (Gracefield Art Centre, Dumfries) contains an inscription in old English—"and we have the payne and traveyle, rayne and wynde in the fields"—a quotation taken from one of the leaders of the Peasants' Revolt. For further reference see Newcastle upon Tyne Polytechnic Art Gallery, *Peasantries,* 50–52.

63 Bradford Art Galleries, *Sir George Clausen,* 50.

64 *Art Journal* (1889): 192. That Lindsay had lost interest in the Grosvenor Gallery after the departure of Hallé and Carr is confirmed in the correspondence between Sickert and Blanche. Around this time Sickert notes that Lindsay had employed Deschamps, formerly with Durand-Ruel, to stage his pastel exhibitions; see Jacques-Emile Blanche, *Portraits of a Lifetime* (London: J. M. Dent, 1937), 301–02.

65 Walter Shaw Sparrow, *John Lavery and His Work* (London: Kegan Paul, 1911?), 61.

66 *Art Journal* (1890): 171; see also *Magazine of Art* (1890): 326.

67 *Saturday Review* (May 10, 1890): 565.

68 This picture was originally *Touchstone,* a scene from *As You Like It,* in 1884 and gradually transmuted into its present form by the time of the Grosvenor show; see Roger Billcliffe, *The Glasgow Boys* (London: John Murray, 1985), 117–20.

69 For a fuller discussion of this work see Kenneth McConkey, *Sir John Lavery* (Edinburgh: Canongate, 1993), 49–52.

70 *Magazine of Art* (1890): 326.

71 *Saturday Review* (May 10, 1890): 565.

72 Unpublished MS. letter dated November 24, 1889.

73 There was a consensus at this time, albeit more implicit than explicit, on notions of perception. Pupils of Gérôme tended to the view that we all see the world in the same way and that this perception was analogous to some of the "truths" of photography. See McConkey, *Impressionism in Britain,* 52.

74 Bradford Art Galleries, *Sir George Clausen,* 52–54; The title *The Girl at the Gate* was borrowed from a story by Wilkie Collins serialized in 1885, the content of which bears no apparent connection to Clausen's picture.

CHAPTER 8. "BEST SHOP IN LONDON"

I am grateful to the staff of The Fine Art Society, in particular to managing director Andrew McIntosh Patrick and deputy managing director Peyton Skipwith, for allowing me access to the gallery records and for answering numerous requests. I am also thankful for the hospitality of Charles Robertson, Gopa Roy, and Patricia Rubin. Two publications of the society at the time of its hundredth anniversary in 1976 have been of paramount assistance: *Centenary Exhibition 1876–1976* (hereinafter cited as *Centenary*), which provides brief essays by various authors on highlights of the society's history, and *One Hundred Years of Exhibitions at The Fine Art Society*, which gives a fairly complete list of the society's more than 2,000 exhibitions since its founding, as well as the names of artists who participated in its exhibitions and the authors who contributed to its catalogues. This chapter covers the society's history until 1890, the final year of the Grosvenor Gallery. Many of the artists mentioned here in connection with The Fine Art Society continued to exhibit there after that date.

1 Quoted in Wendy Baron, *Sickert* (London: Phaidon, 1973), 59.

2 Although there is no record in The Fine Art Society Minute Books (hereafter FAS Minute Books) stating that the company was founded specifically to publish reproductive prints, two important facts support this assumption. One of the earliest acts of the society was to purchase at great expense several copyrights to Elizabeth Thompson's paintings from J. Dickinson and Co. (see note 23); second, from its beginnings, family members who owned the publishing company Longman also owned a large share of the society's stock.

3 A reviewer in the November 4, 1896, issue of the *Sketch* noted: "Practically, the Society invented the fashion of holding one-man exhibitions which are usually the record of a year's work in some picturesque district of Great Britain or the Continent and are generally in watercolours, of which they have acquired, apart from the 'Societies,' almost a monopoly" (quoted in John O'Callaghan, "The Fine Art Society and E. W. Godwin," in *Centenary*, 8).

4 "Art Notes and Reviews: Works by the Late Samuel Palmer at The Fine Art Society's," *Art Journal* 33 (December 1881): 377.

5 FAS Minute Book, April 25, 1876.

6 Before it was published as a book in 1889, *Japan and Its Art* appeared as a series of lectures at the time of the exhibition at The Fine Art Society in 1888, and then as a series of twelve articles, "Notes on Japan and Its Art Wares" by Marcus B. Huish in the *Art Journal*; see "Art Books: 'Japan and Its Art'," *Illustrated London News* 94 (March 2, 1889): 274.

7 For his support of reproductive prints and printmakers, see Huish's impassioned letter to the editor, "The Decay of the Art of Engraving," *Times* (January 22, 1884): 12. Huish's thorough knowledge of the Victorian art scene is reflected in another of his articles, "Ten Years of British Art," *Nineteenth Century* 27 (January 1890): 102–18. Huish died on May 4, 1921. On his life and career see Joseph Foster, *Men-At-The-Bar* (London: Reeves and Turner, 1885), 230; *Times* (May 6, 1921): 13; *Who Was Who, 1916–1928* (London: A. & C. Black, 1929), 529; and J. A. Venn, *Alumni Cantabrigienses* (Cambridge: University Press, 1947), 3:481.

8 See Austin Brereton, *A Walk Down Bond Street: The Centenary Souvenir of the House of Ashton and Mitchell, 1820–1920* (London: Selwyn & Blount, 1920); H. B. Wheatley, *A Short History of Bond Street Old and New from the Reign of King James II to the Coronation of King George V* (London: Published for the Bond Streets Coronation Decoration Committee by The Fine Art Society, n.d.); and O'Callaghan, "Fine Art Society and E. W. Godwin," 5.

9 The importance of the Bond Street address is underscored in an advertisement of January 1, 1883, concerning the relocation to 116 and 117 New Bond Street of Goupil and Company, formerly of 25 Bedford Street: "Goupil and Company have long felt that the situation of the late galleries has been found too inconvenient to allow their seeing patrons so often as they would desire, and they trust that . . . their removal to the most famous of West-end thoroughfares, will insure to them not only more frequent visits from their present numerous amateurs, but also that the new galleries may offer sufficient attraction to draw all interested in the Fine Arts to their establishment" (*The Year's Art 1883*: 5).

10 Quoted in O'Callaghan, "Fine Art Society and E. W. Godwin," 5.

11 RIBA MSS Collection G/LO.1/12, quoted in O'-Callaghan, "Fine Art Society and E. W. Godwin," 7.

12 There were several possible reasons for the society's choice of Godwin. Originally, in the 1870s, Godwin had been selected as an architect for Bedford Park by the developer, Jonathan Carr, brother of J. Comyns Carr of the Grosvenor Gallery, and therefore he was associated with Aestheticism (Mark Girouard, *Sweetness and Light: The Queen Anne Movement, 1860–1900* [New Haven: Yale University Press, 1977], 160–62). Moreover, in addition to the society's relationship to Godwin through Whistler (for whom the architect designed the White House, beginning in 1877), Godwin may have been introduced to the society through board member Colonel Archibald Stuart Wortley, as Godwin had designed houses on Tite Street near Whistler's White House for Wortley's first cousin, Archibald (Archie) Stuart-Wortley (Girouard, *Sweetness and Light*, 177–88, and Mark Girouard, "Chelsea's Bohemian Studio Houses: The Victorian Artist at Home—II," *Country Life* 152 [November 23, 1972]: 1370–74).

13 O'Callaghan, "Fine Art Society and E. W. Godwin," 7. On Godwin and Japanese art see Toshio Watanabe, *High Victorian Japonisme*, vol. 10 of *Swiss Asian Studies* (Bern: Peter Lang, 1991), 185–96, and Nancy Burch Wilkinson, "Edward William Godwin and Japonisme in England" (Ph.D. diss., University of California at Los Angeles, 1987). Wilkinson also sees elements of the "Free Renaissance" style in the façade (ibid., 337). On Whistler and Godwin see ibid., 301ff., Girouard, *Sweetness and Light*, 177–83, and Girouard, "Chelsea's Bohemian Studio Houses," 1370–74.

14 O'Callaghan, "Fine Art Society and E. W. Godwin," 9.

15 "Art Notes and Reviews: Works by the Late Samuel Palmer," 377.

16 Rosamond Allwood, "The Fine Art Society and George Faulkner Armitage," in *Centenary*, 11.

17 The Fine Art Society purchased the copyright from the picture's owner, John Whitehead of Manchester (FAS Minute Book, April 11, 1876, and Lady Elizabeth Butler, *An Autobiography* [London: Fisher Press, 1993], 121). The FAS Minute Book of March 28, 1876, also records that Huish was authorized to pay up to 12,000 francs to the French artist Henri Félix Philippoteaux for his painting of Balaclava.

18 On Elizabeth Thompson's pictures *The Roll Call, Quatre Bras, Balaclava,* and *The Return from Inkerman,* see Rosemary Treble, *Great Victorian Pictures: Their Paths to Fame* (London: Arts Council of Great Britain, 1978), 79–81; Matthew Paul Lalumia, *Realism and Politics in Victorian Art of the Crimean War* (Ann Arbor, Mich.: UMI Press, 1984), 136–45; John Springhall, "'Up Guards and At Them!': British Imperialism and Popular Art, 1880–1914," in John M. Mackenzie, ed., *Imperialism and Popular Culture* (Manchester: Manchester University Press, 1986), 64–69; and Paul Usherwood and Jenny Spencer-Smith, *Lady Butler, Battle Artist, 1846–1933* (London: National Army Museum, 1987), 41–43 and passim.

19 Ruskin made this comment in his *Academy Notes* in 1875 in speaking about the painting *The 28th Regiment of Quatre Bras* (E. T. Cook and Alexander Wedderburn, eds., *The Works of John Ruskin* [London: George Allen, and New York: Longmans, Green, 1904], 14:308). As one reviewer commented, Ruskin seemed to have forgotten, "in his alliterative enthusiasm, that the Royal Academy Exhibition is no longer held in Trafalgar Square, or the line of Pall Mall, but in Piccadilly" ("Balaclava: Miss Thompson and Mr. Alfred Hunt," *Academy* 9 [May 20, 1876]: 493).

20 Butler, *Autobiography,* 121.

21 See the list in the exhibition catalogue, *Miss E. Thompson's New Picture Inkerman, and her Other Battle Pieces, The Roll Call, Quatre Bras, and Balaclava* (London: Fine Art Society, 1877).

22 The sum is all the more astounding since Galloway paid only £126 for the painting (Butler, *Autobiography,* 89).

23 FAS Minute Book, February 23, 1876. Several sources (e. g., Butler, *Autobiography,* 121; Lalumia, *Realism and Politics,* 264; and Usherwood and Spencer-Smith, *Lady Butler,* 41) state that J. Dickinson and Co. changed its name to The Fine Art Society. A brief letter in the *Times* (February 16, 1876: 12) regarding the copyright of *The Roll Call,* located Messrs. Dickinson and Co. at 31 Ely Place, the same address at which the initial meetings of the society were held before its move to 148 New Bond Street. There was certainly a close relationship between the two companies, but its exact nature is not certain.

24 Dickinson is listed as a creditor on January 1, 1879 (FAS Minute Book). This same entry records that the society also owed C. J. Galloway £250 with respect to the copyright of *Quatre Bras,* which implies that even though the society bought the reproduction rights from Dickinson, the society may not have acquired the copyright completely or may have been paying off Dickinson's copyright fee to Galloway at the same time. An entry in the FAS Minute Book in September 9, 1879, records the official transfer of the copyright of *The Roll Call* from Dickinson to The Fine Art Society.

25 Stacpoole is listed as a creditor on January 1, 1879 (FAS Minute Book). See also Anthony Dyson, *Pictures to Print: The Nineteenth-Century Engraving Trade* (London: Farrand Press, 1984), 71. In addition, the society paid £300 for a painted copy of *The Roll Call* to be used by Stacpoole in making the engraving (FAS Minute Book, October 17, 1878, and Dyson, 72).

26 FAS Minute Book, December 5, 1877. The society negotiated with Thompson for *The Return from Inkerman* and its copyright during March and April 1877. After rejecting Thompson's original asking price of 6,000 guineas, the society agreed to purchase the work for £3,000 plus 90% of what the picture sold for over £1,500, provided it was ready for exhibition at the society by April 20, 1877. The agreement included the stipulations that the society would lower the price to £2,500 if it were shown at the Academy; that Thompson would not paint any battle pictures larger than a certain size during 1877–78; that Thompson had the right to price *Inkerman* before June 1, 1877, after which time the society would determine the price; that the society had the right of refusal of any religious subject that Thompson might paint; and that the print of *Inkerman* would be engraved in the same style and size as the other military prints (FAS Minute Book, March 7, 21, 28, and April 11, 1877). Long's picture and copyright cost 3,000 guineas (FAS Minute Book, February 28 and March 7, 1877).

27 FAS Minute Book, January 13 and December 5, 1877, and January 10, 1879; and Dyson, *Pictures to Print,* 14. W. T. Davey produced the engraving of *Inkerman.* An autograph letter from Thompson dated May 9 [1878] to Davey records the painter's satisfaction with the print, in which Thompson praised Davey who "adhered to the character of the heads of the soldiers . . . in your admirable engraving." Thompson continued, "It is evident you have given great attention to the work" (FAS Clipping Book, 32).

28 For the prints after the paintings see G. W. Friend, *An Alphabetical List of Engravings Declared at the Office of the Printsellers' Association* (London: Printed for the Printsellers' Association, 1892), 321, 303, and 20, respectively, and Usherwood and Spencer-Smith, *Lady Butler,* 59, 62, 66, and 68.

29 On the enthusiasm for military subjects in the late Victorian era see Springhall, "'Up Guards and At Them!'" 49–72.

30 FAS Minute Book. On de Neuville's painting see Usherwood and Spencer-Smith, *Lady Butler,* 166. The print was declared at the Printsellers' Association on May 14, 1881 (see Friend, *Alphabetical List,* 85).

31 On the commissions of de Neuville, Wyllie, and Woodville see FAS Minute Book, March 14 and April 11, 1883, and November 14, 1882, respectively. The paintings were reproduced in photogravure and declared at the Printsellers' Association on February 13, 1884 (see Friend, *Alphabetical List,* 166, 193, and 374). Of these three artists, only Wyllie showed at the Grosvenor Gallery.

32 More than two dozen letters from Ruskin to Huish are in the Whitehouse Collection at the Bembridge School, Isle of Wight. Among these letters are several from December 1875 concerning an exhibition of copies by William Ward after Turner. Thus, Huish and Ruskin were in contact even before the society was registered. I am grateful to Peyton Skipwith for bringing this correspondence to my attention (see James S. Dearden, *Ruskin, Bembridge, and Brantwood: The Growth of the Whitehouse Collection* [Keele, Staffordshire: Keele University Press, 1994], 135).

33 Luke Herrmann, "The 1878 Exhibition of Ruskin's Turner Drawings," in *Centenary,* 12. Further details concerning the various editions of Ruskin's *Notes* are provided in *The Works of John Ruskin,* 13:389–536.

34 "Notes on Art and Archaeology," *Academy* 13 (March 9, 1878): 221.

35 "Ruskin's Turner Drawings," *Times* (March 20, 1878): 6. The *Times,* however, was very critical of the installation.

36 "Fine Art: Prout and Hunt," *Academy* 18 (October 2, 1880): 245.

37 FAS Minute Book, December 4, 1878. According to Elizabeth and Joseph Pennell the fund was set up by Burne-Jones, F. S. Ellis, and Huish at the Bank of London by December 10, 1878, and a subscription list was published amounting to £150 (*The Life of James McNeill Whistler*, 6th ed. [Philadelphia: J. B. Lippincott, 1925], 180). Linda Merrill points out that the fund was initiated promptly within three days of the verdict (*A Pot of Paint: Aesthetics on Trial in Whistler v. Ruskin* [Washington, D.C., and London: Smithsonian Institution Press in collaboration with The Freer Gallery of Art, 1992], 275–76).

38 Merrill, *Pot of Paint*, 275–77.

39 "Fine Arts: Pictures of Venice," *Illustrated London News* 81 (November 18, 1882): 526, and "Mr. Bunney's Venice," *Spectator* 55 (December 2, 1882): 1542. Bunney showed one work at the Grosvenor Gallery in 1879.

40 See "Ernest George's Etchings," originally published in the *Architect* in 1873, reprinted in *Works of John Ruskin*, 14:335–38, and "Art: Mr. Ernest George's Etchings," *Spectator* 52 (November 15, 1884): 1514.

41 *Exhibition No. 42. Catalogue of I. A Collection of Drawings in City, Town and Hamlet, by Alfred A. Goodwin, R.W.S. II. A Series of Drawings Made for St. George's Guild Under the Direction of Mr. Ruskin* (London: Fine Art Society, 1886), 8. To this catalogue Ruskin appended a postscript, "Mr. Marcus Huish, at the address of The Fine Art Society, will take care of any donations which may be given towards the work [of the Guild]."

42 Ruskin made this statement in *Ariadne Florentina: Six Lectures on Metal and Wood Engraving*, a series of talks delivered at the University of Oxford in Michaelmas term, 1872 (*Works of John Ruskin*, 22:421).

43 In his preface to the catalogue Haden sarcastically commented about Ruskin's denigration of the medium: "I respect Mr. Ruskin. I admire his honesty of purpose and outspokenness and I shall *not* bring an action against him because he says that Etching is a blundering art" (*About Etching. Part I. Notes by Mr. Seymour Haden on a Collection of Etchings by the Great Masters Lent by Him to the Fine Art Society's Galleries to Illustrate the Subject of Etching. Part II. An Annotated Cata-*logue of the Etchings Exhibited, 3rd ed. [London: Fine Art Society, 1878], 17).

44 A. H. Palmer, *Samuel Palmer: A Memoir, Also a Catalogue of His Works, Including Those Exhibited by The Fine Art Society 1881, and an Account of the Milton Series of Drawings, by L. R. Valpy* (London: Fine Art Society, 1882). The society published two etchings by Palmer: *The Bellman* in 1879, and *Opening the Fold* (or *Early Morning*) in 1880. On these works see Raymond Lister, *Catalogue Raisonné of the Works of Samuel Palmer* (Cambridge: Cambridge University Press, 1988), 246 and 248, respectively.

45 Sir Francis Newbolt, *The History of the Royal Society of Painter-Etchers and Engravers: 1880–1930* (London: Print Collectors' Club, 1930), 12.

46 See "Haden on Etching," *Saturday Review* 48 (October 4, 1879): 426.

47 FAS Minute Book, July 17, 1878. As of January 1, 1879, Haden was listed as a creditor whom the society owed two payments of £375 for his etching *Windsor* (FAS Minute Book). On the two prints by Haden published by the society see Richard S. Schneiderman, *A Catalogue Raisonné of the Prints of Sir Francis Seymour Haden* (London: Robin Garton, 1983), 353, 357.

48 FAS Minute Book, October 30 and November 6, 1878. Brown was hired at the salary of £130 per year.

49 Pennell, *Life of Whistler*, 186; Katherine A. Lochnan, *The Etchings of James McNeill Whistler* (New Haven: Yale University Press in association with the Art Gallery of Ontario, 1984), 176; and Merrill, *Pot of Paint*, 282.

50 As of January 1, 1879, Ellis was owed £150 for Whistler's sixteen plates, payable March 31, 1879 (FAS Minute Book); Lochnan, *Etchings of Whistler*, 178.

51 FAS Minute Book.

52 See Lochnan, *Etchings of Whistler*, 181 ff., and Margaret F. MacDonald, "Whistler and The Fine Art Society," in *Centenary*, 21.

53 David Park Curry, "Total Control: Whistler at an Exhibition," in Ruth Fine, ed., *James McNeill Whistler: A Reexamination*, vol. 19 of *Studies in the History of Art* (Washington, D.C.: National Gallery of Art, 1987), 76.

54 Curry, "Total Control," 77, and O'Callaghan, "Fine Art Society and E. W. Godwin," 6. Whistler received £300 from the sale of the pastels (FAS Minute Book, March 23, 1881).

55 Curry, "Total Control," 77. The society spent £50 in decorating its small room for Whistler's exhibition in 1883. This exhibition realized a profit of £130 (FAS Minute Book, March 14, 1883).

56 FAS Clipping Book, 4. An earlier entry of December 4, 1878, in the FAS Minute Book concerning a competition for frame designs mentions two first prizes of ten guineas each for the best frames for a watercolor and an engraving, and two guineas each for any design that was accepted by the society.

57 In 1883 the society published two books with prints by Whistler. These were *Four Masters of Etching* by Frederick Wedmore, which included *The Little Putney, No. 1*, a print of 1879; and Edmund W. Gosse, *Cecil Lawson: A Memoir*, which included Whistler's *Swan and Iris*, an etching after an unfinished painting by Lawson. Lawson's widow, Constance, who was an artist, was the sister of Beatrix Godwin (the widow of the architect E. W. Godwin), whom Whistler married in 1888 (Robert H. Getscher and Paul G. Marks, *James McNeill Whistler and John Singer Sargent: Two Annotated Bibliographies* [New York: Garland, 1986], 77). The society deliberately limited the printings of its fine art books. An advertisement for publications of the society at the back of the Lawson memoir states, "The rule of the Society in publishing books is to make an issue sufficient only to meet the demand at the time of publication. By doing so they find the subscribers are materially benefited as their books quickly increase in value" (Gosse, *Cecil Lawson*, n.p.).

58 "Art: 'Signor Costa' at the Fine-Art Society," *Spectator* 55 (June 10, 1882): 764–65, and "The Costa Exhibition," *Magazine of Art* 5 (1882): 396.

59 See Treble, *Great Victorian Pictures*, 52–53.

60 Other women artists included in the society's exhibitions were Lady Alma-Tadema, Constance Lawson, Miss Mary L. Gow, and Dorothy Tennant in the exhibition *One Hundred Paintings and Drawings by One Hundred Artists* in 1884, and Victoria Dubourg (the wife of the artist Henri Fantin-Latour), Maud Naftel, Constance Lawson, and Anna Alma-Tadema (daughter of Lawrence) in the autumn exhibition of watercolors in 1888.

All of these women showed at the Grosvenor Gallery. After a two-person exhibition with Hugh Thomson in 1891, the society held three exhibitions of the works of Kate Greenaway (1894, 1898, 1902).

61 Katherine DiGiulio, *Natural Variations: Photographs by Colonel Stuart Wortley* (San Marino, Calif.: Huntington Library, 1994), 29. The copyright was purchased for £300 from Poynter by Stuart Wortley on behalf of the society (FAS Minute Book, May 3, 1876). It took F. Joubert four years to produce the line engraving for which he was paid £1,600 (see the list of creditors in the FAS Minute Book, January 1, 1879, and Dyson, *Pictures to Print*, 71). This print won the praise of numerous critics (*Art Journal* 33 [August 1881]: 256; *Times* [August 1, 1881]: 11; *Academy* 20 [August 6, 1881]: 109; and *Athenaeum* [August 20, 1881]: 249). On the painting *Atalanta's Race*, see Alison Inglis, "Sir Edward Poynter and The Earl of Wharncliffe's Billiard Room," *Apollo* 126 (October 1987): 249–55, and Helen Smith, *Decorative Painting in the Domestic Interior in England and Wales, c. 1850–1890* (New York: Garland, 1984), 63–64.

62 William Holman Hunt, *Pre-Raphaelitism and the Pre-Raphaelite Brotherhood* (London: Macmillan, 1905), 2:341. Craik also lent a drawing on wood, *Rebekah at the Well*.

63 Mary Lutyens, *Millais and the Ruskins* (New York: Vanguard Press, n.d.), 240. Another more distant connection between Millais and the society was forged in 1886, when his daughter, Alice Sophia Caroline, married Charles Beilby Stuart-Wortley, brother of Archie Stuart-Wortley (who had studied painting with Millais) and first cousin of Colonel Archibald Stuart Wortley (by then no longer on the society's board).

64 FAS Minute Book, February 20 and March 27, 1878, and Jeannie Chapel, *Victorian Taste: The Complete Catalogue of Paintings at the Royal Holloway College* (London: A. Zwemmer, 1982), 113–15.

65 FAS Minute Book, July 12, 1878, and April 6, 1881.

66 FAS Minute Book, March 28, 1879. According to Chapel (*Victorian Taste*, 113), *The Princes in the Tower* was sold to Holloway for £3,990 at auction at Christie's on May 28, 1881. Holloway bought *Princess Elizabeth* a month later; its sale for 3,000 guineas is reported in the FAS Minute Book, June

8, 1881. On the *Princess Elizabeth* see Chapel, 115–16.

67 The Tennyson portrait with copyright was commissioned for 1,000 guineas (FAS Minute Book March 9 and April 6, 1881) and sold to the publisher Mr. Knowles for £1,250 (FAS Minute Book, May 11, 1881). The society paid 2,000 guineas for *Caller Herrin'* (FAS Minute Book, August 3, 1881, and February 15, 1882) and sold it to Mr. Dunlop for £2,200 (FAS Minute Book, June 21, 1882). The society paid 1,000 guineas for *The Captive* (FAS Minute Book, August 9 and November 14, 1882) and sold it for £1,750 to the Trustees of the Art Gallery of New South Wales, Sydney (FAS Minute Book, June 3, 1885).

68 The autograph letter is dated November 11, 1880 (FAS Clipping Book, 31). Millais said the engraving after the Tennyson portrait was "most admirable" (FAS Minute Book, February 15, 1882). On the prints after Millais see John Guille Millais, *The Life and Letters of Sir John Everett Millais* (New York: Frederick A. Stokes, 1899), 2:495–97; Alfred Whitman, *Samuel Cousins* (London: George Bell & Sons, 1904), 126, 129–30, and passim; and Friend, *Alphabetical List*, 25, 43, 46, 55, 104, 297, 332, and 375.

69 Friend, *Alphabetical List*, 97, and FAS Minute Book, May 23, 1883. The society paid £350 for the copyright.

70 Millais, *Life and Letters*, 2: 131. A few critics commented on the juxtaposition of the Whistler and Millais shows; see "Pictures by Mr. Millais," *Saturday Review* 51 (March 5, 1881): 307–08. John O'Callaghan also cites the comments of a reviewer in the *British Architect* of February 25, 1881, wherein the differences between Whistler's novel installation of his pastels and the more traditional display of Millais's paintings are noted (O'Callaghan, "Fine Art Society and E. W. Godwin," 7). Millais had shown his portrait of Mrs. Jopling at the Grosvenor Gallery in 1880.

71 FAS Minute Book, July 6, 1881.

72 See FAS Minute Book, March 9, 1881. Jopling later received £50 for his role in the sale of the picture of *Princess Elizabeth* (FAS Minute Book, June 8, 1881) and £50 for his services regarding the portrait of Tennyson (FAS Minute Book, June 27, 1881).

73 FAS Minute Book, October 24, 1883.

74 "A Great Picture," *Spectator* 58 (March 28, 1885): 419–20. The painting exhibited in the 1885 show is now in the Tate Gallery. It was a replica with minor changes of subject that Hunt took up earlier, which is now in the Walker Art Gallery, Liverpool (see Mary Bennett, *William Holman Hunt* [Liverpool: Walker Art Gallery, 1969], 52–54). Hunt seems to have been paid £1,000 by the society for allowing the gallery to show the painting (FAS Minute Book, February 25, 1885). He was also paid £500 at the time of his retrospective in 1886 (FAS Minute Book, March 18, 1886). A photogravure of *The Triumph of the Innocents* was published in 1887 (Friend, *Alphabetical List*, 383).

75 See "The Holman Hunt Exhibition," *Times* (March 15, 1886): 12; "Mr. W. Holman Hunt's Pictures in Bond Street," *Athenaeum* (March 27, 1886): 427–28; and "Art Notes and Reviews," *Art Journal* 38 (May 1886): 158.

76 Richard Ormond, "Leighton and The Fine Art Society," in *Centenary*, 13.

77 Leonée and Richard Ormond, *Lord Leighton* (New Haven and London: Published for the Paul Mellon Centre for Studies in British Art by Yale University Press, 1975), 74. On Leighton's importance to the society's exhibition see "Art: 'Signor Costa' at the Fine-Art Society," *Spectator* 55 (June 10, 1882): 765, and "Professor Costa's Pictures," *Times* (July 5, 1882): 5.

78 The society purchased *Wedded* from Leighton without the copyright for 1,250 guineas (FAS Minute Book, May 11, 1882) and sold it to the Trustees of the Art Gallery of New South Wales for £1,500 (FAS Minute Book, May 24, 1882). Amendola received his commission from the society on September 26, 1884 (FAS Minute Book). On Amendola's sculptures see "The Fine Art Society," *Academy* 29 (June 12, 1886): 422.

79 FAS Minute Book, May 30, 1889. On the prints after Long see Friend, *Alphabetical List*, 103, 232.

80 FAS Minute Book, July 2, 1884.

81 "Art: The Japanese Exhibition," *Spectator* 64 (March 15, 1890): 373–74; "Minor Exhibitions," *Athenaeum* (March 29, 1890): 411; "Exhibitions," *Saturday Review* 69 (March 29, 1890): 380; "Alfred East's Pictures of Japan," *Times* (March 4, 1890): 13; and "Mr. East's Pictures of Japan," *Academy* 37 (March 8, 1890): 175. For a more recent account of East's trip and the subsequent

exhibition see Peyton Skipwith, "An Enlightened Artist in Japan: Sir Alfred East (1849–1913)," *Country Life* 175 (January 5, 1984): 24–25. On the importance of Japanese art to the society see Jack Hillier, "Japanese Art and The Fine Art Society," in *Centenary*, 24.

82   See Kenneth McConkey, *Impressionism in Britain* (London: Yale University Press in association with Barbican Art Gallery, 1995), 121, 166.

83   Peyton Skipwith, "The Fine Art Society and the New English Art Club," in *Centenary*, 31. Among the more recent exhibitions at the society were Bevis Hillier, *The Early Years of the New English Art Club* (1968), Bruce Laughton, *Channel Packet Paris-London: 1880–1920* (1969), and Peyton Skipwith, *William Stott of Oldham, 1857–1900 and Edward Stott, A.R.A., 1855–1918* (1976).

84   FAS Minute Book, May 31 and December 20, 1888, and October 31, 1889. Bing's magazine *Le Japon artistique* (1888–91) appeared in an English version edited by Huish (see Tomoko Sato and Toshio Watanabe, eds., *Japan and Britain: An Aesthetic Dialogue, 1850–1930* [London: Lund Humphries in association with the Barbican Art Gallery and the Setagaya Art Museum, 1991], 149, and Gabriel P. Weisberg, *Art Nouveau Bing: Paris Style 1900* [New York: Harry N. Abrams, in association with the Smithsonian Institution Traveling Exhibition Service, 1986], 25–28).

Checklist for
the Exhibition

by artist. Each entry lists the date of completion, followed by its exhibition date at the Grosvenor. Titles given are those in current use and not necessarily the title under which it was exhibited at the Grosvenor. Several works not exhibited at the Grosvenor are included in this exhibition either to represent the type of work an artist did exhibit at the gallery or to provide contextual information about the Grosvenor and its founders. Dimensions are given in inches, with centimeters in parentheses; height precedes width.

The following abbreviations are used in the checklist:

Bt   Baronet

IS   International Society of Sculptors, Painters, and Gravers

NEAC New English Art Club

PS   Pastel Society

RA   Royal Academy

RBA   Royal Society of British Artists

RBC   Royal British Colonial Society of Artists

RBSA   Royal Birmingham Society of Artists

RCA   Royal College of Art

RHA   Royal Hibernian Academy

RI   Royal Institute of Painters in Water Colours

RP   Royal Society of Portrait Painters

RPE   Royal Society of Painters and Etchers

RSA   Royal Scottish Academy

RSW   Royal Scottish Society of Painters in Water-Colours

RWS   Royal Society of Painters in Water-Colours

SWA   Society of Female Artists (later known as the Society of Women Artists or Lady Artists)

1   *Grosvenor Gallery Season Ticket*, 1887
Printed paper affixed to leather wallet
4 3/8 × 3 (11.1 × 7.6)
Lowell Libson

2   (see plate 1)
Sir Lawrence Alma-Tadema, RA, RBA,
PRBSA, RP, RPE, RWS (1836–1912)
A Garden Altar, 1879, exh. 1880
Oil on panel
15 × 6 1/4 (38.1 × 15.9)
City of Aberdeen Art Gallery
and Museums Collections

3   (see plate 2)
Sir Lawrence Alma-Tadema, RA, RBA,
PRBSA, RP, RPE, RWS (1836–1912)
Ave Caesar! Io Saturnalia! 1880, exh. 1881
Oil on panel
8 3/4 × 18 (21.2 × 45.7)
Collection of the Akron Art Museum,
gift of Mr. Ralph Cortell
Yale and Denver only

4   Sophie Anderson (1823–1903)
Guess Again, 1878
Oil on canvas
38 3/4 × 29 1/2 (98.4 × 74.9)
The FORBES Magazine Collection, New
York, all rights reserved

5   (see plate 9)
Jules Bastien-Lepage (1848–1884)
Les Foins, 1877, exh. 1880
Oil on canvas
63 × 73 3/4 (160.0 × 195.0)
Musée d'Orsay, Paris
Yale only

6   Thomas Buist
*Sir Coutts and Lady Lindsay at Balcarres
Castle*, 1864
Carte-de-visite photograph
National Portrait Gallery, London

7   (see plate 3)
Sir Edward Coley Burne-Jones, Bt, ARA,
RBA, PRBSA (1833–1898)
Laus Veneris, 1872–73, exh. 1878
Oil on canvas

42 × 71 (106.7 × 180.3)
Laing Art Gallery, Newcastle upon Tyne,
England (Tyne & Wear Museums)

8   (see fig. 42)
Sir Edward Coley Burne-Jones, Bt, ARA,
RBA, PRBSA (1833–1898)
The Love Song (Le Chant d'Amour),
c. 1868–77, exh. 1878
Oil on canvas, signed (lower left) EBJ
45 × 61 3/8 (114.3 × 155.9)
The Metropolitan Museum of Art, The
Alfred N. Punnett Endowment Fund, 1947
Yale only

9   Julia Margaret Cameron (1824–1913)
Sir Coutts Lindsay, 2nd Bart., 1865
Sepia albumen print
10 × 7 9/10 (25.4 × 20.0)
National Portrait Gallery, London

10   Sir George Clausen, NEAC, RA, RBA, RI, RP,
RWS (1852–1944)
The Gleaners, c. 1882, final version of
painting exh. 1882
Pen and ink
8 × 10 (20.3 × 25.4)
City of Aberdeen Art Gallery and
Museums Collections

11   (see plate 8)
Sir George Clausen, NEAC, RA, RBA, RI, RP,
RWS (1852–1944)
Haying, 1882, exh. 1882
Oil on canvas
27 × 22 3/4 (68.6 × 60.3)
Art Gallery of Ontario, Toronto, purchase
1937

12   (see plate 7)
Sir George Clausen, NEAC, RA, RBA, RI, RP,
RWS (1852–1944)
La Pensée, 1880, exh. 1880
Oil on canvas
49 × 29 (124.5 × 73.7)
Glasgow Museums: Art Gallery and Museum, Kelvingrove

13   Sir George Clausen, NEAC, RA, RBA, RI, RP,
RWS (1852–1944)
Ploughing, 1889, exh. 1889
Oil on canvas
48 × 72 (121.9 × 182.9)
City of Aberdeen Art Gallery and
Museums Collections

14   Walter Crane, PS, RI, RWS (1845–1915)
Diana and Endymion, exh. 1883
Watercolor (laid down on board)
21 3/4 × 30 3/4 (55.3 × 78.1)
Dundee Art Galleries and Museums

15   John Scarlett Davis (1804–1845/46)
      *The Interior of the British Institution
      Gallery*, 1829
      Oil on canvas
      44 1/2 × 56 (113.0 × 142.4)
      Yale Center for British Art,
      Paul Mellon Collection

16   (see plate 27)
      Evelyn Pickering De Morgan (1855–1919)
      The Grey Sisters, 1880–81, exh. 1881
      Oil on canvas
      38 1/4 × 66 1/2 (97.2 × 168.9)
      The De Morgan Foundation
      at Old Battersea House

17   (see plate 29)
      Evelyn Pickering De Morgan (1855–1919)
      Night and Sleep, exh. 1879
      Oil on canvas
      42 × 62 (106.7 × 157.5)
      The De Morgan Foundation
      at Old Battersea House

18   Norman Garstin (1855–1926)
      The Painter's Wife, 1889, exh. 1889
      Oil on canvas
      18 × 20 (71.1 × 50.8)
      National Gallery of Ireland

19   Edmund John Gregory (1850–1909)
      Sketch for "The Rehearsal," c. 1882,
      original painting exh. 1882
      Oil sketch
      14 × 10 (35.6 × 25.4)
      Indianapolis Museum of Art

20   Sir James Guthrie, NEAC, RHA, RP, PRSA,
      RSW (1859–1930)
      A Pastoral, 1887–88, exh. 1890
      Oil on canvas
      24 3/4 × 37 7/8 (62.9 × 96.2)
      National Gallery of Scotland

21   (see plate 12)
      Edward Matthew Hale, ROI (1852–1924)
      Three Princesses (Les Trois Princesses),
      1881, exh. 1881
      Oil on canvas
      52 × 81 1/2 (132.1 × 207.0)
      Guildhall Art Gallery,
      Corporation of London

22   (see fig. 7)
      Horace Harral
      *"The Grosvenor Gallery, New Bond
      Street—The Entrance,"* 1877
      Wood engraving
      12 × 9 (30.5 × 22.9)
      The Fine Art Society, plc, London
      Published in *The Graphic*, May 19, 1877

23 (see plate 16)
George Henry, NEAC, RA, RP, RSA, RSW
(1858–1943) and Ernest Atkinson Hornel,
IS, RBC (1864–1933)
The Druids: Bringing in the Mistletoe,
1890, exh. 1890
Oil on canvas
60 × 60 (152.4 × 152.4)
Glasgow Museums: Art Gallery and
Museum, Kelvingrove

24 (see fig. 40)
William Holman Hunt, PS, ARSA, HRWS
(1827–1910)
The Afterglow in Egypt, 1854–63,
exh. 1877
Oil on canvas
73 × 34 (185.4 × 86.3)
Southampton City Art Gallery

25 (see fig. 18)
Robert Huskisson (1820–1861)
*Lord Northwick's Picture Gallery at
Thirlestaine House,* c. 1846–47
Oil on canvas
32 × 42 3/4 (81.4 × 108.5)
Yale Center for British Art,
Paul Mellon Collection

26 (see fig. 23)
Joseph Middleton Jopling, RI (1831–1884)
*Sir Coutts Lindsay outside the Grosvenor
Gallery, 1883*
Watercolor
12 3/8 × 7 1/8 (31.4 × 18.1)
National Portrait Gallery, London
Published in *Vanity Fair,* February 3, 1883

27 (see plate 11)
Henry Herbert La Thangue, NEAC, RA
(1859–1929)
The Artist's Father, c. 1882,
exh. 1882/1883?
Oil on canvas
51 1/2 × 43 3/4 (132.0 × 112.0)
Dunfermline District Museum, Leisure
Services, Libraries and Museums

28 Henry Herbert La Thangue, NEAC, RA
(1859–1929)
*The Boat Builder's Yard, Canacle,
Brittany,* 1882, exh. 1882
Oil on canvas
30 × 32 (76.0 × 81.5)
National Maritime Museum, Greenwich,
England

29 Henry Herbert La Thangue, NEAC, RA
(1859–1929)
Portrait of a Girl: The Striped Blouse,
1880–81, exh. 1882/1883?
Oil on canvas
22 × 18 (55.9 × 45.7)
Private collection, courtesy Pyms Gallery,
London

30 (see plate 15)
Cecil Gordon Lawson (1851–1882)
A Hymn to Spring, 1871–72, exh. 1883
Oil on canvas
60 × 40 (152.4 × 101.6)
Santa Barbara Museum of Art,
Gift of Mr. and Mrs. Paul Ridley-Tree

31 (see plate 4)
Blanche, Lady Lindsay of Balcarres, RI,
SWA (1844–1912)
Portrait of HRH the Princess Louise,
c. 1878, exh. 1878
Watercolor
9 3/4 × 6 1/2 (25.0 × 16.5)
Christopher Newall

32   (see plate 5)
Sir Coutts Lindsay, Bt, RI (1824–1913)
Self-Portrait, c. 1864
Oil on mahogany panel
30 × 36 (76.2 × 91.4)
The Maas Gallery Ltd, London

33   HRH the Princess Louise, RPE, later
Marchioness of Lorne, later still Duchess
of Argyll (1848–1939)
Portrait of Henrietta Skerret Montalba,
c. 1882, exh. 1882
Oil on canvas
43 × 34 (108.5 × 87.4)
National Gallery of Canada, Ottawa

34   (see plate 13)
Sir John Everett Millais, Bt, PRA, HRHA,
HRI, RP, HRSA (1829–1896)
For the Squire, 1882, exh. 1883
Oil on canvas
33 1/2 × 25 (85.1 × 63.5)
The FORBES Magazine Collection,
New York, all rights reserved

35   (see plate 14)
Sir John Everett Millais, Bt, PRA, HRHA,
HRI, RP, HRSA (1829–1896)
Portrait of Mrs. Kate Perugini, 1880–81,
exh. 1881
Oil on canvas
49 1/4 × 39 1/2 (125.1 × 100.3)
Mr. and Mrs. Richard P. Mellon
Yale only

36   Sir John Everett Millais, Bt, PRA, HRHA,
HRI, RP, HRSA (1829–1896)
Portrait of the Marquis of Lorne, 1884,
exh. 1884
Oil on canvas
40 × 29 (101.6 × 73.7)
National Gallery of Canada, Ottawa

37   Albert Joseph Moore, ARWS (1841–1893)
Birds of the Air, c. 1878, exh. 1878
Oil on canvas
33 1/8 × 14 1/4 (84.1 × 36.2)
Manchester City Art Galleries

38 Albert Joseph Moore, ARWS (1841–1893)
Blossoms, 1881, exh. 1881
Oil on canvas
58 × 18 1/4 (147.3 × 46.4)
Tate Gallery, London, presented by
Sir Henry Tate, 1894

39 (see plate 17)
Albert Joseph Moore, ARWS (1841–1893)
The End of the Story, 1877, exh. 1877
Oil on canvas
34 1/2 × 12 7/8 (87.0 × 32.7)
Joey and Toby Tanenbaum,
Toronto, Canada

40 Albert Joseph Moore, ARWS (1841–1893)
Forget-Me-Not, exh. 1881
Oil on canvas
15 3/8 × 6 1/4 (39.1 × 15.9)
Mr. and Mrs. Christopher Whittle

41 Frank O'Meara (1853–1888)
October, 1887, exh. 1887
Oil on canvas
39 1/2 × 19 1/4 (100.0 × 49.0)
Hugh Lane Municipal Gallery of Modern Art,
Dublin
Yale and Laing only

42 Sir William Quiller Orchardson, RA, PRP,
HRSA (1832–1910)
The Farmer's Daughter, 1881, exh. 1884
Oil on canvas
41 × 33 (104.1 × 83.8)
Glasgow Museums: Art Gallery and
Museum, Kelvingrove

43 (see plate 6)
Sir William Quiller Orchardson, RA, PRP,
HRSA (1832–1910)
Master Baby, 1886, exh. 1886
Oil on canvas
42 1/4 × 65 1/2 (107.3 × 166.4)
National Gallery of Scotland

44 William Payne
Private View of the Royal Academy, 1858
Watercolor with pen and black ink
3 3/4 × 4 1/8 (9.5 × 10.4)
Yale Center for British Art,
Paul Mellon Collection

45   (see plate 10)
Valentine Cameron Prinsep, RA
(1838–1904)
An Unprofessional Beauty, c. 1880,
exh. 1881
Oil on canvas
26 × 20 (66.0 × 50.8)
South London Gallery

46   John Roddam Spencer Stanhope, RI
(1829–1908)
The Pine Woods of Viareggio, exh. 1888
Tempera on canvas
52 × 42 1/2 (132.1 × 108.0)
The De Morgan Foundation
at Old Battersea House

47   (see plate 20)
John Roddam Spencer Stanhope, RI
(1829–1908)
*The Waters of Lethe by the Plains of
Elysium*, 1879–80, exh. 1880
Tempera and gold paint on canvas
58 1/16 × 111 1/8 (147.5 × 282.4)
Manchester City Art Galleries

48   (see plate 30)
Philip Wilson Steer, NEAC (1860–1942)
The Bridge, 1887–88, exh. 1888
Oil on canvas, signed
19 1/2 × 25 3/4 (49.5 × 42.5)
Tate Gallery, London, purchased 1941

49   Philip Wilson Steer, NEAC (1860–1942)
Water! Water! Everywhere, c. 1885,
exh. 1885
Oil on canvas
15 × 24 (38.1 × 61.0)
Private collection

50   (see plate 18)
Marie Spartali Stillman (1844–1927)
By A Clear Well, 1883, exh. 1884
Watercolor and bodycolor
21 1/4 × 18 1/2 (54.0 × 47.0)
Julian Hartnoll

51   Marie Spartali Stillman (1844–1927)
La Pensierosa, c. 1878, exh. 1879
Watercolor
21 1/4 × 18 1/2 (54.0 × 47.0)
Elvehjem Museum of Art, University of
Wisconsin, Madison, Frederick Leach
Estate Fund, Edward Blake Blair Endow-
ment Fund, Membership Art Purchase
Fund purchase, 1993

52   (see plate 19)
Marie Spartali Stillman (1844–1927)
Love's Messenger, c. 1885, exh. 1885
Watercolor, tempera, and gold paint on
paper
32 × 25 1/2 (81.3 × 64.1)
Delaware Art Museum,
Samuel and Mary R. Bancroft Memorial
Yale only

53   Edward Stott, NEAC, PS, ARA (1859–1918)
Feeding the Ducks, 1885, exh. 1885
Oil on canvas
18 7/8 × 15 1/2 (48.0 × 39.4)
Manchester City Art Galleries

54   (see plate 21)
      John Melhuish Strudwick (1849–1935)
      A Golden Thread, c. 1884, exh. 1885
      Oil on canvas
      28 1/2 × 16 3/4 (72.4 × 42.5)
      Tate Gallery, London, purchased 1885

55   (see plate 22)
      John Melhuish Strudwick (1849–1935)
      Isabella, 1879, exh. 1886
      Tempera on canvas
      39 × 23 (99.1 × 58.4)
      The De Morgan Foundation at
      Old Battersea House

56   James Joseph Tissot (1836–1902)
      Croquet, c. 1878, exh. 1878
      Oil on canvas
      35 3/8 × 20 (89.8 × 50.9)
      Art Gallery of Hamilton, Gift of Dr. and
      Mrs. Basil Bowman in memory of their
      daughter Suzanne, 1965

57   (see plate 31)
      James Joseph Tissot (1836–1902)
      *The Gallery of H.M.S. Calcutta
      (Portsmouth)*, c. 1876, exh. 1877
      Oil on canvas, signed
      27 × 36 1/8 (68.6 × 91.8)
      Tate Gallery, London, presented by
      Samuel Courtauld 1936

58   James Joseph Tissot (1836–1902)
      Holyday, c. 1875, exh. 1877
      Oil on canvas
      30 × 39 1/8 (76.2 × 99.4)
      Tate Gallery, London, purchased 1928

59   Henry Scott Tuke (1858–1929)
      The Fisherman, 1889, exh. 1889
      Oil on canvas
      78 × 46 (198.1 × 116.8)
      City of Nottingham Museums,
      Castle Museum & Art Gallery

60   Stanislas Julian Walery, Count Ostrarog
      Lady Lindsay, c. 1888
      Photograph
      9 7/10 × 7 1/10 (24.7 × 18.0)
      National Portrait Gallery, London

61   (see plate 25)
      George Frederic Watts, RA, RP, HRCA
      (1817–1904)
      The Judgment of Paris, 1874, exh. 1887
      Oil on canvas
      57 × 46 (114.8 × 116.8)
      The Faringdon Collection Trust
      Yale only

62   (see plate 23)
      George Frederic Watts, RA, RP, HRCA
      (1817–1904)
      Miss Rachel Gurney, 1885, exh. 1885
      Oil on canvas
      44 1/2 × 27 1/2 (113.0 × 69.9)
      The Trustees of The Watts Gallery

63   (see plate 28)
      George Frederic Watts, RA, RP, HRCA
      (1817–1904)
      Orpheus and Eurydice, c. 1869,
      full-length version exh. 1879
      Oil on canvas
      12 3/4 × 21 (30.5 × 53.3)
      The FORBES Magazine Collection,
      New York, all rights reserved

64   (see plate 24)
      George Frederic Watts, RA, RP, HRCA
      (1817–1904)
      *Portrait of Lady Lindsay Playing the
      Violin*, 1876–77, exh. 1877
      Oil on canvas
      43 1/2 × 33 1/2 (109.9 × 85.1)
      Private collection, on loan to the
      John Rylands Library

65   (see plate 26)
      George Frederic Watts, RA, RP, HRCA
      (1817–1904)
      The Wife of Pygmalion, 1868, exh. 1881
      Oil on canvas
      26 × 21 (66.0 × 53.3)
      The Faringdon Collection Trust
      Yale only

66   (see plate 33)
      James Abbott McNeill Whistler, PRBA
      (1834–1903)
      *Harmony in Yellow and Gold: The Gold
      Girl—Connie Gilchrist*, 1876, exh. 1879
      Oil on canvas
      85 3/4 × 43 1/8 (217.8 × 109.5)
      The Metropolitan Museum of Art,
      Gift of George A. Hearn, 1911
      Yale and Denver only

67   James Abbott McNeill Whistler, PRBA
      (1834–1903)
      *Harmony in Grey and Green: Miss Cicely
      Alexander*, 1872, exh. 1881
      Oil on canvas
      74 × 38 1/2 (190.2 × 97.8)
      Tate Gallery, London, bequeathed by
      W. C. Alexander, 1932
      Laing only

68   (see plate 32)
      James Abbott McNeill Whistler, PRBA
      (1834–1903)
      Thames—Nocturne in Blue and Silver,
      1872–78, exh. 1878
      Oil on canvas
      17 1/2 × 24 (44.5 × 61.0)
      Yale Center for British Art,
      Paul Mellon Fund
      Yale only

69   (see fig. 59)
      James Abbott McNeill Whistler, PRBA
      (1834–1903)
      *Arrangement in Black: La Dame au
      brodequin jaune—Portrait of Lady
      Archibald Campbell*, 1882–83, exh. 1884
      Oil on canvas
      86 × 43 1/2 (218.4 × 110.5)
      Philadelphia Museum of Art: purchased
      with the W. P. Wilstach Fund

70   Alfred Joseph Woolmer (1805–1892)
      *Interior of the British Institution (Old
      Master Exhibition, Summer 1832)*, 1833
      Oil on canvas
      28 1/4 × 36 1/4 (71.7 × 92.0)
      Yale Center for British Art, Paul Mellon
      Collection

Lenders to the Exhibition

City of Aberdeen Art Gallery and Museums
    Collections
Akron Art Museum
Art Gallery of Hamilton
Art Gallery of Ontario, Toronto
City of Nottingham Museums, Castle Museum
    and Art Gallery
Delaware Art Museum
The De Morgan Foundation at Old Battersea
    House
Dundee Art Galleries and Museums
Dunfermline District Museum
Elvehjem Museum of Art, University of
    Wisconsin, Madison
The Faringdon Collection Trust
The Fine Art Society, plc, London
The FORBES Magazine Collection, New York
Glasgow Museums: Art Gallery and Museum,
    Kelvingrove
Guildhall Art Gallery, Corporation of London
Julian Hartnoll
Hugh Lane Municipal Gallery of Modern Art,
    Dublin
Indianapolis Museum of Art
Laing Art Gallery, Newcastle upon Tyne,
    England (Tyne & Wear Museums)
Lowell Libson
The Maas Gallery Ltd., London
Manchester City Art Galleries
Mr. and Mrs. Richard P. Mellon
The Metropolitan Museum of Art
Musée d'Orsay, Paris
National Gallery of Canada, Ottawa
National Gallery of Ireland
National Gallery of Scotland
National Maritime Museum, Greenwich,
    England
National Portrait Gallery, London
Christopher Newall
Philadelphia Museum of Art
Private collections
Santa Barbara Museum of Art
South London Gallery
Southampton City Art Gallery
Joey and Toby Tanenbaum
Tate Gallery, London
The Trustees of the Watts Gallery
Mr. and Mrs. Christopher Whittle

Contributors

Barbara Bryant is an independent art historian in London.

Susan P. Casteras is curator of paintings, Yale Center for British Art.

Colleen Denney is assistant professor of art history and adjunct assistant professor of women's studies, University of Wyoming.

Hilarie Faberman is Robert M. and Ruth L. Halperin Curator of Modern and Contemporary Art, Stanford University Museum of Art.

Paula Gillett is professor of humanities, San Jose State University.

Kenneth McConkey is professor of art history and dean of arts and design, University of Northumbria at Newcastle.

John Siewert is assistant professor of fine arts, the University of the South.

Allen Staley is professor of art history, Columbia University.

Index

Photographic Credits